Liverpool, for Real

Glenn Bowden

ISBN-13: **978-1482680942**
ISBN-10:1482680947

For Leo

Acknowledgements

The author owes it all to the following people: Barry Jaundrill, Eddie and Joyce, Pam and Gary, Lyndon and Phil, Sam and Meg, Max and Frances, Michael Barlow, Juliana Austen, Graeme Pepper, Kate Ferguson, Chris Middleton, Erin Snelgrove, Kerry and John, Craig McAllister, Dean Robinson, Andrew Ballantyne, Boss Kaiteri, Tomo, Rhea and Oli, James Dunne, Jim Parsons, Frank Dawe, the Jewell of Dubbo, Louis Tabak, Steven Gerrard, and the fine patrons of the Birkey.

1. Arrival.

This is not a grand entrance.

The stone walls darken the windows and swallow the train. They're like the walls of medieval dungeons you see in the movies. If you're sadistically inclined you could clap a heretic in irons, tie a conspirator to the rack and feel right at home here — the pop of a leg joint a nice accompaniment to the drip drip drip of the solemn black walls. For torturous effect, the train stalls. Then continues at a snail's pace. Through the dungeon darkness you go. It's taking forever and just when the suspense has you wondering if it's ever going to happen, you step off the train into space and light. High above is a single vaulted roof of curved iron and glass. You wander through the ticket barrier to the concourse where there's a beautiful big clock, a news agent, and some okay-looking cafes. It's busy, but not *too* busy. With ease you make it outside onto the steps where the ball-cracking breeze sweeping in through the city makes you wish you'd gone to the bloody tropics after all. Never mind. For me this is a kind of paradise. Not even the jackhammer pounding the foot path just metres away can put me off. There are landmarks: across the street and to my right are the neo-classical columns of St George's Hall. To my left, and looming over a big block of something nondescript is the tall, dumb, yet strangely endearing, Radio City Tower. Lime St Station, St George's Hall, Radio City Tower. As Morrissey announced as he walked on stage here not so long ago: '…it's Liverpool…it's perfect!'

Since the conception of this city as my own personal Mecca it has taken me several years, two intimate relationships and plenty of scrimping and saving to get me here. Despite this, my celebratory cigarette on those limestone steps is short lived. Like I said, the wind has ice on it. It blows low and hard, passing through layers as if they aren't there. I'm shrinking.

Although he never got around to actually visiting, Carl Jung had a dream about Liverpool that prompted him to declare it 'the pool of life.' What made it so was the significance Jung derived from the image of a tree 'in a shower of reddish blossoms' - illuminated by a blazing light amidst the cold, sooty streets of his dreamscape. Jung interpreted the dark foggy city to represent the confusion in his life at the time; with the red tree representing *the Self*, the very core of his inner universe. For better or for worse, Liverpool reds inhabit my inner universe as well. So from the station, I go searching. A short walk in the direction of the tower has me at Williamson Square, almost the centre of the city. On the far side of the square an old man sits slumped against a wall. He's strumming a long piece of cardboard in the shape of a guitar. The pigeons in front of him look indifferent; the man has no food and the guitar music is all in his head.

There is, however, a wisp of a tune coming from a busker hidden down an adjacent laneway. Trumpet music makes its way into the square but then loses out to the diarrheic splatter of one of those arty fountain things which ejaculate columns of water from the pavers. A teenager makes use of the ridiculous thing by pushing his mate into one of the columns. The lad's school uniform is soaked. There's laughter and swearing and just metres away the old man looks oblivious, just keeps on strumming.

Faceless shop fronts and an average-looking theatre help border the square yet the overall blandness is saved by a lone stall where over half the items for sale are red. Red scarves, red clocks, red badges and glossy red pictures of mighty red footballers – faces superimposed onto those of Spartan soldiers going into battle, celebrated footballers staring Che Guevara-like into the middle distance - seeing that which is beyond the scope of mere mortals. As if that isn't satisfying enough, I look to the northern end of the square and there they are again – this time blown up several metres high – the familiar faces and figures of the Liverpool Football Club, all styled and merchandised, looking back from the display windows of a large outlet store. I cock my head and sigh. Such a pity I hate shopping. Yet it's funny how all the big brand bullshit and the blatant commercial crap is so much easier to stomach when it's in aid of Liverpool; the club playing the part of big commercial entity in order to compete. I guess that's what all the big companies say, but the essence of Liverpool seems so authentic, so *not manufactured*. I've travelled a long way for it, and right now the merchandise on display simply reasserts that I'm in the right place.

So too the demeanor of the people. In Williamson Square red shirts and scarves pass to and fro and those wearing them have a spring in their step. In a matter of hours my team – I mean *their team* … or maybe *our team* – is due to kickoff. Another episode in the wonderful tale of the world's greatest football club is about to play out on home soil, and, despite my hefty backpack, it's enough to give me a lift as well. I have a ticket with the words Liverpool v West Ham (Wednesday 5th March 2008) in my pocket which means as long as me and that ticket get to Anfield Stadium by 8pm, I stand an excellent chance of experiencing, *in the flesh*, my very first Liverpool game. Oh yes, the ticket is my golden egg; it's all seven numbers (plus the bonus), an Iggy Pop million in prizes. A simple phone call to the Liverpudlian ticket lady on the other side of the world just a week ago confirmed it - a seat in the Kop Grandstand for thirty-two pounds. How this happened I do not know. I was tempted to ask if I'd got in on some overseas allocation but didn't want to jinx it - just put the phone down after the transaction was made to declare gratitude to the football gods, thanking them for their rare show of grace through my good fortune.

Now I'm here I keep it in an envelope inside the inner breast pocket of my green coat. I value the piece of cardboard so much it's making me stupid. And suspicious. Every sideways look, every crooked smile or nervous tic in my vicinity *screams* potential thief. The problem with Liverpool, according to its many critics, is that a significant number of its inhabitants are fulfilling that potential. No doubt the city has its fair share of unsavoury elements. It is a place of economic hardship after all, a place that bore the brunt of Margaret Thatcher's harsh reforms and never fully recovered. In theory, it's every bit the vulnerable breeding ground for all the negative elements it has so vehemently been accused of. But that's just the problem. The accusations against Liverpool come so thick and fast and are so often stated with such venom that the critical thinker could be excused for smelling something a bit off. Perhaps there's something about the city that sets it up a little too conveniently as the scapegoat for a nation's woes. Perhaps the people here aren't the nasty pack of whingers capable of despicable acts that newspaper editors, police commissioners, pundits and politicians make them out to be. Even literary folk (who should know better) have called them vermin and accused them of sounding hideous and uneducated. In 2003, the author Will Self penned an article about a Liverpool exhibition in which, aside from spraying syllables around like a tom cat does urine, he refers to the city as 'a benighted burgh'. If you want to sum up a people from a certain place as being, say, pig ignorant, but want to sound pompous while doing so, 'benighted burgh' ought to do it. The tone of the language alone makes me wonder, is Self's assumption fair, or just symptomatic of someone trying to write while humping a thesaurus? I refuse to buy into it. I may not have been here before and I may not have spent more than a handful of days in Old Blighty but I come expecting great things, for I know *the Liverpool way.* I have witnessed the power of the Kop from afar, heard warmth, humility and defiance in the unified voice of up to 40,000 fans at a time. They sing *You'll Never Walk Alone* at the beginning and the end of every game, and when they're not belting that one out, they're serenading the players, saluting the manager, and chanting their love of Liverpool to a tempo so feverish it can make a TV in New Zealand seem like it's crackling under the intensity 'of a stadium 19,000 kilometres away. Surely the provenance of such a force is the pool of life, not the benighted burgh.

But like Liverpool's detractors, I too have problems. If there's one thing I'm becoming increasingly aware of in this world, it's the spectre of cruel mockery. In recent years, it has duly followed me like a savage stink and is sadly apparent in my track record of putting stock in people that others have written off. In Williamson Square I can all but sense impending mockery lurking in the shadows, ready to pounce on my hopes and rob me of my ticket just hours before the game. The gods of football are known for their cruelty to players and fans alike; they'll turn a hero into a fool in a heartbeat. They'll crush the hopes of the most ardent supporters on a whim. They aren't the 'all-virtuous' gods of the Christian and Muslim faiths; sometimes they seem to derive as much enjoyment from failure as they do from glory. Come to think of it, they're more like Jung's God, whom he envisioned sitting 'on his golden throne, high above the world – and from under the throne an enormous turd falls upon the sparkling new roof, shatters it, and breaks the walls of the cathedral asunder.' As this is something of a football pilgrimage I'd be surprised if the football gods aren't scheming a way to crap on me as well. They'll deprive me, I'm sure of it.

I drop my pack and sit down. As the daylight dims to a darker shade of grey, people look my way, their x-ray vision penetrating the lining of my jacket to zoom in on the magical words, *Liverpool, Anfield Stadium,* and *Kop Grandstand,* printed on the ticket within. It's important to note that approximately ten seconds after Morrissey took to the stage to announce 'It's

Liverpool, it's perfect!' he was struck in the head by a bottle flung from the crowd. The ageing rock star turned on his heels and stormed off the stage. To my knowledge, he hasn't been back since.

My phone rings.

'Hello.'

'What's the crack?' says Kate, my local contact. I have no idea what 'the crack' is so I simply state my position. 'I'm in Williamson Square.'

'It's better at the pub,' she replies.

We meet at Dr Duncan's Pub where Kate and I have the Cain's Liverpool lager while Graeme, her Northern Irish boyfriend, slurps a pint of Guinness. Kate and Graeme have agreed to put me up at their place until they get sick of me. Kate is a cousin of Mike, a friend of mine back in New Zealand, and it's on his word that they are willing to have a southern seas stranger impose upon their space. We chat away for a couple of minutes before I ease the ticket from my breast pocket. I hold it in front of them. 'You don't think it's counterfeit, do you?' They smile and lean forward and say it looks fine. Graeme even remarks how impressed he is at me getting a ticket to the legendary Kop. His right hand looks as though it's about to move so I snap the ticket away. As I said, I've only just met the guy.

I have no qualms, however, when they offer to take my bags while I scoot off to the game. Their kind gesture allows me to hop in a cab to the nearby ground an hour before kick off. There's barely a minute to spare.

The taxi driver (the first in a long line of friendly cabbies) chats away like a long-lost friend. He even apologises for the cold wind, saying the recent influx of Poles brought it with them. Whatever he's on about, I'm not here to be derogatory towards immigrants. If anything, I'm here to cheer them on. They include the stylish Spaniards Reina, Torres and Alonso, Sami the Giant Finn, the Dutchman Dirk Kuyt, and the list goes on. So too the taxi – all the way down Walton Breck Road past crowded pubs, steaming chip shops and grey side streets of grim terrace rows. There's barely a building that doesn't look battered. Anfield looms as the highest and most solid structure for miles.

Despite plans for a shiny new replacement, the old stadium looks impenetrable from afar, indestructible up close. I'm dropped before its hallowed gates where I stand in disbelief at my good run. From New Zealand to the UK via Sydney, Bangkok, and Dubai. From Heathrow to Lime St via Euston. So many planes, trains and automobiles and incredibly, not a single problem - no lengthy delays, no missed connections, no hijacks, no bird strike, no dead air, no mid-air collisions. The food? Fine. The passengers? Pleasant. The turbulence? Tame to the point of timid!

Here I am, on the threshold of my football fantasy, at the gates of this steel and concrete cathedral with not so much as a puddle in my path. A shiver runs the length of my spine. Surely the football gods have something up their sleeves? Is it possible they're saving their best till last, a twisted homage to Jung in the shape of a giant turd crashing down from the heavens?

I look up. The sky is clear. I brandish my ticket, and stroll on in.

Chapter 2. Anfield.

'The past is not dead. In fact, it's not even past.'

- William Faulkner

By entering Anfield I'm consummating my allegiance. It's a big deal. I've never done this before, never been willing to give myself over and truly say 'I'm with them' to any club, organisation, or institution of any kind. Organised gatherings of people for a purpose other than mere entertainment have never been my thing. They're good in theory, but no matter how right-minded, decent or vital the purpose, someone always buggers it up.

I've been rejecting institutions since I was a kid.

The first was the Marshland Cub Scouts where I accrued some two whole badges before deciding I'd rather be at home having a kick-around with my brother Lyndon before heading inside to watch MASH. That Hawkeye Pearce was one loose unit. In contrast, the podgy fella who called himself Akela down at the Scout den was deadly serious. Any grown man who goes by the name of a Jungle Book character and wears schoolboy shorts and a leather toggle cannot be serious. By all accounts, Liverpool FC is a toggle-free zone.

The next institution I rejected was the Pentecostal Church. I had two sets of aunties and uncles (mother's side) who practiced the faith.

When they visited Christchurch they were hell-bent on me realising my potential as a 'great Christian leader.' For a while it seemed like a good idea. My dad had left home and living on a small farm on the outskirts of Christchurch could get a bit lonely. Of the handful of kids that went to Marshland's Primary School not one of them was within decent biking distance to my house. Especially when the dry Nor-wester was whipping its way from the Southern Alps and across the Canterbury plains. That wind could kick dust out of a green paddock, make a willow tree look manhandled, and make a kid's bike go backwards. Studies have revealed that the Nor-wester increases the likelihood of suicide among adults. In Marshland it comes with an added bonus: the sweet rotten pong of the Belfast freezing works delivered right to your back door. Days like that it was best to stay in, back door shut.

I preferred my own company anyway, but for a while there I experimented with an imaginary companion. His name was Jesus. He appeared shortly after my Aunt Joy and Uncle Darryl gave me an array of Christian comic books in which Jesus always knew what to do. His superpowers weren't the greatest – he didn't have a laser that blasted from his chest like Iron Man, nor did he swing from buildings like Spidey – but uttering his name was like abracadabra to a magician, and according to my Uncle Darryl, Jesus was actually real. He was dead but still alive, just like Obi Wan.

Heaven: what a concept! Heaven meant that all my pet cats that'd been flattened on Marshland Rd weren't really dead. Neither was the horse we had to put down and neither was my pet lamb Mork (who died bloated from all the bread I'd been giving him), nor our pet duck Mindy, Mork's favourite companion.

When my grandfather Ted died, I naturally thought that he'd be in heaven as well. As long as you believed in Jesus, you went to heaven. Even though I couldn't recall him ever talking about Jesus or the Bible I just took it for granted that good old Ted was looking down on us.

Soon I was wearing a pendant that read *The Lord is my shepherd, I shall not want*, reading the Bible every night, saying grace before meals, and praying to God several times a day. Whenever the aunties and uncles were in town, I received very high praise indeed.

Then the cracks began to show.

It was the contrast in Aunty Joy and Uncle Darryl's behaviour I noticed first. For the most part they were these incredibly nice and wholesome people who seemed to have all the time in the world for me. They were never angry and never swore. I remember cracking up when hearing them call someone a 'Charlie', or when they said 'flip' when people would normally blurt the notorious f-word, the one I was forbidden to say. But even though my aunties and uncles were happy (and often literally clapping when they talked about Jesus), their attitudes would switch alarmingly whenever they saw someone on TV, or even out the car window, that they didn't like the look of. These people, the ones they lowered their eyes at, had the devil inside of them. And they weren't the only ones. I learned that my cousin's girlfriend had the devil inside of her. So did Tina Turner. And Michael Jackson – in fact, every single member of Live Aid (including my favourite, Bruce Springsteen) were all, despite trying to save Africa - *hell bound*. The devil was working over time.

One Sunday, they took me to a church in the city where, as long as I sang along and mimicked their movements (hands raised, body swaying from side to side while looking up at the ceiling), they all got very excited. Afterwards, when we went back to my grandma Mo's place to meet up with Mum, my aunt Joy beamed at her: 'He's going to be your saviour!' she said, her arm around me. I had no idea what this meant and just assumed it was a good thing, although Mum didn't seem that pleased. That night, I pondered. Does Mum need saving because she's separated from Dad? Is she sick? Is it because we have prowlers? I was sure we had prowlers.

Something was up. When I broached the subject she began by saying that I was free to believe in anything I liked. But, personally, Mum wasn't sure about the existence of God. She didn't actually believe. She wasn't a real Christian! The person who would do anything for me and my brother Lyndon, the person who cared for Mo more than all my aunties and uncles combined, was – as it stood – going to hell.

I knew that was wrong. But then again, how could it be when there was the Bible and churches and so many Christians who believed the same thing? At ten years of age, the answers were beyond me, but the question mark was in place. It hinted at a foul underbelly, and it smelt like the freezing works in a Nor-wester. Then I noticed how my aunties and uncles often acted as though they felt sorry for her, diminishing who she was with their holier-than-thou judgment. I began to resent them for suggesting Mum needed saving, as if Jesus wouldn't see how good she was and accept her all the same.

I decided the comics they'd given me were actually quite naff. Instead of reading the Bible every night, I went back to my Hardy Boys Adventures, twist-a-plot books, and various 'novelisations' of my favourite 80's movies. I noticed that people were actually dismissive of Christianity, whereas before I thought everyone was in on it. Why wouldn't they be?

Then we received a call that the aunties and uncles had been filmed for the evening news. I can't recall exactly why they were on the news but, sure enough, there they were in their new Auckland church, singing and praising the ceiling and doing something really weird called 'speaking in tongues.' *Speaking in tongues.* Footage of adults speaking in tongues should not be shown before children's bed time. Yet the weirdness of it all was ultimately good, for it meant that Mum, as suspected, was safe from the devil. And that the Auckland aunties and uncles were as *crazy as flip.* If you really need saving, it's probably from yourself. That's when I rejected the Pentecostal church, and why it's important that Liverpool FC sing about 'hope' rather than 'belief.'

I went into adolescence with a deep suspicion of adults, so it was natural that I eventually rebelled against everything they tried to teach me. By the age of fifteen I rejected secondary school, effectively becoming a non-student; a verbal agreement with some of my teachers stipulated that, as long as I didn't cause trouble, I could sit to the side and read any books or magazines I fancied. I also rejected a cricket club due to boredom, and a rugby club due to not knowing whether my team mates were serious or not about getting drunk and having sex with a defrosted chicken. (As far as I'm aware, LFC rejects fowl innuendo).

Next to be rejected was a karate dojo, which had been going quite well until the instructor demanded that if we ever saw him in public we were to address him by yelling 'Hey Sensei!' while thrusting a fist in the air - *kyokushin style!* A simple 'hello' or friendly 'gidday' wouldn't do. It was (fist) *Hey Sensei!* or nothing, he said.

Even worse than sensei's ego was that I actually went through with it. I was working in a shop selling science-related gimmicks at the time. One afternoon I spotted his shiny sensei head cruising past the store front. Impulsively, I fisted the air and yelled in his direction. His head swung left. He looked at me; we made eye contact. Without a flicker of recognition, he kept on going. I looked back at the kid I'd been serving. I asked if he needed a bag for his slinkee. He graciously declined. After that, my days attending karate were numbered. The delayed realisation that he kind of rejected me first is very humbling.

So how does Liverpool minimise such shortcomings?

It comes down to the integrity of its past, because the past is still present and perceived as key to a desirable future. Which is why, before I describe the atmosphere inside Anfield Stadium, you need to know about Bill Shankly.

Liverpool, among other things, is often criticised for being too caught up in its own history. The critics are idiots, for those who try and denigrate the fine traditions and heroic achievements of Liverpool can only be ignorant, arrogant, or jealous. I don't mean to cause alarm, but often they're a blend of all three. It's scary, I know, but this is the world we live in.

Compared to that of Liverpool, the histories of some other clubs can seem a bit hollow. It's kind of like comparing that beautiful old house you love, the one you occasionally alter your daily route just to see – the one with the heritage listing, the tasteful features and the solid materials – the one that contrasts so greatly to that soulless stucco box you can't help but see every time you walk out the bloody door. The beautiful old house makes you want to invite yourself in to soak up the ambience, enhance that sense of continuity you got from just walking past.

It might be a little worn in places but hey, that's okay, that's the character; the reassurance that what really matters in life still actually matters. So what makes Liverpool's history like a big old beautiful house, and some others so stucco? It's easy. The others never had a visionary architect, never had a master builder, never had Bill Shankly. If they had, they might also be the proud owners of glorious histories. Then again, when you consider the elements, everything suggests that it was something that could only have happened on Merseyside (Location, location, location!)

Key to Shankly's influence was the institution that represents the club's core identity: *the Kop.*

From the cinders and rubble left over from the completion of a tram line in 1906, the Kop came into existence as little more than a man-made terraced hill at one end of Anfield. If its form was rudimentary, its significance was great, for it was made to resemble 'Spion Kop', a hill located some 10,000 miles away in the South African province of Natal. The summit of Spion Kop (or Spy Hill) was the scene of one of the most horrific and futile battles in the Second Boer War.

No battle before or since has seen as many people slaughtered on such a small piece of land. On the 'acre of massacre' hundreds of British soldiers were gunned down by Boer guerillas. The soldiers had been ordered to take Spion Kop at night. They were told that it was the best vantage point in the valley. But, when the dawn mist cleared, the soldiers were horrified to find themselves utterly exposed, something the Boers took maximum advantage of from their positions in the surrounding hills. A layer of rock barely 40 cm below the soil meant that British trenches were far too shallow to provide decent cover. Instead, they tragically served as the soldiers' graves. Despite the blunders of their superiors, the soldiers' plight was acknowledged and commemorated with football stands throughout the UK.

For twenty-two years Anfield's Kop remained an open-air embankment, 'a huge wall of earth', until it gained a cantilevered steel roof in 1928. But it wasn't until the arrival of the relatively unknown manager, Bill Shankly, that the roof's ability to stay lodged to its stanchions was truly put to the test – not by the winds whipping in from the River Mersey, but by the very people it served to shelter.

When Shankly took over the reins in 1959, the club was grafting away at a lowly pace in the second division. Yet despite its ailing condition, support for Liverpool was strong. Having played at Anfield some years before, Shankly stated that the Kop's unity, loyalty, cockiness and pride had left a lasting impression. They were the exact same qualities he wanted in his Liverpool side. With the city's obsession with football on a par with his own, Liverpool represented a land of dreams for Shankly, the one place where he could take his ideals and build his football utopia: a holy trinity between manager, players, and fans.

The seed of his vision can be traced. Shankly grew up in the Scottish mining village of Glenbuck, where excelling at football was virtually the only way of avoiding a hard, dangerous existence – a life in the pit.

Shankly was employed at the coal mine when he was just fourteen years old. Despite the mine having electricity (before the people of Glenbuck had it in their homes) the conditions were primitive.

Shankly:

> *At the back of the pit you realised what it was all about: the smell of damp, fungus all over the place, seams that had been worked out and had left big gaps, and the stench ...You were supposed to get air but I'm sure there were some places it did not reach. People got silicosis because they had no decent air to breathe.*
>
> *You had to eat where you were working and there was no place to wash your hands...We would see a lot of rats in a mine, though not as many in a pit. In a mine the rats could go down the incline. But they did not frighten the men. Not at all. I have seen rats sitting on men's laps eating.*
>
> *We were filthy most of the time and never really clean. It was unbelievable how we survived. You could not clean all the parts of your body properly. Going home to wash in a tub was the biggest thing. The first time I was in a bath was when I was fifteen.* (Quote from Shankly, by Bill Shankly, 1977)

According to Shankly, the small, isolated community got by with 'fun, jokes, laughs and exaggeration,' not to mention a socialist ethos whereby people looked out for each other, sharing food, clothes, and money with whoever was in need at the time; the recipients doing the same when misfortune beset another.

Despite a mistrust of left wing politicians (especially the Labour men who did little for the mining communities of Ayrshire), Shankly spoke often about the vitality of socialism. Influenced by the writings of Robbie Burns, Shankly's idea of socialism was a distillation of the theory to its purest form:

> *The socialism I believe in is not really politics. It is a way of living. It is humanity. I believe the only way to live and to be truly successful is by collective effort, with everyone working for each other, everyone helping each other, and everyone having a share of the rewards at the end of the day. That might be asking a lot, but it's the way I see football and the way I see life.*

The post war gloom of Liverpool in the fifties – where children played in bomb craters, where half the buildings had either been damaged or destroyed by German air raids, and where rag and bone men were still a ubiquitous sight in the neighbourhood slums – did little to deter Bill Shankly.

While he set to work, the advent of television was giving an unprecedented amount of attention to the players and managers of the English first division. Some obtained a celebrity status almost on a par with the music and movie stars of the day. As they were often from humble working class origins, the sudden exposure did not sit well, some of the football men putting on posh accents and affectations to disguise their meagre backgrounds. No such identity crisis would afflict Bill Shankly: he feverishly set about nurturing what Barney Ronay, the author of *The Manager*, describes as 'the popular notion of a mass communion between supporters, team, and geographical place.'

After releasing twenty-four players from the squad he took over, he selected those he believed would assert his goal of an unbreakable bond between team and fans, assuring his new players of success just as long as they didn't over-eat or, indeed, lose their accents. Shankly, by way of example, was every bit himself in the public eye: straight up, streetwise and sincere. Under Shankly, Liverpool players would have to epitomise teamwork, humility and goodwill, without ever forgetting who they were playing for. When hard man defender, Tommy Smith, complained that his leg was sore, Shankly famously replied: 'Correction. It's not *your* leg, son; it's Liverpool's leg.'

Thus, the sixties proved to be the period when the loyalty of those who trotted along to the Kop on a regular basis was to be rewarded. Alan Edge, author of *Faith of our Fathers*, was there: 'When Bill Shankly provided something on the pitch to shout about and, simultaneously, the Beatles let the world know the city was not simply a port of call, the detonation took place.'

Two seasons into Shankly's tenure, Liverpool won the second division. From there they rose through the first division to be crowned the 1963-64 league champions. On the last day of that season, the cameras rolled up to Anfield to film the deciding match against Arsenal. To find out more about the Kop phenomenon, the BBC sent a reporter from the London-based current affairs show, Panorama. He stood neatly attired in a dark fitted suit, looking very much abuzz from the noise and energy of the swaying stand behind him. In his polished yet excitable BBC tones, his report would become a cherished moment in the history of British broadcasting:

> They don't behave like any other football crowd,
> especially at one end of Anfield ground, on the kop. The
> music the crowd sings is the music that Liverpool has
> sent echoing around the world. It used to be thought that
> Welsh international rugby crowds were the most musical
> and passionate in the world, but I've never seen anything
> like this Liverpool crowd...the gay and inventive ferocity
> they show here is quite stunning. The Duke of Wellington
> before the Battle of Waterloo said of his own troops, 'I

don't know what they do to the enemy but by god they frighten me,' and I'm sure some of the players in this match this afternoon must be feeling the same way.

'An anthropologist studying this Kop crowd would be introduced into as rich and mystifying a popular culture as in any south sea island, their rhythmic swaying is an elaborate and organised ritual. The 28,000 people on the Kop itself begin singing together. They seem to know intuitively when to begin. Throughout the match, they invent new words usually within the framework of old Liverpool songs which stress adulatory, cruel or bawdy comments about the players or the police. But even then they begin singing these new words with one immediate huge voice. They seem mysteriously to be in touch with one another, with wacker, the spirit of Scouse. The spirit is good humoured and generous when they're winning, but not necessarily when they're losing...

Liverpool walloped Arsenal that day 5-0, and Shankly's Liverpool won the first division ('the big league' as he called it) three times in total, the FA Cup twice. The second FA Cup win prompted a civic celebration that saw Shankly ascend the steps of St Georges Hall. Before the 300,000 supporters stretched all the way to (and onto the roof of) Lime St Station, he announced triumphantly: 'Even Chairman Mao has never seen a greater show of red strength.'

The club also had its first taste of European glory by winning the UEFA Cup in 1973. By then, the road had been paved for his assistant, Bob Paisley, to take over and steer Liverpool into a golden era that would make them the most successful club in England with, and by no coincidence, the most famous 'end stand' in the world. Shankly's style of 'socialism without the politics' proving the perfect recipe for the right kind of success. From now on, teams that took on LFC would take on a city.

> *It's not a club, it's an institution and I wanted to bring the crowd closer to the club. People have their ashes scattered here. One family came when it was frosty and the groundsman dug a hole in the goal at the Kop end and inside the right-hand post a foot down there's a casket. Not only do they support Liverpool when they're alive, they do it when they're dead. This is why Liverpool are so great. There's no hypocrisy about it and that's how close people were brought to the club. It was sheer honesty, I brought them in, accepted them in.* (Quoted in 'Shanks – The Authorised Biography.')

After making my way through the cavernous bowels of Anfield I emerged from the corridor of Block 105. There, a fine expanse of rectangular green opened up before me – floodlights warming the turf with a celestial glow. There I was, a little boy in big boy's skin, marveling at all the same angles, installations and idiosyncrasies I'd seen only on TV. One foot followed the other and much to my delight I found my seat to be directly behind the very goal where Shankly claimed the bodies of next dimension fans were buried.

My decision to come early was a good one. Plato said that you can discover more about a person in an hour of play than a year of conversation, and I was delighted to see the players I felt I knew so well go about their warm ups.

Each member of the team possessed an effortless precision and ease of movement almost too well-oiled to be human. I marveled at goalkeeper Pepe Reina's agility and balance as he leapt and dived for the ball. Even Dirk Kuyt – normally about as graceful as a stubbed toe - looked sleek and assured. To finish the warm-up the team took turns at blasting the ball at goal from the edge of the penalty area. Everyone hit the back of the net except the defender

Jamie Carragher (excusable) and we – the lucky souls standing directly behind – *oohed* and *ahhed* at the force of each strike, some of us even ducking when the ball looked as if it would surely burst the back of the net.

When the team disappeared down the tunnel for their final words of advice from manager Rafa Benitez, someone from the row behind me complimented me on my *1985/86 League and Cup Double Champions Season* scarf. I told the enquiring faces how my friend Craig had gifted it to me several years ago, after finding the scarf in the lonely corner of a Christchurch garage sale. They seemed impressed, although one Kopite was more interested in how a Kiwi could just ring up from the other side of the world and secure a place on their terrace so easily. I was busy excusing it as just a fluke when, without warning, the very song that was so integral to my being here stopped all conversations mid-sentence, and we sang: *When you walk through the storm/ Hold your head up high, and don't be afraid of the dark...* When you lift your scarf with both hands above your head and sing *You'll Never Walk Alone* at Anfield, your heart inflates ten times its normal size, a well of emotions bores through your centre, and life suddenly seems infinitely more precious than it did just seconds before. *At the end of the storm is a golden sky/ And the sweet silver song of a lark...* It was around the lark bit where I had to take stock. Pausing mid-song not only made me realise just how superior the voices around me were to my own, it also prevented me from breaking down and bawling my cry-baby eyes out. Yup, when it comes to Liverpool I'm a soppy, sentimental fool. I'm sure there was a time when I wasn't like this. Had Liverpool – so symbolic of life's triumphs and tragedies - made me this way? Who knows, *but know this*: soppy I may be, but let it be understood that I'm also a man from a land of tackle and toil who will forever be terrified of crying around others. Essentially, the Kop is a tool for inspiring the home side and intimidating the away. The last thing they need is some foreign sop taking up space just so he can have a good ol' *boo hoo-hoo*. With every fraction of my focus I kept the floodgates in check, bit down on quivering lips, and surely turned about as red as the lines on my scarf. Okay, so maybe a few drops leaked from the levee, but thankfully I managed to lasso the melodramatic mess dying to get out of me while Anfield, of course, sang on: *Walk on through the wind, Walk on through the rain, Though your dreams be tossed and blown...* With sobs suppressed, I channeled the soppy stuff into a meaningful, almost intelligible burst for the chorus: *Walk on walk on, with hope in your heart/ And you'll never walk alone/ You'll never walk alone...*

A repeat of the chorus and we were done. We roared, the whistle blew, and we roared again. But the singing did not stop there.

Almost immediately, the Kopites launched into a protest song against the club's American owners, George Gillett and Tom Hicks. Since their takeover in February 2007, the Americans had outraged Liverpool fans by loading the club with debt and stalling over the construction of a new 60,000 seat stadium, the building of which would lead to more revenue, in turn helping Liverpool compete in the transfer market. They had also revealed dastardly plans to siphon money from LFC to ice hockey and baseball teams owned in America.

Finances aside, Tom Hicks had the audacity to inform the media that he'd entertained German coach Jurgen Klinsman at his Californian ranch where it is believed they drew up a provisional contract for his replacement of Rafa Benitez. All this had not gone down well. Since Shankly, a code of conduct has been observed at Liverpool, whereby managers are granted the utmost respect and given every opportunity to prove themselves; the Kopites, loyal to a fault. By undermining Rafa, the new owners were failing to adhere to the *Liverpool way*. Before the game, a group called the Spirit of Shankly walked the streets and voiced their disapproval with a song that was simple and clear and really quite catchy: *They don't care about Rafa/ They don't care about fans/ Liverpool football club, is in the wrong hands.*

Despite the turmoil off the field, the team itself looked calm and in control of the game's opening minutes as they probed West Ham's formation for weaknesses. Soon the politics were vanquished by an explosion of cheer as Fernando Torres scored my very first goal at Anfield. A new signing from

Athletico Madrid, Fernando Torres had already proved himself a striker with more than just a cool name.

A year earlier he'd made Scousers swoon at a time when few regarded him as a potential signing. After his impressive form for Spain in the 2006 World Cup, Manchester United, Arsenal, and a host of European clubs wanted the one they called 'El Nino' (the kid) to be their own. Considering the mercenary attitudes of so many modern footballers, most thought a player with his ability would automatically make a bee line to the club with the biggest wallet. What they didn't know was that Torres had his heart set on Merseyside. In May 2007, while captaining his hometown club Athletico Madrid in a game against Real Sociedad, a photo taken of the young striker revealed the words *You'll Never Walk Alone* written on the inside of his captain's armband. Liverpool gasped; Manchester, et al, groaned. *Fernando Torres*: Spanish blood, Scouser heart – the armband said it all. Within months of the photo being taken, the lean Spaniard with the blond hair and unassuming face was smiling before English media looking resplendent in red.

Ten months later, not only was I privileged to see him score, I was also treated to what I'm led to believe was the Kop's debut performance of his very own song. To the tune of Two by Two the Scousers sang:

His armband proved he was a red, Torres, Torres
You'll Never Walk Alone it said, Torres Torres
We got the boy from sunny Spain; give him the ball he'll score again
Fernando Torres, Liverpool's no. 9!
Na-na, na-na, na-na, na-na, na-na, na-na
Na-na, na-na, na-na, na-na, na-na, na-na
Na-na, na-na, na-na, na-na, na-na, na-na, na-na, na-na
Fernando Torres, Liverpool's No.9!

With the tempo rising on the na na-na's every repeat grew louder. Complete with compulsory bouncing from the Kop, the overall effect was magnificent.

On the field, Liverpool was rarely without the ball yet the score remained the same until the second half when – this time actually facing the Kop itself – Torres headed home another. I remember that goal like it was yesterday and sincerely believe it will be etched in my memory until the day I die and maybe even beyond: the gleaming ball floating towards me, arcing before the backdrop of the night sky like a space pod ejected from the mother ship while everything around it stands motionless, frozen in time. I swear if it hadn't been for the net it would've dropped nicely for a return header of my own. A short time later, as if to show the Kop his utmost appreciation, El Nino completed his hat-trick with a neat shot that snuck below the keeper.

We all felt incredibly pleased with ourselves. I was deemed by the kindly folk around me an instant good luck charm. People shook my hand and patted me on the back, encouraging me to come along to as many games as I could manage over my stay. Then, as if we hadn't been spoiled enough, with two minutes remaining, Captain Steven Gerrard struck a trademark 25-yard screamer to remind everyone who was still boss around here.

The crowd dispersed, filing out of Anfield, still smiling, still singing. Finding shelter from the cold wet night became the priority for many, while smitten fools such as myself lingered outside the stadium .The makeshift stalls along Walton Breck Road were doing a roaring trade selling the same gaudy memorabilia that graced the stall in Williamson Square. I bought a game badge from a guy who, while reaching for change, slipped on a groundsheet and landed on his arse like a clown. He climbed to his feet in obvious pain yet smiled at his customers' jibes: *Alright, alright.* Oozing compassion, I told him to keep the change. He looked up: 'Whadda yer know; I just broke me arse for ten pee!'

The streets around Anfield were jam-packed with people and cars. Before working out how the hell I was going to get to Kate and Graeme's, I made a point to doff the proverbial cap to the statue of Bill Shankly outside the stadium store. Inscribed below, a noble legacy: *He made the people happy.*

3. A Brief Comedown.

I woke late the next morning to the sight of my breath, and chilled to the core. The living room I'd slept in was very much the living room of people in their early twenties: coffee table heaped with overflowing ash trays, empty cans of Guinness and a bottle of something called *Buck's Fizz*, which Kate, I vaguely recalled, had sworn by for its speed-like qualities. Add kooky art on the walls, photo montages of good times, and the sour odour of me, the drunken guy on the couch.

Kate and Graeme had already left for work. They'd instructed me to help myself to breakfast the night before. They couldn't have made me feel more welcome, but it didn't feel right raiding the kitchen on my very first morning. A warm breakfast in a neighbourhood café seemed a much better idea.

But first, a shower. The chill of the flat made it imperative that my movements beyond the sleeping bag were fast and efficient. I bolted to the bathroom, undressed, and nearly wept when I couldn't for the life of me coax one measly drop of warmth from its pipes. The room felt like a haunted ice box and had me certain I'd landed in a home of sadists – this being Kate and Graeme's idea of a cruel joke on a person from warmer climes. I braved the shower all the same, cursing through chattering teeth at the sight of my half frozen, rapidly retracting penis.

I left the flat in search of sustenance, hailing a cab to drop me off at the reinvented Albert dock. The restaurants looked pricey. And uninviting, in that up-market, uptight way that makes you feel your money is simply lining the pocket of some cashed-up bastard who doesn't give a rat's arse whether you enjoy your meal or not. Not so long as you pay up like a good little tourist whose one-off patronage helps fuel his loveless, low quality/ high yield, stink status formula.

You bet I was grumpy. I did not come here to be a tourist. Standing at the dock, I was fully aware of its importance – how integral it was to the making of Liverpool. This was the first dock of its kind (non-combustible, made only from brick, stone and iron) and I'd read local author Linda Grant's description of its opening in 1845 and how 'nothing in the whole of England could compare to it in size and splendour, the monumental mass that loomed so large upon the river, the western gateway of the empire.' All that brick, stone and iron should have had me standing in awe of the sheer poignancy but, with a grumbling stomach and a 4 degree Celsius wind funneling up my own western gateway, I just couldn't feel it.

I rounded the Albert dock to see the trio of structures they call the Three Graces (the buildings of Royal Liver, Cunard, and Port of Liverpool) but with only a low sky of mordant grey to offset them they all just looked so weighted, brutal, and glum.

There was a similar shade of grey on the surface of the River Mersey, the dock's rectangular pools, and every building in sight. Maybe if I'd come from a New Zealand winter the contrast wouldn't have seemed so great. What I *had* come from was the city of Auckland, dubbed by writer Janet Frame as a 'paradise of light' in the height of summer. Hot blanket humidity, sticky tar seal roads, and days where there's little else possible but to take a few steps forward, flop to the ground and give yourself over to the sun.

Where was the bloody sun? I wanted to scale the façade of the Royal Liver, reach to the sky and wipe clean the latent menace. 'I'm here to like you!' I felt like shouting. 'Can't you at least look pleased to see me?'

Less than twenty-four hours in The Working Class City and here I was, stricken with a nouveau riche-like desire for instant gratification, for something shiny and bright. If travelling is all about getting to know yourself, could it be that Liverpool had revealed me as a fun-boy phony ... and so soon?

As if to say *you can't handle the history,* the wind pitched its icy hands through the tightly woven fibres of my coat and shoved me towards the inner city. Even my green coat, impenetrable in the past, was no match for the Irish Sea wind. That feckin' Irish Sea wind.

I carried my foul mood along Strand St, took a right up James and onto Lord. But somewhere on Church St things changed. No, the sun didn't come out and grant the city colour. Nor did I suddenly find myself in a quaint garden of roses, tickle berries and gnomes. I did, however, find myself on a strip of mall surrounded by Scousers. Walking, talking Scousers.

'The immediately recognizable features of the Scouse dialect are the congested, nasal sounds reminiscent of catarrh together with a plaintive singsong pronunciation where a sentence starts with a slightly whining intonation, rises questioningly in mid-sentence, ending on a higher pitch,' so says the Scouse English Glossary. I grabbed a Cumberland sausage from a café, sat on a bench seat, scoffed the sausage, and listened.

In many parts of the world, especially in those exotic places, animated conversations often come with florid gesticulations and dizzying head movements. In India, heads virtually swing from necks; in Italy, hands grapple the air. In the streets of Liverpool, it's the spoken syllables alone which provide the animation. Too cold to be talking with hands anywhere but deep within pockets, the syllables were keeping things warm with a dance of their own. They hop from the mouths of Merseysiders, stomp, rise and grind in the course of conversation, giving vivid descriptions to each anecdote and quality repartee in return. This combination of Scottish burr and Irish lilt made the perfect antidote to an oppressive sky. Every snippet and half conversation overheard elevated my spirits no end.

Then, just as I was washing the sausage down with some fizzy lemon drink, a not-so-sporty looking couple wearing 80s shell suits caught my eye. Their quintessential fashion sense insisted they stood out from the rest. They walked quickly with the kind of effortless movement only 100% polyester garments can give. With the assured confidence that comes with knowing you can run, leap, and lunge with maximum freedom at any given moment, they glided from right to left before my eyes. Breaking with the multi-coloured tradition that marked the shell suit's audacious arrival to eighties fashion, his was a monotone of straight pastel blue while she went with an uncomplicated mauve. What a sight! A lightweight, front-zipped, elastic-waisted couple walking with supreme comfort as the foolish world around them rasped and chafed in their denim and wool-clad conformity. He completed his look with a gold earring and slicked back hair. She, with blonde hair and terracotta tan. They were spectacular, perfect in their mutual disregard/ obliviousness to the shell suit snobbery of the world.

It should be noted that she wasn't alone with the tan. There were so many fake tans in town that day that I swear if you could turn down the hustle and bustle at just the right moment, the hum of a thousand sun beds would lull the city into a trance.

Another source of colour was the wildly dyed hair of marauding teens. I gave them, say, ten years before they looked back on photos and screamed *what the fuck!* But, for now, in the streets of Liverpool, just inches above their hormone-doused surliness and alarming outbursts, it was all electric blue, vivid green and emergency red. Say what you like about the kids but collectively they could be modern art. This could either mean something or nothing at all.

Something else that may, or may not, mean something is the designation: Liverpool, 'European Capital of Culture 2008'. By edging out bids from the likes of Cardiff, Newcastle-Gateshead, and Oxford, the Capital of Culture accolade came with much fanfare and what was believed to be a genuine chance of regeneration. Some wondered whether it would deliver little more than a lick of paint and too many construction sites but, in fairness, it was too early to tell.

The chairman of the judges' panel, Sir Jeremy Isaacs, said that aside from having more museums and galleries than any other English city apart from London, what swung the accolade Liverpool's way 'was a greater sense there that the whole of the city is involved in the bid and behind the bid.' His views were supported by the Culture Secretary who hailed it as the most vital and energetic bid, one which 'embraced the whole city.'

It would be naïve to think that every Scouser and his dog were enamoured by the idea, or that a celebration of culture would do much to improve long term unemployment, gang violence, and neighbourhood degradation. But with an estimated five million pound injection for its troubles, Liverpool had either pulled off the biggest scam of the new century or, God forbid, it was actually deserving of the accolade. Either way, not bad for a benighted burgh.

The renaissance the city was purportedly enjoying seemed typical of what Ringo Starr meant when he called Scousers 'the rubber men of England: they have a habit of bouncing back.' But more on that later. For it wasn't long after wiping Cumberland sausage grease from my hands that I received an important call from The Capital.

Just minutes before dialing my number, Richard, a friend from New Zealand then living in London, had opened the Metro newspaper for a quick football fix. As he perused a photo taken of the back of Fernando Torres as he was scoring his 2nd goal – the space pod header – from the night before, his girlfriend looked over his shoulder and spotted a gaping mug that looked a lot like mine.

-'Hey Glenn, were you standing behind the goal with something in your hand?'

-'It's not how it looks.'

-'It looks like a camera.'

-'Then that's the story I'm sticking with. What's going on?'

-'Oh my God Glenn, it's you – you tinny bloody bastard I can't believe it! You've made the papers. You haven't been here a day and you're in the bloody papers!'

My initial euphoria was tempered by the knowledge that my good friend Richard, bless his excitable soul, was notoriously prone to exaggeration and had been known to look you straight in the eye and swear he'd seen UFOs in the skies above New Zealand. It wasn't until I got back to the flat and Kate rolled in with her copy of the Metro that I could take a deep breath, look at the photo in question, and utter two very pleasing words: 'It's me.'

'Oh my God, it's fate!' cried Kate. 'You being here – you're a good luck charm - it's meant to be!' She was delighted until she remembered her allegiance to Everton, the blue half of Merseyside. 'Oh no! That means the reds are going to keep winning and Everton will be crap! It'll be the reverse of when Mick was here.' She said that when Mick (or Mike, her cousin/ my friend/ our connection) visited from New Zealand, Everton went on a winning spree while Liverpool floundered over the same period. It was, of course, all down to his presence.

I had a sneaking suspicion that the success of Liverpool's season lay more in the hands of Steven Gerrard and Fernando Torres but, hey, it was nice to feel important. Surely there's no harm in thinking that in this heavily fated city, a slither of that fate – a slight insignificant slither – had been cast my way. It was right there in the newspaper looking back at me. Graeme (an undoubted reds supporter) downloaded the photo so I could email it around the world.

Once my gleeful chore was done, the night resumed as you'd expect – more Guinness, more good cheer. As we sat marveling at the likelihood of it all Graeme took a stab at the bigger picture. 'It's amazing-like,' he said. Starry-eyed and goofy, he looked at me: 'We're going to win the Champions League!'

'I hope so,' I said.

'You're the good luck charm – just having that spot in the Kop was amazing enough. But the photo as well – none of my friends can believe it.'

'Cool,' I said. 'Do you think there'll be any hot water tomorrow morning?'

'There will definitely be hot water tomorrow morning,' he said.

4. Credentials

Part 1

By now you might be wondering how a guy from a southern land of picturesque mountains, delicious livestock, and rampaging rugby teams manages to become a good luck charm for the greatest football club in the world. Let me tell you, and in spite of how it may seem, becoming a good luck charm doesn't just happen overnight.

Football lore deems it imperative that every self-respecting fan comes with a lovely little story about how they came to support their particular club – attendance at a game, the sounds and smells of the animated crowd, soggy chips and meat pies, and valuable bonding sessions with one or more adults, usually a father. Combine these elements and you have a rite-of-passage peek into The World of Man.

The first encounter with The World of Man is a strong one. It will sear the child's mind – a memory to make him almost discernibly weepy when the tradition is repeated with his own son or, when the crueler side of nature's cycle continues, and the father passes on.

There's no reason why this story can't feature a daughter instead of a son but, let's face it, females are more inclined to spread their sentimentality far and wide whereas man – big, striding, *ooger booger* man – is an emotional incompetent. That's why you better look out when he's drinking and in the mood. Beware! Release of bottled sentiment could make for the most one-sided drunken conversation you'll ever know –the very reason I'll spare you, dear reader, and write this paragraph before I drink my evening solace.

My own lovely little story lacks the presence of a father. Sounds negligent, doesn't it? Actually, it wasn't his fault. He was more of a rugby, racing and cricket man and besides, my first experience of Liverpool came at an ungodly hour on God's day of rest when parents who know what's good for them are still sound asleep.

When I was a kid, the only time you could watch decent football (or 'soccer' as we in New Zealand ashamedly call it) was at the crack of dawn every Sunday. With its snazzy theme tune, goal-scoring action, and genial English host, Brian Moore, *Big League Soccer* was a must see. I watched for tricks and moves I could try out in the backyard, something to practice in time for next Saturday when I took to the field with my own team, the Western Lions. As the Western Lions kit was red, it was only natural that I identified with the red uniformed players on the telly. And, by a truly wonderful coincidence nearing divine destiny, the team featured most were the reds of Liverpool.

From the late seventies and into the eighties there was an unquestionable parallel between the red men of Merseyside and a red team of five-year-old boys a world away in Christchurch. Like Liverpool, anything less than an annual restocking of the Western Lions' trophy cabinet was considered a failure. They scored goals, we scored goals; they won competitions, we won competitions. Instead of striker Ian Rush, we had Ryan Merlow; for midfielder Graeme Souness, we had Andrew Worley; for goalkeeper Bruce Grobelaar, we had me. We only lacked moustaches.

Our coach made up for this glitch in our parallel universe with a handlebar beauty of such rigid strength of follicle it almost looked detachable. Add a heavy forehead, sideburns and a gold neck chain that bounced about his chest as he bellowed orders and you have the defining image of coach Wayne Smith, our fully functional archetype of the 1970s good bastard.

His job? To enforce the fundamentals. He advised us to stay upright rather than bend over when puffed; he taught us the concept of the ball being faster than the player; and he pleaded until he was all but down on his knees for us to stay in position – this being the toughest lesson of all. Trying to convince us kids with our juvenile pack mentality that it was better to pass the ball rather than chase it en masse was something he worked at tirelessly – with minimal success.

The ball was everything. We were drawn to it like flies to a hippy – the sensation of kicking the thing as hard as puny white legs would allow was the reason we were there. *Punt it! Give it a hoof! Boot it! Boot it over here!* Forget accuracy: he with the mightiest kick was king.

Wayne Smith noticed how delirious we became every time he swung his leg and cannoned an errant ball towards goal. To us midgets, the force of his right foot was up there with the hammer of Thor. When Wayne Smith connected, trees turned their backs, brick walls braced themselves, and goal nets shivered. We were convinced our coach was one of the awesome superstar legends of the game. Even the knowledge that he was the dad of our team mate Matthew, lived in the suburb of Shirley, and never actually featured in the Liverpool line-up come Sunday morning, didn't stop us believing. Shrewd as a badger, he promised to display his perceived shooting prowess as a reward at the end of practice, as long as we didn't piss him off. If we did, he'd threaten us with a drop to the B team, the group of kids otherwise known by us little A team elitists as the 'pack of uncos' who practiced on the neighbouring pitch, right on the verge of a paddock of horses. (We looked across the muddy green expanse between us – a vast distance of what was probably 30 metres at most, and shuddered at the thought of it. The B's seemed less inclined to dribble the ball than dribble on the ball; a drop to their level and we might as well turf the boots for tidily winks.)

Every Saturday you could see how much it meant to Wayne Smith for us to do well. He wasn't averse to screaming 'WASTED!' after we'd fluffed an opportunity or, at the other end of the spectrum, hooting and hollering with the parents after we scored.

And he despised selfish play – on and off the field. He even acknowledged the good manners my mother had instilled in me as I waited for everyone else to grab their half-time orange wedge before I took my own. Seeing those wedges disappear before my eyes every Saturday, week-in, week-out, not knowing for sure if there would be enough to go around, had me seriously questioning just where this bloody politeness gig was getting me. That was until the week Wayne Smith winked a bushy eyebrow and told me I was the only kid with any manners. He said it as though it was a good thing. Naturally, I kept them.

Following the annual prize-giving in which we strode valiantly onto the stage to collect our silverware in front of a packed clubhouse, parents and kids were invited back to the Smith's place for an end of season feast. As we filled our greedy little gullets on cheerios, fizzy drink, and mallow puffs, Wayne Smith put on a tape of *Big League Soccer* which he'd recorded on the amazing new contraption that was currently rocking our TV addicted worlds, the VCR: *Video-Cassette-Recorder*. Unraveling the cord which led from the video player to the 'remote control', he implored us to take note. 'This is what you need to think about for next season,' he said, looking hopeful, crouching beside the TV.

As a Liverpool fan he was adamant that the reds' high tempo pass-and-move style of play deserved nothing less than our full attention. 'Look at the triangles,' he'd say, eyes wide as he pointed at the shapes drawn by the movement of the ball. 'Can you see the triangles? Who can see the triangles?' When no one said anything he scanned our faces for a flicker of recognition. With highly-sugared brains pinging off the insides of our skulls it was difficult to sit still, let alone envisage invisible triangles. We were in it for the spectacular goals, the tricky dribbling and the sliding tackles. But Wayne Smith was hell-bent on showing us there was more. He had the vigour of a young chaplain desperate to deliver the message crucial to our spiritual well being: Behold the triangular passing of messrs Dalglish, Souness, and Lee, for therein lies the grace of God. Ay, salvation from the sins of mankind, through soccer.

For Anfield is the kingdom
The power and the glory
For ever and ever,
Red Men.

By the age of nine, and after several glorious seasons playing for the Western Lions, my two constants in life were success with Wayne Smith and success for Liverpool.

Thanks to Shankly and his 'boot room' of managers-in-waiting, Bob Paisley and Joe Fagan, Liverpool did indeed rule for the best part of two decades. But for the Western Lions it was a quicker demise, Wayne Smith's golden run as our coach ending in the mid-80s.

Despite our winning ways, things weren't always rosy with the big coach. Kids being kids, we constantly tested his patience. He was often grumpy, but he was the kind of coach who, the grumpier he was, the more you wanted to improve. He liked to muck about as well, the banging of balls at goal typical of his capacity for fun.

But there was one season when he was less inclined to muck about. Imagine our disappointment when halfway through the competition he stopped turning up and the coach of the B's took over, merging the two teams.

I was certain our behaviour had made him too grumpy to continue and cursed the bad manners of my team mates. In truth, the real culprit was life's grim reality. Wayne's wife, Matthew's mum, was sick. The word 'cancer' was never mentioned. Even if it had been, I still would've struggled to understand why she couldn't just recover.

All I knew was that Wayne Smith would have to stop coaching the Western Lions to spend more time with her. Our great little team, Christchurch's own Liverpool in miniature (minus the moustaches), would never be the same.

It was several years before I saw Wayne Smith again, at a Ranfurly Shield rugby game I'd attended with my dad at Lancaster Park. He was cooking hot dogs in the shops under the stands. He didn't look that different. I was about to say hi and, if need be, remind him who I was, but a bout of shyness got the better of me. I was served by someone else as he ducked out the back. An opportunity 'wasted'.

Part 2

The American author Dave Eggers once wrote that 'the abandonment of soccer (in the USA) is attributable, in part, to the fact that people of influence in America long believed that soccer was the chosen sport of Communists.'

In New Zealand, it wasn't so much the threat of Communism as it was the threat to our nation's fragile notion of manhood which seemed to be the problem. Regardless of soccer's standing as part of the national consciousness of almost every other country in the world, soccer to New Zealand was positively effeminate, a game for poofs and sissies on account of all that rolling around and play acting, the lack of violence or crunching tackles.

It was also seen as a game that had an almost demonic power over people, possessing those who watched it with riotous, unsightly, and heathen-like impulses. Perhaps football in the eighties partly deserved such a reputation. But even in the lead up to my departure to Liverpool in 2008, some considered my relaxed attitude towards the perceived threat of hooliganism as naïve, bordering on reckless. A woman at the library where I worked wondered if I might even turn into one. I informed her that that only happens to Manchester United supporters. She wasn't so sure.

Although past characteristics persist, New Zealand has recently made a transition from being a chronically self-conscious teenager of a country to one which is gradually coming to grips with its place in the world. We have travelled and inspected 'overseas' and come to the realisation that we're okay. We no longer rely heavily on foreign visitors to tell us so, although we love it when they do.

But not so long ago it was a different story. We sought comfort through compliments but, like any little teenage prick you've ever known or ever been, we also gained comfort from being highly critical of everywhere else. The common perception of the world when I was growing up was that it was a headless chook of a place, full of madness and confusion. A good example of the tastes and values of foreign countries gone awry was their preference for soccer, or football, or 'whatever they bloody call it', over our fine, upstanding national game, rugby union.

As children, our mums let us play soccer because there was less chance of being knocked around. Our fathers conceded on the premise that, sooner rather than later, we'd transfer to rugby, the oval ball being the conduit to 'real manhood'. They reassured each other from the soccer sidelines that the kicking aspect of the game would benefit the boy once he got out from his mother's blouse to harden up and take on the man's game.

'Good for the ball skills,' they said, often.

Good for the ball skills - a parent catchphrase taken from the then All-Black captain, Andy Dalton, who virtually 'came out' in public by admitting he'd played soccer as a child. As the All-Black captain, however, the man was impeachable, his words a reprieve for those who considered Kiwi kids playing soccer to be wrong.

To them, football was the sniveling, anaemic, limp-wristed stranger who lingered outside primary schools and offered sweeties to your children. Indeed, I once read an account by New Zealand columnist Steve Braunias, who claimed his headmaster back in the sixties would strap any student he caught playing soccer at lunch time.

Things weren't so bad in my day; for the most part it was just ignored. But there was no denying that, to your average kiwi bloke, football was a game for poofs, pansies, and posers – to see it was to sneer at it. Even as recently as 2005 I found myself in the company of a group of guys who ever-so-casually referred to football as 'fagball'.

Never mind that the game of rugby involves launching yourself at another man's waist. Never mind that every few minutes sixteen players on a rugby field stop running to 'crouch and hold' each other in the incredibly intimate facet of the game known as 'the scrum'; a collective embrace which involves players willingly wrapping their arms around the upper thighs of team mates and pressing their heads between their legs. Some players do this so often they develop a condition known as 'cauliflower ear' – a clotting of blood where the external portion of the ear becomes swollen and deformed. A condition that, by no surprise, is most unattractive to women.

What to make of this rugby player preference of rubbing up to men at the risk of losing appeal to the opposite sex? Could this flagrant disregard for the gaining of heterosexual copulation suggest a rugby scrum is merely an elaborate excuse for a simulated orgy of men in uniform? If so, you could almost see the violence of tackling and rucking as self-imposed punishment for gaining enjoyment from such activity.

If Freud's experiments in which homophobic men were revealed to be more inclined to be turned on when watching male gay porn than non-homophobic men, perhaps it's not such a stretch to regard the game of rugby as a representation of the inner turmoil of the sexually-repressed man constantly at war with his homosexual impulses. To further expose the ridiculousness of the 'fagball' attitude, let's consider the respective origins of each game.

In 1823, an English public schoolboy called 'William' picked up a football in the hope that his opponents would play along by grabbing him around his mid section, before pulling him off (his feet) and piling on top of him. What joy!

Little Willy's desire for more contact with his fellow public schoolboys outside the steamy confines of the boarding house led to the aforementioned 'scrum', the moving embrace known as 'the maul', and the action of 'rucking' your opponent while he's lying helpless on the ground, all of which combine to give us the game we know today as rugby union.

Now let's look at football. Melvyn Bragg wrote in *12 Books That Changed The World* (including the Rule Book of Association Football), that one theory has football originating in the Roman City of Chester where, 'half a millennium after the Romans departed from Britain, the Anglo-Saxons played a sort of football with the heads of the conquered Danes. Some scholars push it back farther, into the time of the Roman occupation, and claim it was a way of celebrating occasional British and Celtic victories against the imperial occupiers, this time a Roman head doing the honours.'

Based on these versions of history, it seems odd that New Zealand, along with Australia, the Pacific Islands and South Africa, would see the game which embraces rather than kicks the heads of its opponents as being the one better suited to the tough, stoical, hard-ass nature of their manhood.

So if you ever hear someone from the southern hemisphere denounce football as a game for fags, be sure to know that what he's really talking about is the triumph of homoeroticism. Warning: if you try and explain this to him he's bound to get upset. If you're male, just nod, smile, and pat him on the back. Keep patting, he likes that. But one pat too many and he'll smash you. That's rugby.

Yet despite rugby's pre-eminence, in 1982 something strange happened – something without precedent which caused New Zealand to put its football prejudice aside, albeit momentarily.

For several precious months it was all about soccer as New Zealand's All Whites played in the FIFA World Cup for the very first time after a grueling qualification process that even we could appreciate.

My *Road to Spain* book and Official All-White 1982 Spain World Cup biscuit tin (which converted into a totally cool yet annoyingly bulky lunch tin) took pride of place alongside my Roy of the Rovers book.

In New Zealand's first game of the tournament we scored two goals against a Scottish outfit that featured Kenny Dalglish and Graeme Souness. Our brave stand was enough to ensure the Scots were eventually knocked out of the competition on goal difference. Horrible for Scotland, wonderful for us. At last, we'd made an impression. Even though we lost the game 5-2, somehow, thanks to a favourable planetary alignment and the mischievous nature of those football gods, we scored two goals. Two whole goals.

Following this 'triumph', the Christchurch Star ran an article about the All-Whites with the headline: Soccer: *Not So Sissy After All.*

On the soccer field, kids were no longer pretending to be players from other countries. For a good year or so we became Steve Sumner, Grant Turner or Steve Wooddin, and our goal-scoring celebrations bore a distinct resemblance to the celebrations performed after those magical goals against Scotland. Oh yes, for fans of the round ball in New Zealand, these were heady days.

It helped that a year earlier New Zealand rugby had let itself down. Instead of uniting our small nation it had divided it – the point of contention being a decision to allow South Africa's national rugby team, the Springboks, to play on our shores. Many saw the New Zealand Rugby Union's backing of the tour as a virtual condoning of South Africa's apartheid regime, which extended to excluding black people from participating in the game of rugby. The New Zealand Rugby Union, backed by our own National government and what seemed like one half of the New Zealand public, thought nothing of welcoming the South Africans and letting the games commence.

Prime Minister Rob 'Piggy' Muldoon's official line on the matter was 'no politics in sport.' And he was exactly right. And that was exactly the reason for the widespread opposition to the tour – South Africa's politics being directly responsible for the exclusion of black players. No government in the world, whether in relation to rugby, football, or even tiddlywinks, should have a say about who gets to play, especially on a basis of racial discrimination.

For those who protested against the Springbok tour (and there were many) the decision exposed the dark underbelly of our national game. It was a mean prod in the already heavily salted wound of black South Africans. Moreover, it was a massive undermining of New Zealand Maori who had been left out of previous tours to South Africa upon their government's request – bar one occasion when they were welcomed as 'honorary whites.'

The New Zealand protesters, many of whom were battered by the police and abused by those who just wanted to see a game of rugby regardless of the implications, did enough to make their point known (even caused a game to be cancelled). It was a wake up call for not only the New Zealand Rugby Union, but sectors of the South African regime they were demonstrating against.

A year later, the hostility still fresh in people's minds, the football world cup provided a welcome diversion, the game finally getting the attention it deserved and, with it, a modicum of respect. By the end of the tournament it almost seemed a shift had taken place. There was even talk of the day when soccer would rival rugby for the nation's affections. What a shame it didn't last.

I've heard a few conspiracy theories about Rugby Union officials making a concerted effort to quell the rising threat that soccer posed, but whether they have legitimacy or not, it's hard to ignore the overriding fact that New Zealanders remained brilliant at rugby and crap at football. The jubilation over two goals in a 5-2 drubbing says it all. By world standards we were still rubbish, and soccer soon receded to its old status – somewhere in the region of hockey. That's right, hockey. The lingering thought from that world cup was a very minor concession – soccer wasn't quite as sissy as we thought, but it was still pretty sissy. Four years later, the All Whites failed to qualify for the Mexico World Cup. A year after that, the All-Blacks won the inaugural Rugby World Cup, played on New Zealand soil.

Once again we were certain that rugby was the best game in the world and we had a shiny gold cup to prove that we were the best at it; a pretty big deal for a country with a population of a little more than 3 million at the time.

As far as playing the game is concerned, the words of ex- All Black and academic Chris Laidlaw ring true: 'We may be small, isolated, lonely and not very confident, but by God we bow to nobody when it comes to rugby.'

It's right about now that I would love to tell you that, throughout this time I stayed true to football, kept playing it to the chagrin of parents and peers, my childhood support of Liverpool enough to pull me through a teenage gauntlet of sneers, jeers and derision from my cauliflower-eared compatriots. That the essence of true manhood was not *going with* but *cutting against* the grain and thus, more circular than oval.

Alas, dear reader, I did not. In fact, not only was 1987 the year the All Blacks cemented their rugby supremacy, it was also the year I turned my back on football. I stopped playing it every Saturday, stopped watching every Sunday, pushed my All Whites biscuit tin and Roy of the Rovers book

(James Murphy said I could have it once he realised he wasn't getting it back) to the dusty depths of my wardrobe. I even, yes, consider it my Judas moment - stopped supporting Liverpool.

Now before you throw this book down in disgust and label me a phony bastard, a football *poseur*, I beg you, please hear me out.

Fast forward three years to a very cringe-worthy moment in my mid-adolescence. I'm lying in an upstairs bed of a two story house in the rural town of Bowral, New South Wales, Australia. In the single bed next to mine is a boy (this is not what you think) called Hamish Monk, another member of the St Andrews College First Fifteen rugby touring squad, and with whom I've been billeted.

I'm into my third year of playing rugby and am one of the youngest members in a squad of twenty. My physical development at the age of fifteen means I'm fast and coordinated enough to be a back, but my true strength is that I possess the ability to fell the biggest bugger on the paddock with the bonus of hurting him in the process. But for all my tough guy status I'm about to be undone by a single sentence downstairs.

Around the dinner table of the nice Australian family who are giving Hamish and I a roof over our heads are Hamish's parents (sheep farmers from Northern Canterbury), my mum, and her partner Gary, who also happens to be the forwards coach of our team. From upstairs, Hamish and I can hear the conversation clearly. The parents are talking about their kids. Mum's talking me up, which is a source of embarrassment in itself until the Australian father takes it to a whole new level by asking her why I became a rugby player.
Mum answers: 'He wants to be a man.'

Hamish Monk squeals and rolls about on his bed: 'Little Glenn wants to be a man! Little Glenn wants to be a man!' He points at me as if there's someone in the room unaware of my ridicule. He doesn't cease teasing me until I deliver the squealing farm boy a very decisive dead arm. The simpleton shuts up, but the damage has been done. Teenage armour has been pierced. Steel plates of staunchness protecting the hormone-fuelled sensitivity within have come unstuck and are lying dented and diminished on the floor between us. My mother's comment has rendered me powerless and the reason it's so lethal is because it's true. Mum was right. All teenage players of rugby want to be big, strong men – rugged as hell and rearing to go. They even like to pretend they already are, until mum blows the façade.

Part 3

So now you know: I'm not worthy. But thanks to the passing of a small plot of trees I have pages to explain.

Please pause for a moment and imagine a long bow sliding its way very slowly across the strings of an old violin. The strokes of the bow create a sound that is solemn and mournful and provide the perfect accompaniment to the sad, sad story that was this boy's shift from round ball to oval, from All White to All Black, and from the mighty red of Liverpool to the red and black of the Canterbury Rugby Team.

I was about eight when, after all the anger, deceit, and buggery bollocks crap that leads to your parents' divorce, my father left home for good.
My brother Lyndon (eight years my senior) went flatting soon after, so it was down to just me and Mum.

Time to step up. According to my Uncle Darryl, my main priority now was to look after Mum. The job came with my very own gun. I lobbied for a .22, but ended up with an air rifle. It would prove sufficient.

We lived on the rural outskirts of the city; our land partially bordered by a meandering creek and a long busy road into town. Even when Dad was still there, he'd had two cars stolen right beside the house, just outside the living room where we watched TV. Once he was gone it felt like the eyes of the wicked world had spotted new prey. Foot prints in the frosted lawn come morning. Silhouettes (often imagined, I'll admit) moving in front of my window at night. Things going bump and me bolt upright in bed, clutching my rifle, trying to discern whether that particular noise – that shuffle, that stomp – was human or horse.

One night, it was human.

It was late. The bastard was bold enough to try the handle of a door down the side of the house.

This was the moment I'd been waiting for. I grabbed my gun – already loaded – and headed down the hallway. Mum got up as well. The commotion from inside must've startled him. By the time I unlocked the door I could hear someone sprinting down the driveway. Still in pyjamas I bounded down steps and fired half a dozen pellets down the sixty metres of darkness to the road. Did I get him? Almost certainly not. Still, it didn't stop me fantasising that somewhere, maybe under a hedge or perhaps in some getaway car heading back to the city, there was a furious prowler picking pellets from his arse.

Sure enough, over the next couple of years my BMX, the ten-speed which replaced it, and a lawn mower were all stolen from the garage. But the house itself was never invaded.

I was bitter over the bikes but, considering all the baddies out there, I felt like I was holding my own.

Nevertheless, the threat remained.

So when I wasn't at school, reading books, watching TV or kicking a ball, it was all press-ups and bar bells in the mirror. My purpose? To become seriously unfuckable like the two men most proficient at defending what was theirs: Schwarzenegger and Stallone. I imagined bad guys storming the house and me shooting and beating up every last one of them like Arnie did in Commando. When I needed stealth outdoors I summoned Stallone, my hunting skills wreaking havoc on the local fauna, my element of surprise proving fatal to stupid imaginary soldiers. But just as the conflicted Rambo swung between victim and predator, I too took a lean to the dark side.

It started with a shovel and a pile of shit. One of my jobs on the farm was to scoop the horse dung that accumulated in the paddocks into a wheelbarrow before adding it to the manure heap. Once the manure was nice and steaming, we bagged it in kleensacks to sell at the front gate. Mum discouraged me from wasting my time waiting for customers (she said I had jobs to do, but I'm sure she just didn't like the look), so we converted an ice cream container to use as an honesty box instead. When it became apparent that not all of our customers were taking the purpose of the honesty box seriously, I would hide half way up a leafy silver birch along from the manure stall and wait. A pair of binoculars enabled a decent look. If I spotted anyone loading their boot and neglecting to slot the full $1 per bag into the box, he or she paid for it with as many pellets as I could cock, load, and shoot at the roof of their precious car while it was still in range. Some foolishly pulled over after the clang of the first ricochet. Another shot would normally send them on their way. But if they got out looking angry, I held my breath and remained very still. Even Rambo wouldn't shoot a man over manure.

Nevertheless there was a thrilling empowerment to be gained from applying my own form of justice. So much so, I took to leaving the binoculars in the house. Without them, I had to more or less guess if the customer had paid the full dollar. I nearly always guessed no. I knew it was wrong. Out of every five customers perhaps only one failed to pay and therefore the law of averages suggests that it was mainly innocents being pelleted.

After every 'watch' I made my way surreptitiously (Rambo stealth again) to the bridge that bestrode the creek a few hundred metres from our property. I hid the rifle in a wall cavity under the arch, just in case the police cottoned on to my antics and came searching for the gun. By doing this, my tracks were covered. Catch me if you can. At eleven years of age, I was the ruler of my domain.

Unfortunately, the rest of the world wasn't so convinced. Much like Liverpool in recent seasons, my form was a little erratic away from home. Mostly I played within myself – a right little sulk.

When I was ten Mum began her relationship with Gary. Apart from owning a pizza factory, Gary was the coach of the Sydenham Rugby Club senior team. By all accounts he was an excellent coach and it was via Gary that I first heard the Maori word, 'mana.' It says something about the importance of this word that it was widely understood and used even in a white conservative town such as Christchurch in the eighties. Gary used it to describe certain players in his team, the ones who never shirked responsibility, 'put their bodies on the line', excelled in all facets of the game, and thus gained the kind of respect that made them natural leaders. But mana wasn't just about authority, influence, and prestige – the trick was not to let it go to your head. I took note of the guys Gary was talking about, both on the field and in the club rooms after the game. They had a different way about them. It's true that you don't need to play rugby to have mana, but to me, and no doubt countless other New Zealanders, back then the two were synonymous. For a kid who tended to regard adults in general as strange and unsavoury, the idea of attaining mana had a certain appeal. By having mana you were spared from that incessant adult eagerness to please or to discriminate. People respected you. You were on a different level, you were cool, you were a no worries mate, a sweet as, a she'll be right. And unlike all the slobber mouths, you could even hold your piss.

(Out of all the rugby players with mana, the man who seemed to have the most when I was growing up was the indomitable All-Black No.8, Wayne 'Buck' Shelford. Widely respected and charismatic as a bull, Buck was an almighty Maori warrior who took the All Black haka to new levels, tackled like a fiend and always made ground with the ball in hand. But what really launched Buck to the top of the mana pops was his decision to play on after

having four teeth smashed out during a game in France. Pretty impressive, don't you think? Imagine spitting out four teeth and deciding, oh well, better get back out there. But wait, there's more. At the bottom of the same ruck some Frenchie ran the sprigs of his boot along Buck's nether regions and tore open his scrotum. Agh! They did what? You read true, no need to go back: they ripped open his scrotum. Ow! It doesn't get any better the second time, does it?

So Buck played on and only noticed in the changing room afterwards that one half of his sacred pair was dangling 5 inches south of the other. Gulp. Not only did he play in nearly every game to win the world cup the following year, he also produced several healthy offspring. Respect.)

It's no secret that kids from broken homes tend to have a greater need for getting to the bottom of things. Parents are acting in ways they don't understand, so it's only natural to search their world for clues to what's going on a little more stringently than kids from happy homes.

And, like any kid, my most effective tool in getting to the bottom of things was my ability to eavesdrop. If you see me as an adult you'll notice that my ears, although thankfully quite flat to my head, are quite large. If they veered a few more degrees I'd be a regular wing nut, a cumbersome dumbo with his big fleshy hearing organs flapping around in the breeze. They're pointed near the top as well. It's as if there's an extra antenna trying to protrude from each ear for better detection. And while some may say it's down to genetics, I wouldn't be surprised to hear a study that claimed the ears of people from broken homes are larger than average on account of all that listening in.

It was while eavesdropping on Gary and a friend one night when Mum and I were staying at his South Brighton house that I overheard *the sentence* that explained everything. As mentioned, the world wasn't convinced I was an all-action hero in the making. Instead, they often looked at me with eyes of pity, as though there was something actually wrong with me, which kind of left me with an impending sense of doom without knowing what an impending sense of doom actually was.

On the night all was revealed I was in bed, presumed asleep.

But as any young professional eavesdropper will know, it's late at night when adults reveal the stuff worth hearing; completely unaware how loud their words slosh about and slip from their mouths.

Gary was having a few beers in the spa pool with a mate when my little nodule antennas detected the waves of my uttered name. They'd been talking about Gary's son Brad until then, and as was usual, the conversation was centered on rugby. Brad's prospects were good, and while he had limited speed due to a gammy hip, he had the right physique to continue playing throughout high school in the position of prop – not a glamorous position by any stretch of the imagination but respected even more so because of it: to play prop you had to be 'hard'.

When the conversation turned to me I sat up in bed and cocked an ear towards the open window. The question was whether I had it in me to give up the sissy sport and choose to play rugby. Wally asked the question of Gary and, as was Wally's tendency, answered it himself: 'He'll never play - not tough enough.' Gulp. The verdict was in: not tough enough. I'd heard similar claims before, but not so loud and clear. This was irrefutable. I'd been dismissed. It explained what was behind all those pitying eyes. Unbelievably, inconceivably, the world had me pegged as a mummy's boy – sheltered and timid, limp-wristed and lame, a not-cut-out-to-make-it little Nancy pants. No mana for me, not a chance. I was doomed.

It was by no small coincidence that I was soon enrolled at St Andrew's College, a strict, disciplined private school where rugby was taken very seriously indeed. 1st XV members were paraded in assemblies like heroes, and to a third former or 'turd' such as I, these hairy, big-shouldered boys really did look like men. Classes were stopped on the afternoons of mid-week fixtures against rival schools so we could gather and support the team with

700-strong student hakas. There was the pomp of pre-game bag pipes before packed stands that included parents and old boys. After the respective teams performed their own hakas the whistle blew for what would often be a highly charged and impassioned spectacle. Meanwhile, on some distant field the school's 1st 11 Soccer team played to a crowd of say, ten, coaches and subs included. Still, to this day, I have no idea if they were even very good. For a kid with a chip on his shoulder, rugby was the way.

I began proving the Wally's of this world wrong by playing for the U14 team. We won the competition and I gained my rugby wings through my said ability to tackle. The key to this wasn't so much technique but the absence of fear. I'd seen that even the best players had a tendency to flinch before making a tackle, so it seemed obvious that as long as I could throw myself at someone without fear of self-harm everything would be fine, I'd be the best tackler on the team.

The same went for brawling. You simply went in with maximum aggression and without fear of consequences. Fearlessness and stupidity are often blurred, but whichever was the case for me, it worked. A few successful street fights against marauding rival school gangs later, and I gained something of a reputation. Friends much smaller (and bigger) than me sought my protection. I was even paid to be present at house parties to take care of any trouble.

As far as rugby was concerned, I made the 1st XV for the Australian tour and kept playing right through school, even had a season at club level in a team that took out the Canterbury U21 competition.

But for a teenager who was fast discovering the many satisfactions of the weird and wonderful, the conservative institution of rugby was never a good fit. I simply couldn't give myself over to it as much as the school wanted me to. The deputy rector even offered to 'take care of my marks' and turn a blind eye to my truancy issues just as long as I played good rugby. The school relied on the symbolism of a strong 1st XV to impress the rich parents of potential students. At times you could be forgiven for thinking that nearly everything the school encompassed was geared solely for rugby, that everything else was just a way to fill in time until we played the next game. But instead of baulking at the offer, I said, 'Sure. No problem,' and promptly made my way from his office to go make the most of my new-found impunity.

When I wasn't cruising the silent streets of Christchurch or smoking rollies with friends down at 'durry bridge', I cut afternoon classes to meet up with my girlfriend, returning to school just in time for rugby practice, thoroughly and happily shagged.

My rugby form naturally suffered but that wasn't the form I really cared about. Compared to an afternoon with a beautiful girl with a bad reputation, trotting around a paddock with 14 other guys seemed pointless. It didn't help that many of my team mates harboured disturbing misogynistic streaks and were more inclined to sleep with a pile of their own puke than a female. They were openly offended by anything that wasn't within the narrow confines of their moleskin pants, stiff-collared shirt and *Achy Breaky Heart* existence.

If you had long hair (and you weren't Billy Ray Cyrus), you were a faggot. If a girl ventured to wear anything other than moleskins and Airtecs (making it difficult to separate the farm boys from the farm girls) she was deemed a slut. And if you listened to music by people they considered 'alternative', then you were a 'try hard.'

Because I was a rugby player whose idea of looking cool wasn't so much about looking like I was off to the barn dance, and because I was into the likes of David Bowie, the Velvet Underground, and early Red Hot Chili Peppers, I was one of the biggest try hards of them all. My friends were all try hards as well; our identities were in part formed by how much we hated their narrow-minded crap. The ruggaheads (or scrummies as we alternately called them) were largely made up of the school's boarders, the try hards being the day boys – students who commuted from home. According to the scrummies, 'day boys' were 'gay boys'. Kind of ironic considering the boarding house was awash with rumours of bastardisation, including the sexual punishments of younger boarders. Non-scrummie boarders lived in fear of what was being committed and subsequently hushed up within the boarding house walls. The scrummies were so seriously foul we avoided being downwind from them. The message was loud and clear: staunch guys had problems.

I gave up on rugby as my vehicle for mana. Respect from ruggaheads was both unattainable and undesirable.

In 2005, Waikato University lecturer Dr Richard Pringle wrote an award-winning thesis called 'Doing the damage? An examination of masculinities and men's rugby experiences of pain, fear and pleasure.'

Having held in-depth interviews with fourteen kiwi males who'd, perhaps unavoidably, been involved with rugby from a young age, Dr Pringle examined how the national game had influenced their understanding of what it means to be a man.

The common perception was that rugby culture reinforced ideas that, in order to be a man, you needed to be tough, aggressive and unemotional – an attitude the subjects disliked yet were hesitant to openly question around peers. Some saw the culture as being stuck in the 1950s while others regarded it as simply immature, the dominion of mere boys.

Dr Pringle's idea for the thesis came from overseas research which revealed that '…heavy contact sports like ice hockey and American football helped produce a problematic form of masculinity. Problematic because they encouraged men to ignore pain, to be hyper-competitive, to drink a lot of alcohol, to think of their bodies as a 'weapon' or object.'

They were more likely to be involved in violence off the field and in rape and sexual assault cases, more likely to hold sexist and homophobic attitudes, and four times more likely to commit suicide, suffer from heart disease, alcoholism, and drug addiction. They were also more likely to die in road deaths or be imprisoned.

Yet despite their feelings towards this pervasive rugby culture, the men Dr Pringle interviewed still followed the game.

And I was no different. The game itself is a good one, especially when the All Black's are on song. But it's kind of like Gandhi's call on liking Christ but not liking Christians; just replace the words *Christ* with *rugby* and *Christians* with *ruggaheads*.

I was never foolish enough to think that football didn't contain its own degree of 'problematic masculinities'. And probably the thing I 'tried hard' at most was to impose my own brand of staunchness on the world around me. Much like my teenage country, I was desperate for recognition from those of whom I was most critical. But once the rugby mindset was shed, I was on my way to realising that by not having staunchness as its dominant characteristic, football had more to offer.

The 1998 FIFA World Cup was like a sign post to home.

Compared to rugby players, footballers looked like they could be cool arse DJs or crazy arse rock stars, and the crowds in turn had an exuberance and vibrancy more akin to concerts than sporting events. The women spotted in the crowd (all of them beautiful) were just as excited as the men. And why wouldn't they be?

Not only did the players look cool, but their talent was unmistakable: from the energy and dynamism of the Brazilian Ronaldo, to the style and elegance of the Frenchman Zidane, to the lightning excitement of the Liverpool striker Michael Owen (who, if I'm to be accurate in my reporting, was in appearance more cheeky choirboy than wild rock star.)

Even from the smoky confines of a Christchurch flat where my friends and I shared couches and spliffs, it felt, it seemed, it appeared that each goal really did have an impact on the world at that time. Maybe that was the pot talking, my heart aflutter with that whole 'everything's connected' buzz, where singular events morph into groovy aspects of the far-out whole so that everything seems more significant than it really is.

Whatever, man. Curiosity was piqued.

After the world cup I can recall watching sports items of Owen scoring time and time again for Liverpool along with the cheeky Robbie Fowler. The latter's goal celebration of snorting the sideline in response to the Everton fans taunting him about being a cokehead setting our flat alight with laughter. Fowler's irreverence reminded me of Liverpool's 1980s goalkeeper, Bruce 'the Clown Prince' Grobbelaar, who will always be remembered for his wobbly-kneed antics during a penalty shootout against Roma in the 1984 European Cup Final. Grobbelaar's stumbling 'spaghetti legs' routine in goal put off the Italian penalty takers; Liverpool won the shootout quite comfortably, thanks to his inspired absurdity: a cigar and glasses to go with his big hair and moustache and *Voila!*: an athletic Groucho Marx.

Yes, glimpses of these new Liverpool players – sportsmen with actual personalities – sparked links within my misty cortex to a time long ago: a time of red success and parallel universes.

But the big jump from watching the odd news highlight to sacrificing my sleeping hours to football was yet to come. The catalyst for this progression was the perfect storm of my friend Joseph, an old house in the seedy streets of East Christchurch, and a bona fide fanatic, Alex.

Even before we met I'd heard plenty about the legend of Alex – a complex character to say the least. I'd seen him at the odd night club and once or twice during the day walking around town with his fashion designer girlfriend. Stories of this forty-something-year-old guy who only ever wore black (unless he was sporting an England football shirt), who grew and sold pot (yet despised those who called him a drug dealer), and who would hire a motel room so he and a bunch of friends could watch football all night, left Joseph and Craig giggling for days.

The more I heard about the guy the more I felt he was someone I needed to meet. It took an age of haranguing Joseph until he felt the time was right. Joseph had already tried to include our friend Bob into Alex's fold, which hadn't gone well. Bob – a few years earlier – had not only slept with Joseph's girlfriend but also managed to burn down the house in which he'd done his dirty deed, a three bedroom weatherboard Joseph rented near the country town of Cheviot. Joseph had forgiven Bob far too easily in an attempt to maintain a degree of spirituality above such corporeal infringements. Alex, however, had a strong moral code and was as protective of Joseph as he might've been a little brother. The only way Bob could hope to impress Alex was by recognizing this and knowing his place.

But Bob's eccentric streak – or whatever it was that allowed him to justify first, the banging, and second, the burning – came with little sensibility. He enraged Alex by recalling that the most amazing thing about burning down Joseph's house was the conversation he'd had with a cow afterwards. Bob narrowly escaped a beating thanks to the calming effect of Joseph, who avoided any nastiness by stalling Alex just in time for Bob to exit stage right. Yup, around Alex, tact was paramount. One mistimed or misconstrued word about his dealing, his late judicial father, or the restraining order placed on him by his ex-girlfriend after he'd attacked the DJ she was seeing on the side and you'd soon see why the man was attending anger management courses on the insistence of the crown.

It was during the European Championship 2000 when Joseph took me to the dilapidated two story house where Alex was more or less residing over the duration of the tournament. The wooden structure, with its peeled paint and rotting timber, was divided into two flats, one of which was being rented by a friend of Alex's, an unhygienic chef called Seb. Alex had set up Sky Sports while using a spare room to store his current stash. With Joseph leading the way, we let ourselves in to a high-ceilinged living room where the tiered seating of lumpy couches and threadbare chairs had been set up to look down on the TV. Sitting atop a window sill was an official Champions League ball partially encased in its colourful packaging. A tournament chart encircled with football-related articles and posters covered a wall, and like a patient game of chess on a corner table there was a meticulously put together

Lego football game, complete with little Lego stands and little Lego floodlights. The room's stand out feature, however, was a 1982 All White FIFA World Cup biscuit tin. I was drawn to it. What a minter! The same as my own from childhood yet looking like it had been purchased just days ago – still shiny and without a scratch, the perfect showpiece on top of the television, lest we forget. *Two whole goals! Two whole goals!*

We caught Alex mid-flight in conversation but he was up in a flash, greeting Joseph with an exuberance of hugs and smiles and me with a welcoming grin. He bounced behind Joseph and actually massaged his shoulders while he was still standing. He then dusted off a chair, sat him down, made sure he was comfortable and fussed over him like a doting grandma. For ten or so minutes he hopped from foot to foot, highlighting everything he liked about Joseph – from his cheerful hobbit-like mannerisms, to his wheezy nasal laugh which he mimicked perfectly, and often. Joseph beamed back at the room and after every compliment, impersonation, and gentle ribbing, responded with a twee sounding 'Thank you, Alexander,' which sent Alex into hysterics.

When he exhausted his affection for Joseph, the stream of energy and words diverted to Seb – the gawky bespectacled chef visibly growing in stature with every antic, quote and attribute Alex chose to share. Then stories of various friends (and enemies) beyond the modest walls of Seb's flat, silly and hilarious stories which left you feeling like you'd gained intimate knowledge of a whole new society.

The subject would then shift with dizzying speed from an outlandish experience 'on a belly full of pills', to the prostitutes he'd paid to accompany him to a Rod Stewart concert. And just when it seemed it was about to get smutty he'd pull it back and wax philosophical about the day mankind finds all the missing socks being the day we discover the meaning of life, or about how much better off the world would be if Henry Kissinger had carried deflated soccer balls in that little black briefcase of his – ready to pump up and kick around with uptight heads of state as a way to relieve the tension of mediation.

He crafted his stories in a way that turned everyone he talked about into harbingers of good or evil bounding through the movies of their own lives. But it didn't take long to realise it was Alex who was in fact bounding through their lives, sprinkling his vivacious fairy dust on ordinary people to make them feel and seem better than they probably were.

On that first night he barely even asked how I was going but I could tell that, like all great raconteurs, he was secretly sizing me up, gaining all the information he needed from my reactions to his ways. It would take nearly a year of knowing him before we would interact in a temperate manner about matters close to the heart; namely, our trials and tribulations with members of the fairer sex. But he did, at least, ask me one important question on that first night.

He asked me who I supported.

'Liverpool,' I said without hesitation. After so many years of consigning myself to the football wilderness, I was amazed at how easily 'Liv-uh-pool' rolled off my tongue. I could've said any team that popped into my head. I could've gone for the highflying Arsenal or the ultra-successful United, but my default setting, I'm so very proud to say, was Liverpool.

'I could tell there was something I liked about you,' said Alex, as if I'd made his night. With that he launched into his childhood infatuation with Kenny Dalglish, recalling the Liverpool forward's brilliance at shielding the ball, the speed of his turns and the blistering shots that left goalkeepers gawping, cemented to the spot as the ball flew beyond them into the net. 'When Kenny scored in the '78 European Cup Final I wrote a letter that just about offered to have sex with him – I honestly did! Did I strop my willy that night - did I what!' *I* laughed out loud. *He* laughed out loud. I still have no idea if he was joking. He said that, on the morning Dalglish last won the first division as Liverpool's manager in 1990, he took a framed photo of him out to a cafe, propped it up on the table and proceeded to order it coffee and breakfast to the bewilderment of the waitress.

Feeling like I'd never strayed, I mentioned how disappointing it was that Joseph was a Man U supporter. As with anything else, Alex didn't hold back: 'I hate those United cunts. I'll never forget the '77 FA Cup Final when Liverpool had to wear those white uniforms that made them look gay. I remember a guy at my school boasting after United beat them. I couldn't help myself; I jumped on him – people had to pull me off! I wanted to rip his guts out and feed the pieces to passing geese!'

He then surprised me with an admission that his support for the reds was no more. Perhaps unsurprisingly, he chose to focus his fanaticism elsewhere when Dalglish quit as Liverpool's manager due to emotional strain in 1991. Dalglish had been with Liverpool for thirteen years. In that time he'd experienced a series of outrageous highs by capturing 8 first division titles, 3 European Cups and 2 FA Cups. It all ended, however, with the horrific low of the Hillsborough disaster and its aftermath. Dalglish felt an admirable sense of obligation towards the families of the 96 victims, and gave himself over in his attempts to help their grieving as he visited every bereaved family and attended every funeral he could. Apparently, Alex felt Dalglish's pain and had to retire his own support for Liverpool due to exhaustion. The club of utter triumph and tragedy wore him out to the point where he was unable to fully support them or any other club since.

Yet his love of watching the game eclipsed that of any other sports fan I've known. Alex watched football with an intensity which could've been channeled directly from the crowd. He over-identified with the players of the team he liked and vilified those he didn't. As with people he knew, he gave the players hilarious catchphrases and over the top personas, and the more you watched the more they seemed to play up to the ridiculous caricatures. With Alex, watching football was like plugging in to a dazzling array of emotions – the drama, the athleticism, the play acting, the swings of fortune and the prevalence of the improbable – football had it all. What a strange sensation it was to feel so alive while sitting on a couch fully dressed!

As I spent more time with Alex, I soon gained contempt for anyone who simply labelled him a drug dealer. The only thing he got me hooked on was football, and over the next couple of seasons we would turn up to Seb's dark smelly house before dawn like members of an underground resistance group meeting incognito to monitor and discuss all the new developments in European football. As when I was a kid, it felt like we were privy to something special, something entirely worth losing sleep over.

Even though Alex couldn't align with any club, he made up for it by investing his considerable energy into supporting England. That's right, En-ger-land. The national side more commonly known as 'that pack of over-paid wankers' or the 'useless bunch of tossers' who turn up to the odd international tournament only to astound their harshest critics by achieving a plodding array of miserable new lows. Although we were all descended from British settlers who made their way to our Maori-inhabited lands in the 19th century, we generally gave scant regard to our ties to the motherland. We lived in a city the colonisers designed as 'a better England' yet we were all very much Pakeha New Zealanders, liked to think of ourselves as easygoing, good natured outdoorsy types of intellectual curiosity, cultural thirst and sporting prowess - everything the blundering British toff or the podgy whingeing Pom was not. Neither Alex, Joseph nor I had even been there. Yet Alex's passion for the English side was heartfelt, fierce, and so utterly infectious that we all felt compelled to jump aboard his bulldog bandwagon and ride it as far we could. When it came to football, England was our collective link to the round ball world. When, in 2001, they beat Germany 5-1 in a World Cup qualifier we went berserk and truly believed we'd witnessed something fantastic, the English display of swift attacking football surely set to conquer all, come next year's World Cup. Without the slightest inclination that the game against Germany would be England's head and shoulders highlight of the whole bloody decade we released Alex's $150 Official Champions League ball from its packaging and thrashed it across the undulating surface of Seb's expansive backyard. It was a full time ritual - getting off the couch for a frantic game of 'headers and crosses' as soon as the first light of day would allow. We played rain, hail or shine and always with bare feet. Aside from good fun, it was our way of offsetting the gnawing guilt of not having real jobs and being stoned and happy instead of mainstream and miserable about having to go to work. And what better way to start the day when you're unemployed than kick the shit out of something expensive?

Alex's seasonal compulsion of forking out big money on soccer balls stretched back to when he saved the pocket money he earned from mowing lawns and cleaning cars at the age of five to pay for an authentic Mitre Soccer ball manufactured in the UK. Once purchased and sent to New Zealand by a family friend living in London, the ball was played with almost constantly, save for the times when Alex would clean it until it was shiny enough to place on the kitchen table next to a photo of Kevin Keegen (Dalglish's predecessor) posing with a Mitre ball of his own.

As it turned out, the way that Champions League ball circa 2001 flew from our numb red feet to skip across the dew-wet grass (or hard white frost) of early morning, you really did believe it was worth all that cash.

And as we crossed it in and blasted it on the volley against a wooden fence that would be in pieces within months, we all secretly hoped we were doing so in the fashion of our favourite footballer at the time. For Alex, it was Alan Shearer; for Joseph it was probably David Beckham; for Craig, it was Zinedine Zidane; and for Seb, I'm not quite sure who it was – Seb and I were never that close. But for me, it was a new player who'd emerged from the Liverpool production line. Right from the start – when he was just a thin, young, street cat streak of raw talent you could tell Steven Gerrard was a class competitor. And with his ascendancy to become the most important

Liverpool player since Dalglish my support for the Merseysiders increased exponentially.

Under the French manager, Gerard Houllier, Liverpool were not only playing well, they had the silverware to show for it. In 2001 they completed a unique treble by winning The League Cup, the FA Cup, and the UEFA Cup with a typical blend of late great goals and high old drama.

But it was the winning of the latter which took me to the point of no return, unearthing something inside me, a renewed awareness of a valuable truth.

For whatever reasons, the final of the Uefa Cup in 2001 against Alaves had somehow slipped under the radar. To think of ever missing a cup final involving Liverpool now seems inconceivable. But back then, while I was enjoying my rediscovery of the club, it was at a level I was still able to keep at arm's length, wary of its potential to distract me from what I then considered more meaningful pursuits.

When I turned up to my grandmother Mo's place to do her gardening on a brisk morning in June, I couldn't help but notice delayed TV coverage of the final, about to kick off. Mo was a great watcher of sport; whether rugby, cricket, golf or tennis, she would sit regally in her chair – its fake fur throw and raised platform giving it a throne-like appearance. A marble-topped side table beside it ensured she was in reach of the four things that got her through the day: a pack of cigarettes, a glass ashtray, a well-thumbed TV guide, and a cup of tea – enthusiastically replaced at 5 p.m. with a glass of beer or a whiskey.

It's fair to say that old Mo, who hated being referred to as 'nana' or 'grandma', transcended her grand maternal role and was easily one of my best friends. Mo had gained what seems to me the only real benefit of old age – a sense of the things that really matter, and her home, with its reassuring familiarity and its happy garden (which included a glasshouse of unbeatable tomatoes) was something of a sanctuary, an easy enough distance on the outskirts of Christchurch for me to come over and help out – or even just hang out – a few times a week.

Mo's life had been one of making ends meet – raising five children on the money from the family market garden to supplement whatever building-related job my late grandfather Ted had going at the time. Thirty years ago he'd worked at the sawmill across the road. But recently the mill and its yard had been subdivided and replaced with rows of charm-free homes. Mo had experienced some great and some not so great neighbours over the years, but the new lot were more inclined to ignore her, seemingly indifferent to the wisdom and welfare of an old lady.

We enjoyed each other's company, and the more open I was about my views on everything from drugs to death the better our conversations flowed. She indulged me at any given opportunity, and on this particular morning she was more than happy for me to delay getting stuck into the garden until after the game.

Once comfortable, we soon found ourselves enthralled in a high scoring contest. Liverpool led throughout the game with fine counterattacking goals, only for Alaves to claw back and level it in the latter stages. Liverpool then reversed the momentum of Alaves' late charge to emerge victorious in extra time, a golden goal to make the final score 5-4. After such a satisfactory conclusion we finally got to exhale, flopping back in our respective chairs as though we'd both been through the proverbial wringer. Mo asked me if Liverpool's games were always like this.

'Always,' I said, grinning back at her. And then, as if the game itself wasn't enough, the team spontaneously sang with the crowd as though they were belting out the finale of their own Broadway musical.

I already loved that Liverpool's anthem was You'll Never Walk Alone, the soulful touch it bestowed in both victory and defeat. But after the final against Alaves, YNWA was sung as though its message was not only crucial to everything that had led to this point, but everything beyond it as well. The sight of the players embraced in a line and singing their hearts out with their faithful fans caught the back of my throat.

'There's something special going on there,' said Mo, fishing for a handkerchief up the sleeve of her cardigan. She was right. Neither of us had seen anything like it before. With this one unified act of grace, Liverpool transcended the bounds of a mere football club. Neither of us was religious but here we were, glued to the box on a wintry working day, having what felt like a religious experience – no televangelist required. To steal a line from the American writer, George Saunders, it was as if we were 'sensing the eternal in the ephemeral' via a theme of hope to which time is irrelevant and to which the words 'belief', 'god', and 'heaven' seemed blissfully unnecessary. Just hope. Hope is all.

From that day on Mo followed Liverpool. When we talked on the phone after I'd moved from Christchurch up to Auckland she often made a point of letting me know she'd been watching. The fact that not all Liverpool's games end in golden goal victories and spontaneous player/fan sing-a-longs didn't even deter her. She got it. So did I.

When she passed away in 2004 (just shy of her 90th birthday) I flew down to be with Mum and Lyndon and do what I could to help with the arrangements. Naturally we were gutted, but we knew we'd done our best – Mum especially – to ensure a quality of life throughout her final years.

But when Mum and I went to the funeral home and I suggested that the congregation should sing You'll Never Walk Alone, the funeral director shook his head and said it wasn't a good idea. They'd had it before. People find it too hard to sing, he said. Makes them feel awkward.

I was tempted to push the matter, state authoritatively that *this* Christchurch congregation would be different, that we would raise the roof with a heartfelt rendition to shame the apathetic bastards before us. Surely, once the singing began, people would recognise the song's power, that despite the horrible reality of Mo lying breathless in her wooden box there was still hope – there is always hope, and it's hope that gives the big absurdity its beauty, makes the pointless mystery somehow bearable.

Then again, maybe not. Our extended family was disjointed to say the least. Pettiness and resentment simmered away beneath a gruff exterior. Too much and too little going on to lose ourselves in song, especially one that requires a bit of effort. The funeral director was right. It wasn't a good idea.

Thankfully, Mo and I wouldn't need them. As long as Liverpool remain healthy, as long as they sing true, they help keep bonds like ours very much alive.

5. Liverpool v Newcastle

Saturday 8th of March had good luck written all over it.

I even had the gall to turn up to Anfield for Liverpool's game against Newcastle without a ticket. I'll admit to some quiet desperation as I wandered up and down Walton Breck Rd looking for a seller, but I needn't have worried.

As time ticked precariously close to kick off, the pale, narrow face of Tony the Tout picked me from the loiterers. 'Looking for a ticket, mate?'

'Maybe,' I said, playing hard to get. He ushered me across the street to the far side of a parked car, a discreet distance from a couple of policemen standing next to the Shankly Gates. Upon handing over the princely sum of seventy quid, I strained to find the tone of someone who shouldn't be trifled with.

'This the real thing?' I said. Tony the Tout made that expression you see in gangster movies, the one where the crim winces at the implication his dealings are anything less than virtuous.

'No worries mate, no worries,' he said, patting my arm. He wore a black leather jacket with a hood over the collar. His build was light and wispy – the perfect build for bolting down laneways and scaling wire fences. As he spoke, his wheeler-dealer eyes scanned passing faces. He glanced over his shoulder and passed me the ticket. I inspected it like I knew a thing or two, nodded my approval, shook Tony's hand, and took off through the gates towards the turnstiles.

As luck would have it, I got in without a hitch. Annoyed at having missed YNWA, but glad to be back inside Anfield and heading up the stairs of the Kop, I was pleased at how natural it felt to be doing so. Tony the Tout was all right. It wasn't quite the seat I'd had against West Ham (right up the back as opposed to right down the front), but my elevated position provided a concentrated view over the heads of Liverpool's most passionate. The field of perfect green stretched from the base of the terrace in the shape of a trapezium, the other stands cut from sight by the framing effect of the overhang roof and steel walls. It was pure, unadulterated Kop.

The game had an added interest in that Newcastle's manager was Liverpool's legendary goal scorer of the early seventies, Kevin Keagen, while Michael Owen had recently signed as 'the toon's' striker. Even though he was in the wrong colours, just seeing Owen in the flesh at Anfield was a buzz. It might even be nice to see him score, as long as Newcastle lost. As it was, Liverpool's ex-glory boys didn't get a look in. Despite the current boardroom disputes, the reds played the game with a zest that defied the shoddy state of affairs behind the scenes.

The first goal, I don't mind saying, was all lucky charm; a freak rebound saw the ball loop beyond Newcastle's keeper and into the goal. With the bounce of good fortune Liverpool seized the initiative. When a Newcastle clearance found the head of Xabi Alonso deep in Liverpool's half, he sent it up field to Torres who headed it in the path of Gerrard. With a trademark surge, Stevie G nodded it twice on the move before executing a diagonal pass that dissected defenders and rolled sumptuously towards the edge of the penalty box for the Spanish striker to run onto. The keeper rushed from his goalmouth in an attempt to narrow the angle of what would surely be a first time strike. But in a moment that would bewilder everyone but himself, the flying Fernando let the ball run. Just when it seemed a goal-scoring opportunity had been lost he finished a move that – to my knowledge – has only been attempted at the highest level by the great Pele. After fooling the keeper into thinking he'd have to block the shot, Torres shimmied to his right. With the keeper unable to adjust in time (and in that moment of being unable to adjust surely wishing he'd just pounced on the ball) the swerving Fernando was around him without even touching the ball, and with the goal at his mercy. He slid feet first to land the deadly strike and did the one thing Pele failed to do in the same position three decades prior. He scored. Pele had hit the post.

As the Liverpool crowd sang about the boy from sunny Spain, Torres returned his captain's favour in the second half with a dinky little pass that left Gerrard with the simple (simple!) task of chipping the hapless keeper for Liverpool's third.

It was, as they say, a beautiful thing: Gerrard and Torres, a match made in heaven.

For so long Stevie G had pined for an equal in the no.9 shirt, someone with whom he could conjure great acts, someone to relieve the burden of being Liverpool's only genuine match winner. Many a potential suitor had come to Merseyside since Michael Owen's departure in 2004. Many had proven – as one great English writer might say – 'far from agreeable.'

Top of the famous flops was the Senegalese striker, El Hadj Diouf, whom Liverpool soon found out was better at gobbing in faces than scoring goals. He gained the unwanted distinction of being the first Liverpool player to wear the number 9 shirt and go an entire season without a goal (although he did manage a degree of accuracy in shooting balls of spit at Celtic fans the same season). Liverpool gladly sold Diouf to Bolton, where he was soon making headlines by spitting at an 11-year-old Middlesborough supporter before hoiking one at the captain of Portsmouth - both in the same month.

Another potential partner was the Welsh striker, Craig Bellamy. It might have worked out had Bellamy not allegedly threatened team mate John Arne Riise with a golf club after he declined to sing karaoke with him at a 'team bonding session.' Bellamy went ways towards making up for his indiscretion (and even set Riise up for the winner in the very next game against Barcelona), but he always came across as a tad unhinged. Eventually, 'the Nutter with a Putter' had to go.

Then there were the 'almost men', the *shoulda woulda coulda* players such as Milan Baros, who needed the ball on a silver platter in order to score and, even then, only if it was the superior Britannia grade rather than sterling.

After him, there was another Fernando, Fernando Morientes, who came from scoring 72 goals for Real Madrid only to lose several yards of pace on the flight to John Lennon Airport. Baggage handlers, fans, and coaches alike were at a loss as to where it had gone. After a season the search was called off and, with his pace still missing, Morientes soon retired.

Another almost man was the Frenchman, Djibril Cisse, who really coulda been great if he hadn't snapped his leg in one of those ghastly bones-sticking-out-through-the-sock freak accidents that make you thankful for the safety of your couch. Defying his doctors, Cisse made an amazing recovery and was playing again in just over five months. As well as being the coolest looking man in football, he had the grand temerity to purchase a countryside property that came with a title, making the black Frenchman with the dyed patterned hair, rock star clothes, and full body tattoos, the *Lord of the Manor of Frodsham.* Soon after, in a move I'm sure raised a chuckle among Liverpool supporters, Lord Cisse banned fox hunting on his ground, a moral stance that made him the bane of the Cheshire Forest Hunt and the darling of the Animal Rights Coalition. But despite his lightning speed on the pitch, Cisse lacked the crucial knack of running off the shoulder of the last defender, a knack that is often the difference between a good and a great striker, and perhaps the reason why Rafa Benitez eventually sold him to Marseille. His last goal from open play, however, was a stunning display of grace and agility, a volley against West Ham that set Liverpool on their way to another marvelous comeback in the 2006 FA Cup Final; it was a goal I'll forever love him for, a goal the other 'almost men' could only dream of scoring. Unfortunately, the day the transfer to Marseille was agreed, Lord Cisse suffered another horrific leg break. He recovered well once again. So well that I'm happy to say he's now considered something of a legend in Greece, popping in goals aplenty for Panithinaikos and adding a large tattoo of the club's four leaf clover emblem to his thigh, a way of thanking them for the opportunity. When you consider the line of gobbers, nutters and slow pokes before him, it was a shame to see such a noble gent as the Lord of the Manor of Frodsham depart.

But, in little more than seven months, Torres had made the long line of almost-men seem like distant aberrations. Liverpool had finally found what they were looking for – a golden boy who scored at a faster rate than the almost-men combined. And who did he thank for his run of form? The club, the manager, and The Kop. He spoke of how much he loved playing with Stevie and with due respect to their respective female partners, the two of them all but tied the knot that day against Newcastle. I was just one of 43,000 witnesses on hand to consummate the marriage. Fernando not only wore the armband 'that proved he was a red', he spoke of how a number of his friends had been tattooed with *We'll Never Walk Alone* and that he and his wife enjoyed reading books about the club's history in bed together. Liverpool, he vowed, was the only English club he'd ever play for. He loved Stevie, he loved the Kop. We had little reason to think the marriage wouldn't last.

Lingering inside the stadium before a burly attendant politely told me to move along, I walked back into the city, jumped in a cab, and made my way to a party Kate and Graeme were at in the suburb of Aigburth. I was greeted on arrival by a large Northern Irish contingent, nearly all of them happy reds. We talked at length about the game and our happiness over Stevie and Fernando's magical pairing. They wanted to hear about my experiences on the Kop and didn't hesitate in making it known what a 'jammy bastard' I was by getting my mug in the paper.

As I'd noticed with Kate and Graeme, their friends rarely used sentences without the word 'crack'. This was 'the crack', that was 'the crack', and there were varying degrees of crack. You had your ordinary everyday 'crack', your better quality 'good crack', and your top of the range 'great crack'.

Unlike its street drug namesake, it was only ever used in a positive sense and although I'm unlikely to ever use the term myself, it was fun to be around those who did. Sometimes it was the only word in their *duh-dee duh-dee duh-dee duh-dee duh*-diatribes that I actually understood.

In addition to the smoking, the drinking, the laughter, the me trying to understand them, the them trying to understand me, I got a sense that, despite their pasty complexions and complaints about the weather, they were all very proud of their adopted city.

They spoke of its grand history and said that, if each of them were to take me on tours of their favourite aspects, it would be a different experience every time. But when I told them that I'd found the sight of the docks and the Royal Cunard building a little depressing on my first morning, the bonhomie was momentarily lost. When I tried to back pedal by saying that it was probably a combination of jetlag, no breakfast and a cold shower that was to blame, they nodded in unison but – I could see it in their eyes – their doubts remained. Thankfully, that great Irish tendency of getting extremely excited at the drop of a hat returned when Cookie insisted I watch YouTube highlights of Northern Ireland's World Cup qualifying campaign. In particular, a guy called Ian Healey who'd scored a flurry of goals in wins over England, Sweden and Spain. Cookie instigated a brief but boisterous sing-along to the tune of *Glory Glory Alleluia!* that went: *We're not Brazil; we're Northern Ireland!* followed by the proud declaration that 'Ian Healey is god for Northern Ireland, and crap for everyone else – and that's why we love em!'

Football-related excitement extended to delayed coverage of an FA Cup tie between the fat cat Chelsea club and the lowly ranked Barnsley FC. Every red in the house already knew the result and loved the fact that the flat's only Chelsea fan, Davy, was watching his team in the front room, oblivious to the humiliation about to unfold. Davy had requested that no one tell him the final score but had a hunch from his flat of gleaming reds that it wasn't going to end well.

I sauntered into the front room to watch the last twenty minutes. Buried in the couch, Davy was the picture of a man desperately trying not to be pissed off and only half succeeding. As we were meeting for the first time, he even offered a few *nice to meet you* pleasantries – big of him under the circumstances. With knowledge of where my loyalties lie, Davy was surely aware that I was secretly relishing Chelsea's imminent loss just as much as my fellow reds gathered in the kitchen.

It's one of the added pleasures of being a football fan that, on top of basking in the glow of your team's victories, you get to revel in a rival's demise. For a Liverpool fan, the rare spectacle of a Manchester United loss is the ultimate. As for Chelsea, it's only since the Russian oligarch, Roman Abramovich, bought their way to the top of the league that the pleasure derived from their (also rare) failures has come a close second.

Chelsea fans had taken to the new regime with gusto, often referring to their club as 'Chelski' while wearing big furry Russian hats and waving 100 pound notes at the working class fans of other clubs. Their new status was money-based and meaningless. They were gleeful and gauche – everything typical of the nouveau riche and, even more typically, they didn't care a jot. I wanted to use this against Davy, stick him with a sly insult, one barbed little comment that would linger and irritate for days, something he would stew on at night, a comment that – even though it was directed at his club – would somehow feel personal. But I had to be quick - the clock was ticking, the final whistle about to blow. *Think Glenn! Think!* Alas, nothing decent came to mind. Truth be known, watching Barnsley play only reminded me of the sorry state I was in three weeks earlier when they'd beaten Liverpool in the same competition.

I'd watched the game before work at my new Auckland flat.

It was another lacklustre display from the reds in a new year of mixed – mainly bad – results. As I had already paid for my flights to the UK, their poor run of form had frightened the bejesus out of me – the thought of turning up Merseyside to see a drab, disjointed display almost too much to comprehend. Before footage of the Barnsley players celebrating at the final whistle, I thumbed Craig's number into my phone with the jittery pace of a slighted teen. One ring and he answered: 'What was that all about?'

'They're a pack of overpaid prima donnas!' I yelled back it him. 'I can't believe it – they were fuckin' useless. Why am I going to the other side of the world to see these pricks! I could be going to somewhere nice and sunny – I don't need this - what the fuck am I doing?'

Craig didn't answer. I could almost hear him rolling his eyes.

'What if I turn up and they play like they did today? What am I going to do...Craig, you there?'

Craig put his own exasperations on hold to put me right. 'Look, it's bad but it's *not that bad*. You're doing the right thing. Just wait; they'll turn it around in the Champions League – it could be a completely different story in a few weeks. You gotta go - you know how it changes.'

'I know, but that's the bloody problem – the inconsistency! The in-con-bloody-sistency! Just when they get your hopes up and look like they can beat any team in the world they come out and play like a rotten bag of arseholes! A rotten bag of bloody arseholes! Look, hats off to Barnsley and all that but, fuck, man – a little consistency, it's not much to ask – you know?'

Perhaps peeved that I'd smothered his own current-state-of-Liverpool complaints with self indulgent bullshit, Craig got curt: 'Just go,' he said, effectively ending the conversation.

Being upset over a football game can mean one of two things. It can either be a healthy venting of life's frustrations or a sign that the frustrations are taking over. Football was once described as 'serious nonsense', something I took to mean as no matter how serious the nonsense is, it's still just nonsense. Try telling someone whose life has been destroyed by war and oppression that your day has been ruined by your team being kicked out of round 5 of the FA Cup. They'll probably summon the last vestige of their will and strength to poke you in the eye with a stick.

My reaction to Barnsley beating Liverpool was less about Liverpool than it was about matters of the heart. Two months earlier my girlfriend had left me. After our year of living together, Erin departed Auckland to return to her hometown of Sydney. Her excuse was that she couldn't fit in, that Auckland was lacking vitality, charm and a decent beach close to the city. Typical bloody Australian. More worryingly, she also questioned the make-up of my Auckland-based friends. She said that, although she still loved me, she struggled to connect with anyone else. Auckland was driving her mad and, with her sudden departure, our short great love affair was over.

At first, I blamed her – her lofty expectations, her all-consuming anger. I had never met anyone who felt things as vividly as Erin. Depending on the situation she could either explode with delight or burst into flames. The first six months of our living together had been some of the most blissful months I can remember; the second six, the worst. It was as though the flames of her temper had enveloped her until she could handle it no more, her leaving Auckland – a fairly watered-down city as far as I was concerned – an act akin to the dramatic escape from a raging inferno.

Soon after she left, however, I began to see Auckland differently. I was going through that post breakup paradigm shift in which everything good turns bogus – Erin's whirlwind exit exposing holes where there had previously only been cracks.

Aspects of my friends' personalities grated on me – every flaw, misplaced sentence or lazy attitude all part of a greater, insidious malaise.

I decided to cut contact and withdraw from my friends altogether – something that was a lot easier to do than anticipated. Every time I went out, I got angry. I took to drinking alone on the old wooden balcony of my new flat, cursing the soulless city of hollow hypocrites and well-to-do wankers before me. I recalled that the only reason I'd come here in the first place was to recapture another girlfriend who'd left me in Christchurch, yet beckoned me north in order to be with her. She'd cuckolded me before I could make the move, yet I did so all the same, eventually successful in my quest to win her back – an act more of vanity than good sense. I eventually learned to like Auckland but now I felt foolish for doing so. Here I was, confined to my new flat with its mysterious odor that I could never locate and a flat mate who was growing increasingly resentful that I, in my rebounding state, wasn't prepared to fuck her. Sure, I was desperate, but sex with a flat mate should only happen if it's unavoidable. Sex with a flat mate whose desperation is even worse than your own is a recipe for ugly.

The only place that I could actually find some peace was the library where I worked. I genuinely liked the people there. They were warm, sincere, and for the most part, silent.

All I wanted was a little consistency. Something close to happiness was obviously too much to ask – I needed to lower my expectations. Besides, happiness was a fallacy, a lie, something for the mindless people with strong families and excellent teeth. Not for me. A steady, unswerving plane of melancholy, something slightly more artful than misery would do. As long as I could purge hope for anything more I would find my even keel – no more the dumb puppy dog need for love, no more setting myself up for a fall. I would become *Man Alone*. Or Mr. Man Alone, to you. Mr. Man Alone would shun society for remote country where he could be dark, brooding, and intellectual while shuddering under the 'latent menace of the land.' He'd spend his days writing down the incredibly deep thoughts he'd had after staring across the unfeeling, eternal vastness of the natural world. He'd grow a big beard and hope to attract lice. He'd view the very few humans he saw on his many wanderings as if they were an entirely different species from him and it would all be so confronting he'd have to quickly run away, back to the sparse confines of his shitty fibro house where he could spend the next three days peeking out from the plastic curtains.

And that's what Mr. Man Alone just might've done if that particular summer hadn't been as warm and colourful and visually joyous as it was. So what did Mr. Man Alone do? He failed. Instead of casting himself off to a solitary existence he went through with previous plans to go to Liverpool. He went to high profile football matches and to a party in a suburb called Aigburth where he enjoyed the company of young Northern Irish people while nodding his head and tapping his toes to their impeccable taste in music.

He did this on the back of three more or less *happy days* on Merseyside. Despite himself he stumbled into a short period of consistency. It was the good kind of consistency, but apparently not good enough. The phony Man Alone had always wanted more. He further betrayed hitherto ambitions of solitary melancholy by ringing Erin to say 'hi' and that he missed her, and, if she still wanted him to, he hoped to come live in Sydney and be with her. Turned out she was receptive to the idea and somehow the hope of happiness had cast its spell on him again, wiping away all doubts to make him believe in the impossible – that his great volatile romance with the Aussie girl (truly a different breed) could actually last. The dishonor of selling-out didn't even register.

At about 4 a.m. the party ended in spectacular fashion. One of the flat mates had gone up to his room to discover someone had puked in his new shoes - pretty much filled them to the brim. He stormed into the living room, shut down the music, and announced what had happened. Standing on a chair, he demanded the culprit step forward. 'I'm not angry. I'm not angry,' he lied, his head shaking like a fist. 'I just want to know who it was. I'm not going to do anything, I Just Want. To Know. Who it was!'

The puker in question had either left or was now sober enough to know that, in this situation, the cowardly option of keeping mum was also the wisest.

We stumbled out, barely suppressing laughter as we headed for the door. Walking the Aigburth streets, we exchanged drunken theories on who the puker could've been.

Imagine my surprise when a very tall guy named Mick accused me on the basis that I was a) an unknown quantity and b) a kiwi. He entertained the thought that shoe spewing is common practice in New Zealand and made my entire race sound like a bunch of nasty, conniving convicts likely to commit such an act several times a day. I suggested he might be confusing New Zealand with Australia but he didn't seem to care. He said that they – the group of friends – should be wary of what else I might do.

'If you weren't so tall I'd piss in your ear,' I told him.

Mick glared at me with an intensity that made it hard to tell whether this was all in jest or if he actually had a problem. He was, without a doubt, a very strange character.

When he told me earlier in the evening that he was a Manchester United supporter – not a common thing in these parts – I'd explained my theory about United supporters all being morally corrupt. You can't back a tyrant without being morally corrupt, I said, referring to the manager, Sir Alex Ferguson. Funnily enough, big Mick didn't put much stock in my theory and the vibe ever since hadn't been great. I'd either struck a raw nerve or he simply didn't like the cut of my jib. As far as the shoe puking was concerned, I had proof of my innocence - my pile was in the garden.

6. Riot, Romance.

It's a sign that you've watched too much football when your eyes fade from focus and the players become blurry dots that move into fluid shapes and groovy patterns on a canvas of green. You don't really know what's happening; you just let the moving composition meditate your mind until you snap, look away, and see scrambled dots imprinted on air.

It was Monday morning. Time to do something else. As wonderful as LFC TV was, there was a city to explore, stuff of cultural significance ... not necessarily draped in red.

Mondays for me are better off silent, so I was grateful my walk along Ullitt Rd into town via the suburb of Toxteth was without incident. Apart from the odd boarded-up window, Toxteth seemed at first glance like a pretty average neighbourhood. But as with anywhere in Liverpool, an important moment in history is never far from the mind.

Had I been here in early July, 1981, I would have been in the midst of a nine-day riot that left one civilian dead, 450 police officers injured, 500 people arrested, and 70-odd buildings demolished or burnt to the ground. Streets barricaded with overturned vehicles. Gangs of black and white youths hurling petrol bombs at lines of shielded police. Looting, looting, and more looting.

The Chief Constable of Merseyside, Kenneth Oxford, blamed it on a 'small group of criminal hooligans who were hell bent to provoke police into a situation that would give them an opportunity to attack what is visibly a symbol of authority.'

A Toxteth community leader, however, suggested to the BBC that the unrest was more the result of long term tensions. 'What happened last night was just an eruption...We've been saying for a long long time now that something's got to be done in terms of jobs, in terms of economic future, in terms of giving the black community some future in society.'

Under the 'sus laws' police were able to instantly search anyone they felt suspicious of wrongdoing. They were laws the UK police apparently abused, especially when it came to policing black communities, and were later cited as being an element that contributed to the Brixton riot earlier that year. The Chair of the Merseyside Police Committee, Margaret Simey, claimed to be aware of the heavy-handed tactics of the Liverpool police force preceding the Toxteth riot, and stated that the local community 'would be apathetic fools...if they didn't protest.'

It was no coincidence that the unemployment rate in 1981 was the worst it had been in Britain since the 1930s, largely due to Thatcher's ruthless determination to alter the state of the economy and reduce a soaring rate of inflation. She implemented a monetarist policy which involved halting government spending and dismantling the majority of the country's factories. The decimation of UK manufacturing caused unemployment levels to double from one to two million in her first two years in power. Soon the number of unemployed would rise to 3 million. With the industrial north bearing the brunt of the blow, communities like Toxteth's never fully recovered.

Almost three decades later, with unemployment still high, many issues of the eighties remain. However, policies of 'light-touch policing' – implemented soon after the riot – have lessened the possibility of another. The major problems now? Cocaine, guns, violent crime.

   The biggest beneficiary from the riots was arguably the Liverpool underworld. According to Observer journalist Mark Townsend, organised crime gained in strength 'after a group of white, middle-aged, former armed robbers brokered a strategic alliance with young black gangs following the Toxteth riots... As Britain's first drug-dealing cartel, strong links to corrupt port officials and haulage contractors ensured its status as an accomplished smuggler. Under the control of a shadowy former docker called 'The Banker', it became the richest gang in the UK.'

As I wandered down leafy Princes Ave things seemed quite orderly on the surface. I passed the Rialto Complex that had been built to replace the Rialto ballroom, a once grand venue firebombed by the rioters, its cupola roof reportedly illuminating the night sky with its copper glow. It was a scene that prompted a reworking of an old folk saying: *Red sky at night/ Toxteth's alight.* On from there I headed into truly fancy streets of beautiful Georgian terraces, the kind which receive far less attention from the press than their boarded-up neighbours. Then, more or less on the cusp of Toxteth and the CBD, the majestic Anglican Cathedral. From the notable facts attributed to the cathedral (it's the biggest in the UK), the one that impressed me most was that it had escaped major damage in the blitz, despite its sheer mass and prominence on the Liverpool sky line. Even though a bomb crashed through its roof, the angle of its drop saw it fly through an adjacent wall to explode clear of the building. Just a few hundred metres away its little brother, the St Luke's Church, wasn't so lucky. Its roof, stained glass windows and bells were all destroyed by an incendiary bomb dropped by the German Luftwaffe just after midnight on 6th of May 1941. Apart from the overgrown garden and trees that have since flourished inside its gothic stone shell, 'the bombed-out church' has remained virtually untouched ever since, a scarred, sacred beauty borne of destruction.

After nosing around the interesting shops along Bold St, I cut back along Lime St, past St George's Hall to a smaller neo-classical gem, the Walker Art Gallery.

In a room packed with old European statues and busts, my attention was drawn to a panel carved by long dead sculptor, John Gibson. It shows the beautiful Psyche flying through the air with her butterfly wings (newly acquired in the underworld), while the randy Cupid (his wings big and feathery) follows in hot pursuit. One panel later and he'd be all over her like a rash. Psyche's story of finding love is one most of us can relate to in that, only after extreme ridicule, longing and despair does she finally gets her man – 'her god'. Gibson's carving portrays the ultimate fulfillment of high romance. Nice for some.

I might have regarded the image as a promising sign of things to come. As it was, the thought of it not working out with Erin and having to return to the ridicule, longing and despair of 'high romance gone wrong,' had me in need of a drink. My decision had been made, and while I had no intention of changing my mind, I also had no idea if it was right.

Dr. Duncan's seemed the best option.

I took my pint of lager to a small, dimly lit table on the upper level overlooking the bar. Sitting at a table below me was an old couple, both pushing eighty, both immaculately attired, and both completely trolleyed.
Until now, I had no idea that such wrinkly, frail human beings could be this drunk and still alive.

'If I want to drink another glass of wine I'm able to,' said the elderly woman. Her husband indicated he didn't fancy the idea one bit. The woman wasn't about to give up. 'What am I allowed to drink then?' she drawled.

No response from the man.

She looked bemused. 'Think you'd be happier if I came out on my own...'

The old man didn't rise to this but came to a conclusion of a different sort: 'I need to use the bathroom,' he said.

Woman: 'You can use the disabled toilet, you know.'

Man: 'I don't tell you to be careful going to the toilet, do I?'

The lady gathered her thoughts. 'Am I allowed a half pint of lager?'

The gent huffed. The lady looked sad. 'I love you. I'm sorry I said the wrong thing but I couldn't live without you,' she said. He looked at her, she looked at him and, despite their sheer drunkenness, that was all it took to reassure each other – they were back on. With that, the gentleman teetered to a stand and took a few unsteady steps to the bar only to return to the table moments later empty-handed. With no indication why he'd done so, he sat down.

'What would I like?' she said. He got up again and made his way back to the bar where several middle-aged men made way for him. As one of them turned for the stairs the lady took his arm. 'I went on my first date with that man fifty-nine years ago. What do you think of that?'

'I'm very impressed. And you've still got the look of a love-struck teen,' said the man. They laughed. She let him go. Keen to know how they'd remained together for so long, I replenished my glass and said hi to the couple on my way back up the stairs. By the way they looked at me, it didn't take a mind reader to realise they could barely understand a word I was saying and, instead of advice on how to maintain a relationship, I got a speech from the gentleman (who introduced himself as Tony) on the evils of capitalism.

As he was talking, wife Lily leaned forward at regular intervals to ask, 'Are we keeping you from your friends?' No matter how many times I answered in the negative, she insisted on repeating the question while old Tony continued his rant. When he had finished, Lily revealed that at the time of their first date she was a military nurse treating the soldiers on their return from Dunkirk. Like her husband, she declared she also had little time for wealth. 'I don't care about money. My family talk about compensation but it won't bring my hearing back.' Then, 'Are we keeping you from your friends?' This time, just to keep things simple, I said that it was nice to meet them both but, yes, it was high time I returned to my 'friends'. Tony shook my hand and wished me all the best. Lily leant forward. 'I've enjoyed your company, but you do come across as someone undecided.'

7. The Great Spirit

The frustrating thing about Liverpool since the 1980s is that the sides picked to represent this great football club haven't always contained the greatest players.

I touched on this in Chapter 5 by mentioning Stevie G's failed suitors.

Sadly, that group of almost men was merely a handful from a basket of bad eggs. One or two were definitely rotten but the majority, I say with some relief, were only slightly cracked.

The *wonderful thing* about Liverpool since the 1980s is that despite their charitable inclusion of ordinary players, the club is still renowned for pulling together to become the ultimate collective unit, the ordinary ones excelling with the help of proper management, excellent organisation, and the spirit of the Kop.

But the reds have a very particular psychological tendency that prevents the ultimate collective unit turning up every week. It's based on 'loss aversion', the theory that people care more about avoiding a loss than making a gain. Loss aversion states you'd be far angrier at losing $100 than you would be happy at finding $100 – the reaction to the loss being greater than the reaction to the gain.

The principle is prevalent in competition. According to studies, even Tiger Woods is more likely to hole a putt to avoid being over-par (considered a failure) than he is to hole the same putt when he's going for a birdie (considered a gain). Thus, Tiger Woods tries harder to avoid a loss than make a gain.

Liverpool's loss aversion is slightly different in that it normally only kicks in when the stakes are impossibly high, when the consequence of loss is despair. This is why, unless they're up against a staunch rival, they tend to under-perform in the Premier League (where there's the rest of the season to make up for a poor result), as opposed to the Champions League (where two consecutive bad results will have you out of the competition). The Champions League is the most illustrious competition in club football where the standard of play (with the top teams packed with international superstars) is superior to the World Cup. The Champions League is where every ambitious footballer wants to be seen. The money clubs earn for progressing in the league is ridiculous. The good thing about the money being ridiculous is that along with the tournament's aura of prestige, the stakes soar beyond the distant stars.

If a game is billed as 'do or die' – as they often are in the Champions league - and if Liverpool are deemed by the critics as having 'little to no hope,' then the concoction of 'maximum loss aversion' and 'maximum Scouse defiance' kicks in.

With the necessary elements in place, average red players become better than they actually are, their victories over much-fancied teams deemed 'thrilling' and 'miraculous'. For a true Liverpool supporter the experience is all the better because it harks back to Bill Shankly's ideal of players doing what they can do well, helping each other out, excelling as a whole – aspects of that socialist ethos crucial to 'the Liverpool way'. And as straightforward as it seems to you and me, it's a concept many struggle to grasp. I find myself explaining it all the time and those who *don't get it* don't get it because they actually *don't want to get it* and they infuriate me.

I was with a group of friends at a Thai restaurant in Auckland when it happened. Seconds before my 'friend' spoke ill of Liverpool he'd been talking about finance matters, the property market, interest rates – that kind of thing. It's a topic I struggle with at the best of times, let alone on a Saturday night. Worryingly, talk of gaining assets, various stocks, and what and when to buy was now a regular topic with my Auckland friends. Having taken the plunge into the corporate world, they'd recently gained incomes that put them into what they referred to as the 'upper bracket'. Being in the upper bracket meant owning a 90s model European car that frequently clapped out, dining in Auckland's smartest restaurants just to show you could, wearing designer woollen jumpers as opposed to sloppy old hoodies, and apparently discarding any remnants of a social conscience.

My Auckland friends and I had known each other since our teenage years in Christchurch. Back then they were the funniest, craziest, most sensitive and thoughtful friends I'd ever had. Talk of the free market during university days would more likely involve an analysis of its pitfalls and its propensity to do more harm than good. Roughly ten years later, the mindset had changed dramatically. Now they had spending power, they were in on it. Society was no longer something to be challenged; it was serving its purpose to make private school-educated white people wealthy.

I considered them far more interesting than their corporate jobs allowed them to be, but what truly worried and annoyed me was that they took it all so bloody seriously. $100,000 a year, they said, was the benchmark of a decent lifestyle. Any suggestion that such a focus on financial achievement was more a symptom of an unhealthy degree of status anxiety and they'd look at me as though I reminded them of their earlier immature selves, of those dark ambiguous days before the perceived safety of commercial conformity.

Money was the way forward now. I got a sense they almost considered it irresponsible of me to be writing a novel and therefore earning and spending as little as I did. I was not only letting the economy down, I was naïve, failing to realise that I was falling behind. And while I was falling behind, they were falling into a trap. Serious talk about money matters on a Saturday night (irony-free) suggested they'd already been snared.

Mind you, the fact I hadn't stopped talking about Liverpool's victory in the Champions League Final two months prior was no doubt as grating to them as their finance talk was to me. I was the only Liverpool supporter at the table and, I admit, it wasn't unlike me to use the game as a metaphor to underline what really matters in life. It happened to be what I was talking about to the person beside me when 'the friend' broke from his riveting discourse on big business to ask: 'Am I boring you?'

I shuffled in my seat: 'You are actually.'

'What are you talking about that's so interesting then?'

'Champions League Final.'

He rolled his eyes. 'Liverpool were lucky. It was a *fluke*.'

'No it wasn't.'

'So you know more about football than me, do you?'

'If you think Liverpool's win was a fluke than I definitely know more about football than you.' And so on. Childish stuff, I know. Thirty years old and quick to the quarrel, we got stuck in. We argued each other from across the table, to and from the bar, and – much to the relief of patrons trying to enjoy their Tom Yum Gai – out onto the street.

'You're just biased,' he said, shutting the door behind him. I was sick of being called biased. So sick of it I'd been making a concerted effort for a long long time now not to be biased. Instead of blurting things in favour of Liverpool, I'd been holding back to consider the true validity of my statements. In a few precious seconds of sound reasoning, I could judge if my intended blurt was actually warranted, or groundless. By doing this I'd cut down on pro-Liverpool blurts by around 10 per cent. Damned if anyone had noticed.

Seeing this was essentially a game of one-upmanship, I countered his accusation of bias with an accusation of pride. He didn't like that at all. But what really annoyed him was the unwavering righteous pleasure I took from the nature of Liverpool's win.

For me, the triumph against AC Milan in 2005 was proof of what Socrates said, that "virtue does not come from wealth, but...wealth and every good thing that men have...comes from virtue."

But who am I to play the preacher? You have to see it for yourself. So without further ado, here it is, the 2005 Champions League Final...

Setting: Olympic Ataturk Stadium, Istanbul

Date: 25 May 2005

Crowd: 80,000

If it had been a contest decided on looks then Liverpool wouldn't have stood a chance. It wasn't that the reds were especially ugly; it was more that the players for AC Milan were – in the words of my then girlfriend – so 'impossibly hot'. You couldn't deny it. They were tanned, taut, and glamorous; even their cheek bones looked designer labelled. Their sparkling white uniforms could've been cut from the cloth of saints – it almost seemed a sin to get them dirty. What made it even worse for Liverpool was that AC Milan were as good as they looked.

If they came with a sense of entitlement they had every reason to do so. They had won the Champions League Final two years before, feasted off the incomprehensible riches and adulation which followed and, instead of becoming addicted to prescription drugs and bacon sandwiches, just kept on winning. They won the Serie A the very next year and were now heavy favourites to destroy Liverpool and take their club's tally of European Cups to seven, just two short of Real Madrid. Although Liverpool was the third most successful club in this tournament, they were currently a team of limited experience. They had a habit of making things difficult for themselves, often relying on the inspired play of their captain – and only genuine star: Steven Gerrard. Even Liverpool's manager, Rafa Benitez, admitted it was like pitting a Mini against a Ferrari.

The final was held on the arid outskirts of Istanbul. Gerrard later described the stadium as looking like a 'spaceship abandoned in the desert'. As the players lined up for the biggest game of their lives everyone knew that in order to win Liverpool would have to be spectacular. To confound the prophets they would have to play beyond themselves and maybe, just maybe, the gods of football would look kindly upon their trying souls, shrug their holy shoulders and let the underdogs have their bone.

Fifty seconds into the game and Liverpool were in trouble as the captain of AC Milan, Paolo Maldini (who looked like the head vampire of the hippest vampire clan in the coolest vampire movie ever made), languidly swung his leg and volleyed the ball into the back of Liverpool's net.

Not only was it one of the most effortless-looking goals you'll see but it was also the fastest goal in the history of the competition, and from one of the most unlikely players in the team. The delighted Maldini roared as though he was no longer allergic to garlic. Milan celebrated with a brief huddle before running back past a head-scratching Liverpool to halfway.

Befitting their reputation, Liverpool responded bravely. After all, it was only one goal, a little disheartening, but hey, it wasn't as if the Turkish sky had fallen on their heads.

Any possibility of nipping one back while Milan's guard might be down was halted by their masterful defense and ease on the ball. The way that circular bag of wind pinged, flew and popped from player to player you could've accused it of favouritism – a bouncing little groupie giggling away at the reds' efforts to win her as she curled around the boots of her superstars.

Their status secure, Milan's skill and verve had them back on attack and threatening to score within minutes.

As if being down a goal so soon wasn't bad enough, Liverpool's cause wasn't aided when their Australian midfielder, the ever-limping Harry Kewell, pulled up lame with a recurrence of that perennial passion-killer, the groin injury. It was a setback that came with a whiff of mockery, Kewell's exit from the field unnecessarily prolonged by his substitute's sideline scramble for his boots. For some reason, Vladmir Smicer had been warming the bench in his socks. (Having coached a children's football team, I know firsthand the importance of stressing the fundamentals of the game. Having to remind the kids to put on their boots was never one of them.)

For Liverpool fans, the sight of Smicer still tying his laces came with a horrible sinking feeling. When he finally took to the field, the whiff of mockery became so pungent you could smell it in New Zealand. Not surprisingly, Milan resumed with even greater purpose and it wasn't long before the ball was back in the Liverpool net. This time the would-be scorer was Milan's champion striker, Andrey Shevchenko. Often referred to as the Ukrainian David Beckham due to his glamour boy looks, Andrey Shevchenko's scoring prowess was such that he'd netted twice as many goals as Liverpool's top scorer that season. He slotted the ball and made off to the corner flag waving his arms wildly at the crowd. Only when he turned around did he see that the linesman had ruled him off-side – his goal wouldn't count.

It was the kind of decision that, in another game, may have upset the dominant team, rallied the underdog, and swung the momentum their way. All it meant here was that it would be truly amazing if Milan didn't score again. They pushed forward with a menace that shook Liverpool's defensive line again and again and, sure enough, a combination of slick passes orchestrated by the Brazilian, Kaka, led to Milan's second goal.

Being two goals down in any game of football is of grave concern. Being two goals down to Milan, who had gone six months in this competition without conceding a single goal, was frightening. Add the statistic that not since 1962 had a team come from two goals down to win the final and you start to feel a bit dizzy. Add to that another goal, as AC Milan did just five minutes later, and you're pretty much screwed.

One nil, bad; two nil, terrible; three nil, toxic.

Rather than just another point on the board, Milan's third was a statement of intent which served to underline their class. Kaka, once again, was the provider. Known for his proselytizing of his Christian ways, even your hard line atheist would struggle to deny that his perfect pass to Hernan Crespo was anything but divine. Without needing to break his stride, Crespo ran onto Kaka's pass and dinked the ball beyond Liverpool's keeper so it bounced merrily into the goal. The commentator described it as 'beautifully engineered and exquisitely finished...' and the faces of everyone in red said it all: Screwed. With a resounding silence, the sky came crashing down.

Half time. And not a moment too soon. The players walked into the changing rooms where, for the time being at least, they could hide. Sooner or later though, they would have to come back out. And then what? Further humiliation from the model men?

Steven Gerrard: 'The dressing room fell quiet for a couple of minutes. We sat there lifeless, our dreams seemingly shredded. Misery clung to everyone in that room. Harry sat there with an ice-pack on his groin. Christ, he was a mess – a lump the size of a tennis ball. Gradually, players began to speak. No recriminations. No blame. Just general laments. "Fucking hell, lads, what's going on?"...Some of the guys were in pieces. Surely there was no way we could score three goals against Milan, not after the way they played first half? "Let's just stop this being 5-0," said Carra. "Let's not have a massacre here."'

Rafa Benitez, who had done exceptionally well to get Liverpool this far in his first season with the club, announced the changes for the second half.

Gerrard: 'Having sorted out the tactics he went to work on our minds...helped change our mood from defeat to defiance. Let's go out fighting, not with a whimper. Rafa kept mentioning the fans. Outside, that huge electronic scoreboard that read 'Maldini 1, Crespo 39, 44' stared at our fans. Proof of Liverpool's terrible performance was written large up there. Looking at that scoreboard, most Liverpool fans must have felt the race was run and lost... Yet against all the odds, against all the evidence of Milan's superiority, our fans were singing loud and proud.

"Listen," I said to the players. "Listen to that."

The singing of 40,000 Liverpool supporters floated down the tunnel, into the dressing-room and into our hearts. Unbelievable...All the players looked at each other in amazement and pride...By singing You'll Never Walk Alone the fans sent a message to eleven shattered men: the fans will be with you, through the wind and rain, through times of adversity like this. No matter how much the players hurt, we'd never walk alone.' (From Gerrard: My Autobiography.)

John Maguire, a Liverpool fan present on the night, recalled his experience to the football magazine, Four-Four-Two: 'I usually hold my hands open when singing You'll Never Walk Alone, but this was the clenched fist version. There were veins popping out everywhere, tears were rolling down faces, dripping off chins, eyes bulging and drenched with emotion. This was the daddy of all YNWA's, and it worked.'

Steven Gerrard scored first.

Freed from the shackles of reason and plausibility, the Liverpool side took to the field and ten minutes into the second half Gerrard leapt high for a crossed ball that looked to be flying harmlessly into Milan's box. Seemingly hanging in mid air, Gerrard twisted his king scouser cranium for the ball to glance from his brow, over the keeper, and into the top right-hand corner of the goal.

Too soon to celebrate, he ran back to half way, urging the crowd for more of what they'd given them at half time. The fans obliged. According to everyone there, the Ataturk Stadium became the loudest place on earth.

The second goal was quick to follow.

This time it was from the boot of none other than Vladmir Smicer – the very player whose socks had emitted the whiff of mockery so early in the first half. His low, long range drive skimmed just wide of the keeper's despairing dive and hit the net barely an inch inside the left post. Liverpool fans went into a state of delirium. Milan's sober mob looked on in disbelief. Moments later, the gulf in contrasting emotions would only widen. Just six minutes after scoring Liverpool's first goal, Gerrard made another pulsating run into the penalty box. The ball was at his feet and would've been in the back of the net with flames on it had his heels not been clipped by the excitable Italian, Gattuso. The whistle blew. Gattuso pleaded. He and his team mates crowded the ref but all the momma mia melodrama in the world couldn't save them. The decision stood: a penalty kick for Liverpool.

As Gattuso and Co continued to act like spoilt children experiencing their first denial, Liverpool mid-fielder, Xabi Alonso, stood up to take the shot.

They say there is no greater test of a player's mettle than the test of taking a penalty kick. The high expectation to score makes the prospect of failure terrifying. Alonso was normally as composed as the Spanish symphony but with every passing second the mounting pressure piled layers upon his brow. Indeed, Alonso had every reason to be nervous.

Six foot five inches of shot-blocking Brazilian stood looking back at him. Dida had been dubbed 'God' in his homeland and 'a saint' in Milan after his three penalty saves won Milan the 2003 final. Could Alonso actually get one past Dida? Was it even possible? The continuing complaints from the Milan players, the jeering from their fans and the presence of the cameras broadcasting his every move around the world (to 3 billion people across 200 countries as it turned out) did not help. Yet with apparent disregard he took several strides towards the ball, and struck it pretty well. The placement wasn't bad either. But Dida read it all the way and pounced sideways to block the shot. Despite this, Alonso reacted well. Really, really well. Before you could yell 'Bloody hell, fuck it!' or 'Fuck shit fuck!' (or any suitable variation) he jumped at the loose ball and slammed it into the underside of the net. 3-3. Pandemonium ensued. 3 goals in 6 minutes!

The comeback to confound the prophets and defy the gods was complete. The watching world shook and screamed – the impossible had happened and now it was Liverpool's game to win. They held onto the momentum with tenacious tackling and proficient passing, forcing Dida to be at his best to stop a fourth. Players who looked out of their depth in the first half were now taking on Milan with a potent vigour fuelled by The Great Spirit! Every time a Milan player had the ball he was confronted by a red shirt. Every time Liverpool had the ball they threatened Milan's goal. Somehow the Italian side did enough to keep the scores level till the end of normal time.

The pace and intensity thus far meant the additional half hour was a period of 'heavy legs and scrambled brains.' The momentum swung back to Milan yet both teams came agonizingly close to finishing the game off. Then, the final whistle was blown; the final whistle which meant the victors would now be decided by that dreaded method of conclusion – the p-p-p-penalty shoot out.

As the chosen ones prepared themselves for the moment that could possibly overshadow their whole career, the commentator reminded viewers of a study undertaken at Bristol University that revealed an increase in heart attacks following penalties in the '98 World Cup semi-final between England and Argentina. 'In other words,' he warned, 'hold on to your hearts, people; it's about to happen again.'

As the camera flipped from haunted looking player to haunted looking player, it paused on a manic, arm-waving rant by defender Jamie Carragher to the Liverpool goalkeeper, Jerzy Dudek.

Jamie Carragher, who'd defied strains and cramps in his efforts to stop Milan scoring a fourth (a performance in equal parts heroic and masochistic), expressed before the game how desperately he wanted to win so he could forever bore his children with the story. Born and bred in the Liverpool suburb of Bootle, Carragher is said to possess an encyclopedic memory of his club's history and it was a part of that history he was relaying to Jerzy Dudek before the shootout.

The last time Liverpool won the European Cup was back in 1984. It too was settled by a shootout and was the scene (described in chapter 4) in which the clown prince Grobbelaar pretended to be a nervous drunken wreck in goal; his stumbling, wobbling, 'spaghetti legs' routine proving just the distraction needed to put off his opponents.

On a famous European night over twenty years later, a very red-faced Carragher implored Dudek to do the same. As outlandish as the idea was – acting like a halfwit to win the greatest cup in club football – it kind of made sense. Whereas Dida had sheer physical presence emboldened by a legendary reputation, the only thing imposing about Dudek was his nose, a real Polish honker that took up much of his face and looked forever to be turning a corner.

Proboscis aside, Dudek had copped plenty of flack for his erratic form throughout the season. A confounding mix of sloppy and superb, he was a true Polish paradox: superman saves one moment; kryptonite cock-ups the next. How could he be so good and yet so bad? God only knows. But Dudek had one fan in particular whose faith in him mattered more than anything else. In 2004, Pope John Paul II, who was a goalkeeper in his youth, met members of the Polish national team. He told Dudek that he was a great fan of his and followed Liverpool whenever they played. Surely, with that kind of faith, Dudek wouldn't lose it again.

Unlike so many keepers who blame their own failings on their defenders, Dudek knew when he'd let the side down. Behind that healthy honker was an open book of self-deprecation. This showed, above all, that the man had humility. And only a man with humility by the freakin' truck load could do what he was about to do.

But could it really work twice?

The first penalty taker was yet another of Milan's Brazilian imports. Serginho had come on as a substitute in the second half only to be promptly snuffed out by the close marking of Steven Gerrard. If that, and the roar of 40,000 Scousers, wasn't enough to dent Serginho's confidence, then the sight of a waving, bobbing Dudek was. Serginho put his spot kick high into the crowd.

The second penalty taker for Milan was the seemingly unflappable Andriy Pirlo. In a show of good faith, Dudek handed him the ball and retreated to the goal line. Once back in position he dipped, shimmied and shook like a rare exotic bird looking for love. The fact that he was illegally off his goal line when he saved the meagre shot went unnoticed. Blame it on the madness. Still, another shot, another save.

Meanwhile, in between Dudek's performances, Liverpool scored twice to take a 2-0 advantage (in the best of five).

Unfortunately, Milan's next two penalty takers managed to ignore the Dudek hoodoo. Liverpool missed one but got another which brought the shootout to a head – Shevchenko up next. If he missed, it was over.

The pin-up Shevchenko was such a sure bet. He'd been here, done that, had the shirt to prove it (which was a lot like the one he was wearing). He'd only failed to put the game to bed earlier due to two freak saves by Dudek – the first a dive to his left, the second a point-blank double reflex block to put ninjas to shame. Surely he couldn't deny Europe's best striker a third time? And surely it was time for Dudek to quit with the spaghetti legs and apply his full concentration into the very serious matter of stopping the ball. Really, this was no time to be fooling around. Aside from the cup, there was 50 million pounds of prize money to be won, some significant coin! You can't be fooling around when that kind of money is on the line – think of the financial security it would give, think of the clout it would gain in the market, what it means in terms of future investments – you have to take these things seriously Dudek, you have to take them seriously!

For Dudek's final performance of the night he stood with his knobbly knees wide apart and shook his upper body like Elvis in decline.

Shevchenko's shot was weak; Dudek's hand was strong. The earth gasped – a short, sharp intake of oxygen before the ecstasy took hold and the high of the reality kicked in: Liverpool, European Champions once again.

The Guardian rated it the 'greatest football match of the decade'.

The Daily Telegraph called it the 'top sporting moment of the decade', while the Times rated it Number 2 in its Top 50 'wish you'd been there' moments (Number 1 being the 1966 winning of the world cup by England.) No one said it was a fluke.

Yet more important than what anyone said was what it meant to Liverpool, where over a million people wearing red came out the day after the win to celebrate as a double-decker bus paraded the team with its European Cup.

It was just like the good old days. According to Kate and Graeme, who were positioned somewhere between Lime St Station and St George's Hall, it was the biggest and happiest gathering they'd ever experienced without drugs. Strangers hugged, sang, and joked. Kids doing the spaghetti legs was a common sight in the Sefton and Toxteth streets for months to come. To underline Socrates quote about wealth and every good thing that men have coming from virtue, it was reported by Sport Business International magazine that Liverpool's triumph was the catalyst for a €47 million cash injection for the city the following year through increased consumer spending, tourism, sponsorship and commerce. And the reason I bring this all up right now, dear reader, is because on a Wednesday night nearly three years later I watched Liverpool prove they were something special in Europe yet again by beating Inter Milan (AC Milan's fierce rivals) to progress to the Champions League quarter finals. Because travelling to Milan was beyond my means, the comfort of watching the game in a Lark lane pub with Kate and Graeme and friends provided a pretty good second best.

It was a sumptuous turn and strike by the wonderful Fernando that provided the winning goal, catapulting us from our seats. But as usual it was the team's all round performance that was even more meaningful, even more heartwarming than what was fast becoming the common spectacle of Fernando's brilliance. Liverpool dominated another star-studded Italian team with exemplary teamwork and an irrepressible hunger for the ball. At the end, among the many camera shots of the crowd, one paused on the travelling Kop where several burly Scousers held a banner in the rain. It read: IN MY LIFE I'VE LOVED THEM ALL.

8. A Beautiful Prejudice

After a week that involved an enjoyable tour of Anfield, more galleries, and much more drinking, it was time to remember I hadn't come all this way to be swanning around the place like some high falutin' fancy Dan.

Liverpool was treating me well, but real gain doesn't come from an endless parade of pleasantries. Oh no, it was time to crawl from my comfort zone and do something unpleasant. It was time to go to Manchester.

Chris, an old Christchurch friend of my brother Lyndon, had been living in Manchester for several months. As a longtime fan of Manchester United he'd been lured to the city by his company's offer of season tickets to Old Trafford. With his girlfriend away for a weekend hen's party, Chris promised a laddish tour of Manchester and its surrounds.

So on Friday afternoon I packed. I packed toiletries, clothes, reading material, a couple of pens, a notebook, and prejudice. That's right, prejudice –

the stuff the bigots, the fundamentalists and the fascists are so hot on. Dirty old, mean-as-hell, shit pie in the face *prejudice*.

If you're *tut-tutting* at me then, please, take a look in the mirror. We all harbour prejudice to some degree whether we admit to it or not. There is good and bad in us all; it's only natural that our nastier selves have occasionally thought ill of something our better selves would have shown greater consideration. Prejudice comes from our capacity to learn, a wariness of others gained from an instinct for self-preservation. It's almost as though we're hardwired with an allocation of prejudice that we can either spend lavishly or nullify with empathy and education. Some of us strive to do the latter, but that involves time and thinking. Many are short of time and choose to spend what time they have by doing as little thinking as possible. The problem with these dumbies is that they end up spending their prejudice on such run-of-the-mill targets as people with a different skin colour, religious belief, political ideology, or of a different gender, sexuality or class. I like to differ. I sidestep these commonplace discriminations by focusing my allocation on one tribe in particular – the vilest and most putrid tribe of all: them bastards Man. United.

Considering how hung-over I was after drinking the previous night in a club called Heebie Jeebies with a guy called Spider and a busker called Baz, my brain was too jaded to counter my prejudice with reason. The neurons weren't firing – I was dumb and therefore resigned to letting my prejudice off his leash to sniff out the crack of Manchester folly and piss on everything it holds sacred.

The Liverpool fans reading this book will know exactly what I'm talking about. For those with little knowledge of why Manchester United are regarded as the evil empire, here's a brief outline.

Let's start with the man in charge. As previously mentioned, Manchester United is managed by the piggy-eyed, ruddy-faced tyrant known as Sir Alex

Ferguson. His reign at Manchester began in 1986 when he declared his aim was to 'knock Liverpool off their @#$%ing perch.'

Before that, he'd worked for the Scottish club, St Mirren, where he was accused of intimidating a secretary. The altercation was noted during an industrial tribunal prompted by Ferguson after the club had dismissed him. The reason St Mirren sacked Ferguson was that there was no official discussion of his planned, not-so-secret move from St Mirren to Aberdeen. Another breach of contract occurred when Ferguson talked to at least one of his players on the sly about joining him at his new club. The tribunal upheld St Mirren's claims while noting that his behaviour towards the secretary – which included not talking to her for six weeks, confiscating her keys and only communicating with her via a teenage assistant – was 'particularly petty' and 'immature'.

UK journalist Michael Crick wrote in his biography of Ferguson (*The Boss*, Pocket Books, 2002), that the St Mirren saga revealed in Ferguson 'the bullying, the desire for total control, the obsession with money, the dishonesty and pettiness.' (If Crick wasn't a self-proclaimed Man United fan, you might accuse him of bias). But picking on the secretaries of Scotland would seem like a warm-up for what was to come. As if being petty and immature wasn't enough, he was soon recognised as a master of psychological warfare – an 'arch haranguer' – who belittles and berates those who threaten his goal of football supremacy. His targets include rival managers, journalists who ask the wrong questions, match officials who make unfavourable decisions, and even his own players – the ones who played the games that won the titles.

In a TV interview he stated that the United midfielder, Paul Ince, was a 'bottler' and a 'fucking big-time Charlie.' In his autobiography he wrote that former United player Gordon Strachan 'could not be trusted an inch'. He then criticised David Beckham's choice of wife which, regardless of what you think of Posh, seemed a little unnecessary, seeing he'd already put the boot in, or rather *kicked a boot at* his star player.

The said boot had been lying on the changing room floor before the raving manager – upset at the game just played – swung a foot at it. The boot caught Beckham just above the eye causing a cut that required stitches. It made headlines – even bettered the time Ferguson smashed a tea set. But after the boot incident, any possibility of Beckham spending another season at the club he had served since he was fourteen years old became untenable. In a matter of months he'd be sold to Real Madrid. Beckham remained relatively quiet about the affair while others who have been given the proverbial boot have gone public: Jaap Stam complained of a 'total lack of normal decency and respect...' Ruud Van Nistelroy said he felt as if he'd been 'stabbed' and Gordon Strachan, in response to Ferguson's claim of him being untrustworthy, wrote that it was the manager who couldn't be trusted, that he constantly ranted and bullied him in front of the team. 'The screaming and shouting did not cease – it just got worse and more personal.'

Not that you should feel sorry for any of these players. Not at all, for at some point they've all been willing accomplices in the win-at-all-costs belligerence which underlines United's success. And every success in turn just adds to their almost unbeatable self-belief.

In the nineties the self-belief could be seen in their youthful, attacking style of play. Since then, a 'smash 'n' grab' policy is what they more often rely upon. Dull and unimaginative for much of the game, they inevitably come out winners through a scrappy goal or a bad refereeing decision against an opposing team that has thoroughly outplayed them. Mind games, malicious tackles, the intimidation of match officials – like the mercenaries of countless wars, plunder is their glue; winning at all costs, their pledge.

This Machiavellian mentality of 'the end justifies the means' may sound harmless enough in a sporting context. But figure in United's global reach, the fact that nearly every bus you're on or office block you're in (no matter where you happen to be, bar Liverpool or New Zealand) will no doubt contain at least a handful of United fans that applaud such unpleasantness every week and you'd have every right to feel concerned. The wayward strains in the fabric of our society may well be linked. They may even be *united*. If you think that's taking it a bit far then, at the very least, consider all the backstabbers and brown-nosers, the tell-tale tits and tossers, the bastards and bitches, the weasels and rats, the glory hunters and gold diggers, the conmen and the connivers that inhabit our world and you'd have cause to wonder – is Manchester United really necessary? Do these types really need more encouragement?

A recent *Times* article claimed Ferguson had been spotted at Manchester airport with a book under his arm entitled *Lenin, Stalin, and Hitler – the Age of Social Catastrophe*. The publisher's spiel states that the tome 'explains how the pursuit of their (Lenin, Stalin, and Hitler's) "utopian" ideals turned into dystopian nightmares.' Hitler, according to author Robert Gellately, 'wanted to be a man of the people, to be loved, the opposite of Lenin and Stalin, who thought the views of the public could go to hell.'

By reading this text was Ferguson taking pointers, tossing up which style was right for him? Funnily enough, Ferguson has been credited with bringing a socialist ethos to Manchester much like Shankly did with Liverpool. His ruthlessness and shoddy treatment of his own players is portrayed by United-loving pundits as an example of his so-called guiding principle that 'no man is bigger than the club'. When a player – no matter how talented – becomes too big for his boots, Ferguson will apparently dump him with a view to the greater good. Yet the theory has undergone some major inconsistencies in recent times. When Christiano Ronaldo and then Wayne Rooney stated they wanted to play elsewhere Ferguson did everything he could to convince them otherwise; in Rooney's case, actually doubling his salary to a reported €220,000 a week.

And considering his abuse is directed at not just 'big time Charlies' but pretty much anyone who dares question him (Ferguson bans media he doesn't like from his press conferences), the image of a principled statesman pales even more. If Ferguson was ever a political ideologist of the left-leaning variety, than surely his behaviour would suggest that he's either lost all sense of reality or, at some point thought, fuck it - dystopian nightmare it is. As Stalin once said: *Ours is a just cause – victory will be ours!* I wonder if Sir Alex ever fancied himself with a bushy moustache?

United's success in the nineties coincided with a big influx of money that came with the newly developed premiership, including the introduction of massive television revenues from Sky Sport. Of all the clubs in England it seems only Manchester United can talk proudly of their 'club's brand' without blinking an eyelid. They seized the opportunity to brainwash the globe through the power of advertising – catapulting its brand through merchandise and team junkets to the four corners of the earth while everyone else was still getting their heads around the words 'football', 'brand' and 'selling power' being used in the same sentence. Some may argue that this is just the way of the world, that United's striving for brand supremacy was an example of great initiative. Indeed, it did increase their own spending power beyond that of any English club. But unless you're a fully-fledged capitalist spouting 'greed is good' than you will know, such financial gains are only made at the cost of something that doesn't have a dollar value.

In 1991 the club was floated on the stock exchange. Significant capital was raised. But once conglomerate status had been acquired things began to change. "When they priced out some of their most loyal supporters," wrote Oliver Kay in The Times, "United were looking for fans with deep pockets, not loud voices. Significantly, they are regarded not just as fans but as customers, willing to spend three quid on a match programme full of adverts for MUTV, MU Finance, MU Mobile and the club's myriad commercial partners, and to buy merchandise in the Megastore."

"The real money though comes from supporters in the corporate seats, of which there are little more than 9000. United boast in excess of 1000 executive boxes – Liverpool just 32 – which gives you some idea why the North West rivals are so mismatched when it comes to commercial revenue.

United's match day income is more than 3.5 million pounds per game, well over double that at Anfield. If that additional revenue comes at a price in terms of atmosphere, it is one that the Glazers (United's American owners) are willing to pay...'

The drawback of their exponentially increased support base through branding is that the 'new fans' wanted to be associated more with success than history and tradition.

At the start of the 2000/2001 season, United mid-fielder Roy Keane made a famous gibe at the 'prawn sandwich brigade' – the growing section of the crowd that prefers the hospitality on offer to actually supporting the team. The kind of fan, he explained, who sits in silence and waits to be entertained. Even Ferguson, as recently as the current season at the time of writing, complained that the atmosphere at Old Trafford was more akin to a funeral. Considering the track record of the American tycoon, Malcolm Glazer, and considering the kind of influence he's had on the club since taking it over in 2005, how could Ferguson expect any different?

An article on Glazer, the "cranky yank", appeared in the Daily Mail soon after his ousting of three key members on United's board. It claimed that Glazer, "orange-bearded and given to belting his trouser waistband ludicrously high like Mr Bean," was the kind of guy for whom money always came first. "He's like a machine – money, money, money. There's no other dimension," said one of his sisters, Jeanette. "I defy you to find one place where he has been charitable," said another. When their mother died, Glazer engaged in a legal battle with his siblings for control of her legacy, an action which led to the judge branding him "a snake in sheep's clothing". This on top of being dubbed the "slumlord" for attempting to rip off tenants with illegal fees at his US trailer parks.

The man who bought Manchester United without having set foot anywhere near Old Trafford, issued no statement of intent to woo fans upon takeover. Instead, he put up prices, putting season ticket holders – supporters since childhood - in a position where they felt compelled to sue their own club.

But really, who cares about them? My concern is with the repercussions that United's commercial revolution has had abroad.

A 2005 article entitled "Masai divided over Man Utd" claimed that even the Masai of southern Kenya have been negatively affected. Journalist Paul Willis stated that, "as in any local bar with satellite television, some would say there are too many Manchester United fans. Now, fed up with fellow warriors worshipping Wayne Rooney, Karatina Sangkok is leading a revolt against the Red Devils' sporting imperialism."

"We were sick of Manchester United fans dominating the village," said Sangkok. The tribesman went on to say that he'd set up an opposing supporters club in the hope that United's evil grip will be lessened.

The view from the train to Manchester was about as unspectacular as Kate and Graeme had said it would be. A few boring hills, the odd muddy waterway. Boggy fields of dull grass. The insipid outlook was occasionally broken by the factories and funnels of faceless industry – which usually meant a town of uniform terraced brick and damp hard streets just down the line. Another constant was the naked deciduous trees that, in their absence of leaves, had sought to cover themselves by snaring discarded plastic bags that flapped and billowed helplessly in the breeze. As usual, the culprit of this common gloom was the low grey sky. All in all, a beautiful day for prejudice.

As we got closer to Manchester, I noted the commuters who were heading home and took the opportunity to let my prejudice off his leash to sniff out the moral corruption.

Seated on the opposite side of the compartment was a pleasant-sounding businessman on the phone to his wife. He was catching up on her day with the kids when he cheerfully enquired whether young Charlie had taken an interest in his birthday present of a brand new football. Harmless enough on the surface but, as he spoke, the businessman shot me a knowing look, making eye contact in a chummy you-know-what-I'm-talking-about-mate kind of way. My prejudice seized upon his lazy assumption. This man's expectation that the world would be automatically in line with his way of thinking was clearly an indicator of the kind of torment he was putting his family through. It's the old story: overbearing father insecure about his own inadequacies pushes son to succeed in order to make himself look better. Then, having built his son up he knocks him back down again in order to feel powerful. The cycle continues until the son grows up and moves to a developing country to help orphaned children whose lives have been ruined by the cruel regime of an insecure despot. 'Okay honey, see you soon,' he said, ending the call. What a bastard.

Then there was the well-dressed, slightly attractive lady opposite me on the phone to her mum to say she'd be over soon, who, despite just a table separating us, didn't acknowledge my presence once. Not once! Even before she stood up for her stop my verdict was in: Snob! Who did she think she was not giving me the light of day? Saving herself for David Beckham was she? Good luck, princess – he's taken! And as for the guy who took his place? Trust me – you're not his type.

My prejudice was off to a flying start.

As per Chris's instructions, I got off at Manchester Piccadilly and took a second train to East Didsbury. *East Didsbury.* I ran the name over my tongue making a mental note to only say it with as little saliva in my mouth as possible. If ever there was a proper noun with globules of spittle waiting to be launched from between its syllables, East Didsbury is it.

Barely a minute from the train station and East Didders reminded me of the posher parts of Christchurch where the grass is sometimes grown to be looked at rather than touched, and where many of the Pakeha majority claim irrelevant ancestral links to first families (and hate being called Pakeha).

It was fast becoming dark when a friendly male face in its early twenties pointed me towards the Didders Pub where Chris had organized for us to meet. In keeping with my prejudice, I received the directions and hurried away, suspicious that someone so helpful in Manchester would surely want more than a simple 'thank you' in return.

I continued on the leafy road of private schools and established gardens. I then stumbled upon the place where the seeds of the Liverpool/ Manchester rivalry were planted. It was the Gothic architecture that caught my eye first, then the plaque that proudly declared that this – the Towers of the Lodge - was the very spot where the decision was made by town representatives, local businessmen, politicians and civil engineers to create the Manchester Shipping Canal.

This was Manchester's response to Liverpool's position as a world-class port. The "Big Ditch" as it was known upon completion in 1894, would stretch fifty-eight kilometres from the landlocked city of Manchester to connect with the Irish Sea, bypassing Liverpool's docks in the process. As well as being at the forefront of the Industrial Revolution as a cotton manufacturer, Manchester would soon double as a major shipping port in its own right. Having long accused Liverpool of charging excessive dues on imported goods, the reaction from Merseyside wasn't good: the Mancs were muscling in on their jobs. Unable to stop the canal from going ahead, the two cities have been locked in a duel for economic supremacy ever since.

If you could keep score on such things it might look something like this: Manchester £44,089 million; Liverpool £7626 million. The two figures are the cities respective GVA's (Gross Value Added); a measure of the value of goods and services produced in each area in 2006. While Liverpool's story is as rich as they come, its dropping behind Manchester in an economic sense is arguably the price it has paid for its rebellious nature.

Globalisation saw the decline of both cities. The advent of shipping containers contributed to Liverpool's 1970s dock closures while Manchester's port closed altogether in 1982. Changing modes of trade and transport meant that whoever adjusted quicker would be the better off. When Thatcher's policies decimated the industries of coal, steel, ship-building, cars and manufacturing, Manchester cottoned on fast (pun!) and reinvented itself as a service sector-based economy. Brick and stone buildings were replaced by glass and steel structures purposefully designed to encourage firms, corporations and companies from around the world to base themselves in Manchester.

Liverpool, on the other hand, took umbrage with both Thatcher and big business and dug its heels in the sand. While Manchester spruced itself up and put on its best shit-licking grin, Liverpool chose to fight. Led by a clique from within the elected council (in the form of the Militant Tendency's Derek Hatton), Liverpool became notorious for speaking out, going on strike, and causing all manner of disruption and disobedience in the face of what it saw as the dark, Tory forces at play. Once so important to its country's wellbeing, Liverpool (like other northern towns) was wounded by severe cuts to jobs, housing, education and welfare, and was told by the Tory government to get used to the reality, to *know its place*.

Brian Reade: 'Its economy, like the port, was shrinking and inward investment stagnated. The population fell, men were told at forty they would never work again, and kids left school with little hope of a career unless they got out of town. Crime escalated, council coffers were hammered and social problems became chronic. It was reckless neglect by a government using Liverpool's free-fall as a lesson to others about what happens when councils become increasingly bolshie and trade unions refuse to dance to their employers' tune. Memos leaked from Tory cabinet minutes showed that the city, like the unions and the IRA, had become an enemy within... There was a manic spirit about the place. Liverpool may have been perceived by a London-centric media as dying on its arse, but with football teams in the ascendancy, its groups still dominating the charts, its writers churning out the drama that filled the telly schedules, and its leaders standing up to a vicious dictator, Scousers felt invincible, superior and amazed that the rest of the country wasn't with them.'

Liverpool did not roll over, but it did get left behind – and due to a woefully inefficient public sector, suffered doubly for its transgressions. When John Pilger visited in the mid-80s he compared scenes on Merseyside with images from the Great Depression: 'An icon of the 1930s was the photograph of a miner and his son scavenging for coal. In the 1980s, the unemployed and their children scavenge on a twenty-acre rubbish tip near the River Streets known as Bidston Moss. They slither and climb on their hands and knees over hills of filth, fish finger packets, bacon rind, tea bags and dead dogs in their search for saleable scrap: a discarded telly, an old copper, wearable clothes. Only the polythene bags tell you this is the 1980s, not the 1930s.'

The depth of its decline means it'll be a while before Liverpool catches up in the GVA rankings. Then again, history would suggest Liverpool doesn't much fancy becoming a Manchester-style metropolis anyway. With a reformed council, growth in the education, knowledge, and research sectors, and with the Capital of Culture proving a great incentive to further highlight its historical identity (and thus increasing tourism numbers), Liverpool could be designing its own style of comeback – one with its personality intact.

The busy outdoor section in front of The Didsbury Pub is a great spot for imagining the sinister side of potential United fans. The fact that many here actually support Manchester City instead didn't deter me. I was just imagining the murderous past of the frail old lady waiting for a taxi (the cold-fisted grip of her walking stick screamed Black Widow!) when Chris arrived with his breezy upbeat self and all but blew my prejudice away. He declared it too bloody cold to be moping around outside so we went in, found a table, and caught up over several pints in the century-old warmth of the inn.

When I offered to pay for the second round, Chris said that he was under strict instructions from Nicky that I wasn't allowed to pay for anything while I was here. It was, Chris informed me, a rule they had for all visiting Kiwis on account of the strength of the pound over the New Zealand dollar; the latter worth about as much as a mouldy bean. My prejudice suddenly felt content to stay quiet by my side.

We got talking about the well-being of family and friends back home, shared a mandatory bitch about the UK weather, and rejoiced at the sheer high of experiencing the culture of our adopted clubs. I asked Chris if he'd planned my walking past the Tower of the Lodge to provoke some kind of response but he seemed oblivious to the little piece of history that had taken place just down the road. There was a temptation to use this as a platform from which to lambaste him about being an ignorant United fan but, with my next pint on the table and my wallet still undisturbed, I felt best to let it slide.

Instead, I brought up how different football culture was to the rugby culture we'd grown up with – the singing in the stands far preferable than simply standing around looking staunch. The subject hit a nerve. 'Rugby isn't staunch! Staunch is following your lower league team all over the country in the wind and rain. That's what football supporters do – that's staunch,' he said. Despite our opposing taste in football clubs, we were on the same page, more or less.

Over the next couple of hours the beer flowed with equal ease from tap-to-glass-to- gullet, and when it became time for a change of scene we made our way via Chris's apartment to *the Woodstock*, a mansion cum multi-storied drinking extravaganza where indulgence seeps from the leather, drips down the stairwells, and cavorts in low-lit corners. Towards the hour of peak intoxication when anything can happen – especially if you're not completely foul and your accent sounds mildly exotic to drunken girls who didn't come out to go home alone – Chris yawned, and suggested we head off. He'd had a full day. Besides, he said sheepishly, Nicky had another instruction: *Behave*.

The call for Saturday was a drive into the Pennines. Chris was keen to show me that there was more to them there hills than the monotony I'd seen from the train. Around midday we took off in his VW Golf for what began as a pleasant jaunt into the Cheshire countryside. I was enjoying Chris's company and, in light of my buoyant mood, my prejudice plonked onto the back seat where, under-utilized and a little neglected, he circled a spot to snooze. Because we where driving through the county whose main purpose had been to supply its industrial neighbours with dairy and meat, I'd nearly considered not bringing him at all, thinking there'd be little worth growling at.

Little did I know that we were entering the infamous triangle formed by the townships of Wilmslow, Alderly Edge, and Prestbury; a triangle known as 'Gold Trafford'. Back in 1999, even before the current crop of flashy Manchester United players donned their pearly boots for their glamorous club, writer AA Gill deemed this area 'smug central'; a place 'where Manchester United footballers bring their tin-opener-voiced, pony mad, disco-found brides to set up home.' Apparently, the twisting thirty mile-per-hour lanes of Gold Trafford are home to more Ferraris than anywhere else in Britain. It's even mentioned on the Wilmslow website that, thanks to the current dearth of traditional shops, you'd have better luck buying a super car here than a sausage.

We were somewhere around Prestbury when Chris dropped gears and shot the Golf up a lane of privet-hedges, landscaped gardens and electric gates. Prejudice pricked his pointy ears and raised his head from his paw.

'I'm sure this one's Rooney's,' said Chris, pulling up outside some crass, characterless monstrosity. He encouraged me to get out and take a closer look. What did he want me to see? Rooney himself? We both knew he was due to be playing that afternoon in Derby. Maybe his wife Colleen? That's a bit creepy.

'You go ahead; I'll stay in here,' I said. But rather than perving on Wayne Rooney's wife, Chris was imploring me to behold the wealth – the massive amount of money on show in the form of all that gaudy, gauche, sanitized and oversized LUXURY. According to Chris, Rooney's trophy house had its own cinema. There was also a sports stadium built into the sprawling garden. It was out of view but he assured me it was there. All I could see was a hangar-sized garage, a few too many pillars, and what looked like a swimming gazebo. The place was proof that Rooney was apparently maintaining something of a United tradition of bulldozing early 20th century mansions to make way for the mock Georgian and mock Tudor mockeries that best reflect their massive spending power and minimal tastes. Chris loved it. He was unapologetically in awe of what 'the boys' earned and what they spent it on when they weren't kicking footballs. He admitted to leering into the slightly-tinted windows of passing Ferraris, trying to spot the fancy footballer behind the wheel, virtually applauding this culture of frivolity with a *good on ya lad* grin.

Once again I had that same old feeling of missing something – not quite getting it, that feeling I often had with my friends in Auckland. Whenever I see a shiny flash car I tend to look away in an effort to deny the smug bastard driving it the satisfaction. You can't tell me there's not an unhealthy degree of self-importance that comes with driving a €100,000+ car. By all means, enjoy the quality, the precision, the handling, but until the driver proves otherwise, my gut reaction will always be: *wanker*. Jealous? Perhaps. It's hard to tell. If I had that kind of money I like to think I wouldn't succumb so easily, that I'd always remember there are better ways to spend it. (I'm like Spike Milligan in that sense – being a millionaire wouldn't change me; I'd just really like the chance to prove it.)

From the place that might have been Rooney's we drove on to observe another three estates – one of which Chris thought might belong to the 'Prince of All Preeners', Christiano Ronaldo. As you'd expect all three were big in every way – big columned entrances, big circular drive ways, big-arse gazebos – but none of them seemed capable of housing Ronaldo's ego. Meanwhile, my prejudice was up on his haunches, salivating at every structure as they served their purpose of fuelling his stereotype of the flashy United footballer. Chris went on about the car 'Ronnie' was importing (the most expensive in England), the bath tub that so-and-so had bought and the monstrous gaming system that required a whole wing of what's-his-name's house. I couldn't keep up.

I tried explaining that what was going on here underlined a crucial difference between our two clubs. Not that Liverpool players aren't immune to such excesses – but on Merseyside these things are more frowned upon than celebrated.

But no matter how I tried to put it, Chris refused to think that 'my lot' were any different to his. The poor bastard was just too far gone. If he loved the glamour puss culture, then United was the club for him and there was little I could say that would sway him either way. Besides, I was enjoying our voyeuristic ride just as much as he was: his happy approval, my happy disgust. My prejudice was all the better for it; his tongue was out, his tail was wagging and his coat was as shiny as any of the neighbourhood Ferraris. And just when it seemed it couldn't get any better, Chris all but threw my prejudice a bone. It was a result of my harking on about Liverpool's inspired singing that saw Chris come out with a few songs from Old Trafford. The first he recited was about Sung J Park, the South Korean player who many United fans thought had been signed for the sole purpose of gaining more support and thus more revenue from his highly populated homeland. To believe such a thing and still have respect for your own club is difficult to fathom. But then there's the song itself (sung to the tune of This Old Man): *Park Park Park wherever you may be/ You eat dogs in your own country/ It could be worse/ You could be Scouse/ Eating rats in your council house!*

Right now you're probably just as disgusted as I was. If that's the case then you'll probably need to brace yourself. Chris had more, much more.

Build a bonfire/ Build a bonfire/ Put the scousers on the top/ Put the city in the middle/ And we'll burn the fuckin lot! Ghastly! Then there was the one about Michael Shields, the young Scouser who was jailed for attempted murder in Bulgaria after the 2005 Champions League Final.

Michael Shields has got 10 more years/ Now he's getting bummed by queers/ 10 more years with no parole/ Now he's got a sore arsehole/ Fuck the scouse!

Hmm. The fact that there was a very good chance of Michael Shield's innocence was obviously not important.

'Why are United fans so bitter?' I asked.

'They're all like that, aren't they. I've heard the scousers are the worst of the lot,' said Chris.

'Doesn't seem that way to me,' I said. 'I've heard the songs – didn't hear anything about Manchester. As far as I can tell, Liverpool's songs are mainly about lifting the players.'

'You're just biased though, aren't you? They're all just as bad as each other.'

Biased, yes. In this instance, guilty as charged. But while Liverpool gets the rose-tinted glasses and Manchester gets the snarling prejudice, I surely hadn't been so blinkered to let any vitriol towards Manchester go unnoticed. If anything, I would've welcomed it. After all, I clearly recall letting out a chuckle when I learned on my Anfield tour that the United team bus had a canister of CS gas thrown at it when entering the ground back in 1986. Point being that, if I can find the funny side in that, then surely I would've been fine with a bawdy old song about the baddies of Manchester.

I asked Chris for more. When he struggled to think of any Manchester songs that *didn't* in some way mention Liverpool, a crazy thought popped into my head: was it possible that, despite their current football and economic superiority, Manchester was actually jealous of Liverpool? That behind their vitriol and slagging of 'Liverpool slums' (a bit rich considering 'Gunchester' has some of the worst violent crime rates in the UK while Greater Manchester has pockets of deprivation with 50% unemployment), that the Merseysiders had something Manchester envied beyond bragging rights of league and European titles? Something which transcends dollar value, something we might call *the Liverpool way*? It was too early to tell. Just a tasty thought in the meantime.

After a coffee and a quick look around the quaint little spa town of Buxton, we were soon back on the main strip of Didsbury, scouring the pubs for one where we could watch United's game against the down-and-out cellar dwellers, Derby County.

Inexplicably, none of the UK's main sports channels were playing Liverpool's game against Reading at Anfield. Seeing as it was a premiership encounter that didn't hold any real weight, I'd decided not to go, in order to save money for more important games coming up, including the match against United at Old Trafford the following weekend. We finally spotted a sign promoting United's game against Derby at a corner pub about half way down Wilmslow Rd.

This was my first and maybe only chance to see the nefarious Manc right up close in his preferred environment. Bearing in mind Chris's comments about Mancs being no worse than the rest, I decided in the name of balanced reporting, to leave my prejudice at the door. Unsurprisingly, the poor little whining bastard wasn't happy. He snapped at my finger. I pointed at the doorway where I needed him to stay put. The crowded pub consisted of two rooms partially divided by the bar itself, the cracked plastered walls decorated in orange, white and green as a precursor to St Patrick's Day.

Mentally prepared, I wondered if my level of anticipation was something akin to what David Attenborough might feel when venturing into the close confines of the steaming jungle in search of the great apes.

Like Attenborough, I trod lightly. I was not of their kind. Even as we ordered beers I kept my movements slow and avoided all eye contact. The flatness of their heads suggested that this particular group of primates had less developed frontal lobes – therefore, anything out of the ordinary could be seen by these creatures as a threat, any irregular behaviour enough to spark a fit of animalistic rage.

Grooming didn't seem to be a high priority for this troupe, and it seemed my downfall might be the lingering scent of the body wash I'd used that morning. It was a classic amateur faux pas. Having overlooked that at some point in the day I could be in close proximity to members of the Manc tribe, I'd used the fancy body wash that Nicky had left in the shower. Not a wise move when you could be in the midst of a tribe commonly known as 'scum'. And sure enough it didn't take long before the two Mancs in front of us tipped back their heads to sniff the air. They turned forebodingly to see what had triggered their sense of smell. Honey and jojoba? I tensed up – but wait, no, a packet of salt 'n' vinegar crisps, freshly opened. *Phew*... The crisps were devoured automatically as the attention turned back to the screen on the far wall. For the sake of experiment, I considered emitting a cheery 'Go Liverpool!' to see just what these creatures were capable of. But, as any scientist will tell you, the rule in the field of accurate observation is for the observer to remain as invisible as humanly possible at all times. I stayed true to this ethic and, as a result, my patience was rewarded; I was treated to a rare and wonderful sight of which I savoured every minute. It's not often you get to see United struggling, as they were that day. Derby County was bottom of the table. If United won the game they would go to the top. Chelsea had thrashed Derby 6-1 the week before so it was expected this game would also be a rout. Not so. With the rain pelting down, Derby showed great resilience and for seventy-five minutes did just enough to keep the score locked at 0-0. United dominated the game but, with every chance that went begging, the frustration was plain to see. The crowd inside the bar groaned and growled, gesticulating wildly at the screen - turning on their players with alarming flippancy and venom. 'Fuckin' useless,' and 'pack of cunts' were the terms I deciphered from the thick Mancunian accent (a guttural version of Scouse).

They also kept referring to someone they called 'Ronnie'. I'd heard Chris mention this Ronnie character earlier in the day. I'd wondered if it was just an odd variation of Rooney until it dawned on me that 'Ronnie' was their cute little nick-name for Christiano Ronaldo. A smile crept across my face. I'm aware that supporting Manchester United requires a fairly high degree of delusion, but this was beyond anything I could imagine. Many English hold onto a notion of themselves as being loyal, stoical and honest, with a dogged fighting spirit. I have no problem with that – it's the stuff that wins the big wars, if not the World Cups. But to try and instill these qualities on a preening, pouting, Portuguese pretty boy by calling him 'Ronnie' was almost too absurd to be comical. Christiano Ronaldo is many things, but a regular

Bobby Bulldog ain't one of them. Better still was the fact that, up on screen, 'Ronnie' was doing a fairly good impression of hapless, a rare role for him indeed. His shots at the Derby goal hit the bar; his passes were repeatedly intercepted. Time and time again his chiseled, lachrymose face looked up to the heavens, imploring the football gods to allow something more than the constant downpour and the terrible slick it was making of his heavily-gelled head. Perversely, the chiseled one's antics were being copied by his very unchiseled followers in the pub. It was then that I realised that instead of United fans making Ronaldo more Ronnie; Ronnie was *making them more Ronaldo.* The misshapened and shapeless mimicking the super model athlete. Think the cast of the Biggest Loser doing the Zoolander blue steel without even knowing it. Add the spoilt brat eyes, the down-turned 'I want bitty' mouth, the rattle-tossing fists thumping down on fatty upper thighs, then put them in front of the football in a Manchester pub and you have a very strange sight indeed. It was so good I was about to whistle my prejudice inside before looking down to see the little bugger was already in, barking and biting at the shuffle of shoes around us. Sadly, the spectacle didn't last. The football gods let Ronnie have his goal and everyone was relieved. United ended the game victors and went to the top of the table. It was a shame it had to end that way, but my prejudice and I got more out of the experience than we could've hoped for. As the locals sat down to their boozy analysis, we headed for the door. Prejudice, tongue out, trotting along behind me, nipped half-heartedly at the flap of passing trouser cuffs. The little bugger had pretty much had his fill and was beginning to feel the satisfying tiredness that comes at the end of an eventful day. He did, however, have one dastardly little deed left in him. As we stepped onto the footpath, he paused and happily cocked his leg at the door.

9. The Birkey

Thursday night back in Liverpool. Restless. Kate and Graeme have friends over. They're taking *Guitar Hero* to epic proportions. They're truly amazing at it - virtual rock gods every one of them. So when I reluctantly get up to play, they think I'm having them on, unable to comprehend how anyone could be so bad. I try to make it less embarrassing with an overload of self-deprecating humour. It doesn't work. Guitar Hero's not for me – I couldn't have sounded worse with two legs of ham strapped to my wrists. Someone urges me to have another go and all I want to do is ram that stupid plastic guitar down his gullet. Eat it, moron.

But that's not the entire reason I feel restless. It's been a strange week. On Monday I returned from Manchester. That night we celebrated St Patrick's Day in the kind of raucous bar-hopping fashion you'd expect in Liverpool; all well and good.

Then, on Tuesday, I spent two nights in Blackpool – two nights I'll never get back.

My reason for heading to the 'archetypal British Seaside Resort' was based on a recommendation from Stephen, a patron of the Leys Library where I worked back in Auckland. While I was checking out books for Stephen one day, he said that some years back he'd ended up in Blackpool because it was the maddest place in England he could find. Stephen had needed somewhere mad because he was a clown. Literally. Big hair, oversized shoes, and a painted smile. Blackpool was the only place where Stephen could earn alright money by performing in such a manner. He made Blackpool sound like the perfect mix of freaks, fun, and fantasy. And I trusted him.

First impressions weren't good. Strolling past the staid blocks of hotels along Blackpool's promenade, I made it to a derelict theme park where I surmised that the sound of gloom is the repetitive clang of an idle rollercoaster, rocking in the breeze of a bleak English day. So I went to the pub.

The Blackpool residents I spoke to at The Albion only shaded my impression. Apparently I was a decade or two too late. Place is full of dangerous wankers, said Ricky, a friendly middle aged man with a faded *London Skins* tattoo on his neck. Ricky's acquaintance at the end of the bar agreed; the fun had left town. And when fun leaves a town like Blackpool with its fake Eiffel Tower and its 'Big Un' rollercoaster, all you're left with is the dreary tackiness, a surplus of Blackpool rock, and kill-me-now-because-I-can't-fake-this-smile-any-longer cabaret. But currently the worst thing going for this seaside resort was the weather – so foul it made the ocean bulge like a tumour and the township's buildings appear frozen to the ground.

In saying that, I spotted what appeared to be English families having the time of their lives. Through the salt-smeared windows of my hotel room I witnessed the delirious cackle of a tipsy Mum, the ruddy-faced smile of a wet T-shirt dad, and the screaming joy of their kids bouncing from puddle to puddle, trying to splash each other while holding down hoods to keep out the rain.

Hugging the radiator, I felt like a wowser.

'What's going on here?' I said down the phone to a highly amused Erin back in Australia. 'It's late, it's bloody cold, and people are having fun as though hypothermia doesn't exist. What's going on?'

Erin had travelled to this part of the world some years ago. She said she'd warned me. With my every demand for an explanation, the harder she laughed, until all I could do was cast my muddled mind to the storm and let the cuckoo birds take control. Bugger it, I thought, wishing her goodnight. If it's good enough for them, it's good enough for me. Off I went into the tempest, a couple of hundred metres down the promenade, hoping to find a bar that I could heroically enter and down shots of whiskey like a rugged cowpoke who's made it through the storm. Alas, nothing. Every bar I'd seen during the day was shut – even the 'rough ones' I'd been warned about when checking into the hotel. I cursed this crackpot town and the faraway clown who'd sent me here. None of it made sense.

But wait.

I was heading back to the hotel when I spotted an oasis of light in the distance. I dropped my shoulder to the storm and stumbled towards the source. Angsty, wet, and soon to be bedazzled, I walked into the foyer of the Lynlene Hotel. I took a left into the ballroom – the light and all it illuminated looking just as welcoming as it did from outside. The dance floor was packed with geriatrics. Their immaculate white hair with its hairspray sheen fair shimmered beneath the ballroom's globes.

They smiled, bobbed and swooned to the dulcet tones of a crooner up on stage – working the audience with his syrup-laden syllables, his booming baritone and his invisible big band. It was magnificent! I hadn't seen so many elderly people having this much fun since Cocoon. Those who weren't dancing were red-faced with raucous laughter and, within minutes of sitting down, I was making friends with the incredibly friendly duo of Brian and Mo McClure. They queried me – in the nicest possible way – as to why the hell I was here. They insisted I have some of their liquor. I raised the vessel, anticipating what was surely the elixir of eternal youth, but what actually turned out to be lager. It tasted like one and the same.

We chatted away until a rendition of something by Frankie Valli set up every flaming fogey in the house for one last surge before midnight. When I left Brian and Mo mid sing-along, I almost felt a sense of pride in the knowledge that, against the odds, I might have just experienced the best Blackpool has to offer. Yes indeed, fun times in tacky town. A very Frankie Valli kind of fun, but fun nonetheless.

Was it enough to have me stay another night? Don't be silly.

The next morning I got up in time to catch the free cooked breakfast they had going downstairs. Apparently I was the only guest of the hotel who'd bothered. There was also a good chance I was the only guest. Still, the grandmother of the family that ran the hotel was more than happy to cook me up whatever I liked. When she brought the meal to my table, she narrowed her eyes at me. 'Are you (so 'n' so) from Coronation St?'

The look on her face when I had to reveal that I wasn't so 'n' so from Coronation St almost made me feel guilty for being boring old Glenn from New Zealand.

She shrugged. 'Typical. No one famous ever comes here,' she said and hobbled back to the kitchen.

For the next several minutes I sat alone, chewing on sausages, eggs and beans, wondering if it would please her if she knew I'd written a novel. Maybe I could lie by saying I was famous in New Zealand; would that make her happy? But the only sign of life for however long it took to finish breakfast was the barely audible din of morning television from behind the kitchen door. I slipped into my coat, gathered my bags, and left the hotel without a soul to notice.

It was at the train station where I discovered Blackpool had a farewell surprise for me. The station's toilet was dimly lit by low neon bulbs – a deterrent to the use of intravenous drugs, denying junkies adequate light to locate a vein. Apparently, they were keeping away the cleaners as well. The stench was unbelievable. Almost vicious in its pungency, it burrowed its fetid beak into my nostrils, causing me to gag. I willed my bladder to empty faster than water from a balloon but the stench succeeded in sticking its talons down the back of my throat to pull out a slop of undigested sausage, beans and eggs, dispersing it across the floor where it added a fresh layer to the coating of lumpy muck already there. I cleaned myself up as much as I could and left the toilet feeling no guilt whatsoever. Five quid says grandma's breakfast is still there today.

After Blackpool you'd think the relief of just being back at Kate and Graeme's flat would be enough for me to relax. But the ridicule of being *Guitar Zero* only exacerbated the restlessness. Then what I considered to be the underlying reason surfaced like a bubble: Kate and Graeme weren't Scousers.

Sure, they were Scousers in spirit, but not by birthright. Even though the majority of Kate's family came from Liverpool, she'd actually grown up in Worcestershire – Malvern to be exact. Graeme, as we know, was Northern Irish as were most of his friends. So where are the Scousers? I asked.

'Scousers are just Irish who can swim,' said Kate. She was alluding to the Potato Famine in the 1840s, when hundreds of thousands of Irish people attempted to cross the Irish Sea in leaky vessels known as 'coffin ships'.

The Irish, with the Scots and the Welsh combined, are a big reason for Liverpool's reputation of being the least English of English cities. The historical significance of Kate and Graeme is that they are the new generation whose decision to live here is partly motivated by Liverpool getting back on its feet. In turn, their input is exactly what the city needs to continue in the right direction.

Kate was a community worker helping underprivileged youths discover their own path. Graeme worked for Sony, whose presence in Liverpool, along with a few other big companies, provides work opportunities outside the public sector. Much needed, considering the public sector accounts for around 40% of Liverpool's employment.

A few decades ago, people their age would've been encouraged to abandon the city and head south. And even though Kate and Graeme were clued up and in sync with their adopted city, I felt that, in order to get to the heart of Liverpool, I would need to be mixing more with those who'd grown up here, more native than naturalized.

'You need to get in with some old timers, like,' said Graeme.

'You need to call cousin Eddie,' said Kate.

Just a few years shy of fifty, it would be unfair to call Eddie an old timer. He was born on Scotland Road, an area just north of the city centre once known for its predominance of Irish Catholics, overcrowding, and hard living. When I dialed his number, he answered as though he'd been waiting to hear from me. Thanks to Mike he already knew who I was. Any time was good for him, so we agreed that I'd pay a visit Friday night.

Crosby village, where Eddie lived with his partner Joyce, was several train stops north of central Liverpool.

The door to their place was blue, one of an all-brick terrace row that verged on the footpath of Harvey Lane. His instructions upon arrival were to walk right in – 'Don't bother knocking – it won't work,' he'd said on the phone. Ignoring Eddie's advice, I knocked anyway. I couldn't help it. How do you turn up to a stranger's house without knocking? You don't. You can't! Sure enough, no one came to the door. After a considerate thirty-second wait in the cold wind that was funneling its way down the lane, I knocked again. Nothing. It was plainly obvious that no one was coming out, yet there I was, paralysed with politeness, seemingly unable to override a basic rule of my upbringing despite so many years of attempting to be my own man. Ever since I was a teenager I had done a myriad of things my mother would have – and had – disapproved of. I'd taken up smoking, experienced great intimacy with wayward women, consumed illicit drugs, been tattooed, gotten into fights, driven dangerously, hung out with unsavoury characters, *been* an unsavoury character, preferred the unshaven look, not cared if my clothes had holes in them, grown my hair really long, and even left the house without a hanky. Yet here I was, once again bound by her code of etiquette, just as I was the first morning at Kate and Graeme's. As I waited streetside the whole silly little debacle had me learn two things about myself: firstly, that home invasion would never be my thing and secondly, if I stayed out here any longer, the only thing politeness would provide is frozen buttocks.

In the country where manners were invented, the idea of walking in unannounced felt so peculiar. But, of course, this wasn't really England; it was Liverpool, and with the help of an embarrassing amount of determination I reached for the handle, turned it, and crept on in. *Scandalous!*

There was a small entranceway, two closed doors and a narrow flight of stairs around to my right.

The muffled sound of music and laughter made choosing the right door a piece of cake. It opened up to a small, smoky living room that at first seemed packed with at least a dozen people but, now I think back, contained merely eight colourful Scousers.

Like many of his ilk, Eddie looked about a decade older than he was. His first gesture was to hand me a smoke. 'You haven't been knocking, have yer?' he said, as if it'd been a test.

'No-no,' I said, unsure why I was lying. 'Nice to meet you Eddie.'

The table expressed their collective delight at the sound of my accent.

They all took turns at saying 'Ehddee', but were tactful enough not to push it. Before I had a chance to sit down, they complimented me on my first novel, a copy of which they owned courtesy of Mike's stay several weeks before. The Liverpool supporters in the room were especially impressed. Eddie procured it so they could pass it around to see if I really had written in my author's bio: 'Glenn's major goal in life is to die, and be reborn a gifted striker playing for the mighty Liverpool football club.' While this provoked great guffaws among the red supporters, in equal measure it put the room's blue supporters on the defense. They fixed me with what seemed like prepared lines about Everton being the first club on Merseyside, Everton being the only club in the premiership that had never been relegated, and Everton being the true 'people's club'. Their zeal was admirable and, once I had received my Everton education from Joyce's ex son-in-law David and his father Brian, a salt-and-pepper fox called Barry asked me if I was intending to stay the night.

Before I could edge in a reply, Barry encouraged me to say yes, and announced that by meeting Joyce I was in for a treat – she was one of the greatest people I was ever likely to meet. Joyce laughed and with a barrow-load of smoker's gravel in her throat stated that 'any friend of *our Michael's* is welcome to stay as long as they want.'

I replied that I'd only turned up in the clothes I was wearing. She looked confused. 'What did he say, Eddie?'

The hovering Eddie explained Joyce's trouble with understanding any accent other than Scouse, not to mention the trouble anyone not from Liverpool had understanding her. When they'd travelled to New Zealand two years ago to stay with Mike and the family, Eddie said he'd spent most of his time acting as translator. 'Heads were turning my way every time somebody said something. It was like I was working for the United Nations, but we were all speaking English.'

With Eddie's help, I explained to Joyce that I'd be happy to stay the night.

When the visitors had gone and Eddie was passed out on the couch, I too had sleepy, drunken notions of crawling upstairs into bed. Joyce, however, was mortified at the idea. When I seemed ambivalent about going out, she declared there was no way I was spending my first night in Crosby without going to the pub. When I said that it really wasn't necessary, she questioned my moral fibre. So off we went arm-in-arm into the bluster of the night to Stamps bar - a lively two-storey joint of bare brick walls and boundless character - where it soon became obvious she was something of a cult hero.

We caught the end of a covers band playing between the curved bar and a spiraling staircase. We downed kookily named local lagers while Joyce introduced me to everyone she knew; which *was* everyone – bar flies and bartenders alike.

I learned that it wasn't just Joyce's lively banter and ability to drink a camel under the table that made her popular. I was told that it was something of a Stamps tradition for Joyce to wrestle the microphone from whatever band was about to play so she could warm up the crowd by singing 'Angels' by Robbie Williams. Now, it must be said that a life of cigarettes for breakfast and boozy cackles by lunch hadn't left Joyce with the most delicate of voices. But I wouldn't doubt for a second that her high notes possessed a certain charm – a bit like a Chinese violin that, no matter how much care an old smiling soul puts into playing it, still sounds slightly broken. Apparently, anyone who didn't look to be appreciating such charm would cop it right then and there – Joyce breaking off mid-performance to declare those people at the back who didn't sing along to the 'Angels' chorus a bunch of soulless bastards. Through sheer force of personality, Joyce's fans far outweighed her detractors.

When the staff at Stamps surreptitiously recorded her one night to replay her performance in the bar the following day, she was inundated with compliments from friends and strangers alike.

Now, Robbie Williams has never been my cup of tea, but, when it came to the cult of Joyce, I was an instant fan.

The next morning, with Eddie working and Joyce visiting her ailing sister, I took the advice of everyone around the table the night before to check out the iron men of Crosby beach. The so-called 'iron men' is an installation by the artist, Antony Gormley. I was taken aback by their resounding praise for it, especially their friend Mick (yes, another Mick) who stated outright: 'I forkin' love them – I forkin' love the oyren men.'

After a twenty minute walk from Eddie and Joyce's flat on a better-than-ordinary morning, I came upon the verge of low lying dunes. There was a car park and a rec centre with a giant brown circular roof that looked as though it could start spinning any moment to whisk everyone inside light years away on a b-grade space adventure.

Not far through the dunes the path opened up to a vast stretch of beach where the first thing to catch my eye was a row of offshore wind turbines. The fact that the distant white propellers caught my attention first says something about the subtlety of Gormley's installation. Like an optical illusion, once you see one you see them all. You feel a bit dopey for not seeing the iron men en masse straight away. All up, one hundred iron men dot the Crosby foreshore. Covering a mile, the space between them gives the impression that they're individuals – albeit sharing the same predicament. You find yourself trying to see what they can see. It's the cold grey breadth of the Irish Sea they're staring at but what these rusted figures are supposed to be contemplating is ambiguously summed up by the work's title: Another Place. I could see how another place carried significance for Scousers past and present. Maybe it symbolised a yearning to leave – in times when the city was offering little more than a difficult existence. For me, Another Place (strangely enough) wasn't anywhere in particular, more a catalyst for thinking on broader terms about the concept of the unknown, of how coming to grips with the unknown binds us together and splits us apart. Some of us try to replace the unknown with fantasies of heaven and hell. Many try and distract themselves from even contemplating the unknown by focusing on the material; others shrug and seem resigned to a 'let's wait and see' approach while some seem comfortable with the idea of the unknown offering nothing else but sudden oblivion. The iron men, though cast from the same mold (of the artist's actual body), seem to be at different stages of life or, at least, more exposed to life's extremes depending on their proximity to the sea. Some are so far out they become completely submerged by the high tide. Then the water pulls away revealing their heavily barnacled bodies – old souls no closer to the answer, but perhaps more accepting that, if there's one to be found, it's somewhere out there, somewhere beyond the shores of our present existence.

I put my arm around one of the figures closer to the dunes. It's not an easy thing to do. I felt as if I might be interrupting something. I also felt that, by merely touching the iron man, he might actually come to life – straight from a scene in Dr Who. But I had to do it. The iron men represent so much of what it is to be human. If nothing else, it was a show of solidarity. A poem I have since read by Harold Pinter seems to describe the experience pretty well:

I know the place.

It is true.

Everything we do

Corrects the space

Between death and me

And you.

I left Crosby beach with a great sense of wellbeing.

Back at Harvey Lane I waited for Barry, whom Joyce said would come over at about one o'clock to 'look after' me. I did some push ups and a few stretches on the living room floor – an attempt to persuade my booze-soaked body from turning to putty just yet.

When Barry arrived he seemed suitably chuffed that I was playing Eddie's CD collection of Beatles 45s up loud, and, after around three seconds of wondering what to do, we decided the afternoon was probably best spent down at the pub.

The first stop was the reliable Stamps where Barry pulled out a homemade poster from inside his overcoat, unrolled it, and pinned it to the notice board. It was an open invitation to 'the Big Camp'. The Big Camp was the brainchild of he and Eddie, who'd mentioned it the night before. 'We get all of Crosby to go camping together,' he said.

'Whereabouts?' I asked.

'We don't know. But everyone will be there. It'll be boss,' said Barry, gazing back at Eddie.

'Big dreams, these two,' said Joyce, shaking her head.

The Big Camp, I learned, was an annual affair in which everyone climbed aboard 'the Big Camp bus,' headed rural, got out, put up a few tents, and got pissed – not necessarily in that order. Last year the bus broke down the day they were meaning to return. They rang the 'auto man' to come and fix it, but, after he left, the bus broke down again. By the time the mechanic returned, Barry, the designated driver, had had a few too many so it was a matter of waiting for him to sober up before they could get going again. Sure enough, once they did, the bus ground to another halt. 'Campin',' said a whimsical Eddie, 'it's what we do.'

After Stamps, Barry took me up to Crosby mall and into a narrow modern bar called Cads. He introduced me to the musician Georgie James, otherwise known as 'Old Blue Nose.' I'd already learned a bit about Georgie James from a promo poster in Eddie's living room that read: 'Old Blue Nose Is Back, the unmissable, the incredible, spine-chilling, toe-tapping, good natured, one and only, honest to goodness, no messing, yes it really is Georgie James…'

When I asked the celebrated Georgie why he had seven wedges of lime floating in his vodka and soda he said that a new wedge with every drink was a good way to keep tabs on how many he'd had. He leaned in: 'But I took some out at the bar, because I don't want to look like a pisshead.'

Being a blue nose (Everton supporter), Georgie was disappointed at me being a red, but led me out the back of the bar through a large swinging door for a smoke and a chat all the same. Georgie had been friends with the Beatles (they'd even been to his wedding), but he was more intent on telling me how much he enjoyed New Zealand lamb and all about his son who'd played for Everton as a youngster and could've gone all the way if it hadn't been for his gammy knee. When I asked Georgie if he was playing any gigs while I was here, he showed me his bandaged hand. He said he'd slammed it a few weeks ago in the heavy door behind us. He became downcast about not being able to play his guitar and, with more than a tinge of regret, said that he'd worked his whole life as a tradesman but had finished up with nought to show for it. Playing music was what kept him going and life without it was driving him to drink.

We went back inside and I was just settling into Cads when Barry slipped his overcoat back on, pushed back his salt and pepper hair, and suggested we go somewhere 'a bit more happening.'

'Happening' seemed a bit lofty for a quiet village on what was now a bitterly cold Friday afternoon, but Barry said it as though he meant it. We walked past a supermarket, negotiated a huge roundabout, and headed down Cooks Road to a large, traditional-looking pub called the Birkey. We veered left through the front door into a roomy wood-paneled bar that, besides a pool table, a jukebox, and something called a fruit machine, was completely devoid of humans. It took a while to get the barmaid's attention – she was tending to an adjoining room that made up half the ground floor. Unlike our side of the bar, the other half had patrons. Barry wasn't fazed. He said we were better off staying put.

We had a game of pool, which I ended up winning largely thanks to Barry not being able to compose himself after my educating him on New Zealand's 'honest attempt' policy when a player is on the black. 'Honest attempt?' he said gleefully. 'Honest attempt!' He looked like he was about to burst.

'You don't play honest attempt?' I said.

'Are you havin' me on? Honest attempt in Liverpool? Every game would end in a bloody brawl!'

He challenged me to a game of pinball of which he was the reigning Birkey champion. And promptly kicked my arse. Barry admitted to being a pinball fiend virtually since the game was invented. The way he made that machine flash, jingle and bleep like a robot on ecstasy gave me little reason to doubt him.

In the meantime, a few locals began to file in, including the buxom Sue who bounced up to the pinball machine with the sole intention of putting Barry off his game. She finally succeeded by grabbing his head and burying his face into the soft depths of her ample cleavage. Barry came up for air with a grin the width of an Everton goal mouth.

Things were starting to happen.

We sat around a table with Sue, her surly teenage daughter (whose name I forget), her off again-on again partner Drew, and another girl called Steph. Within an hour of doing so I'd sung *Mr Mojo Risin'* at the top of my lungs with Barry and Drew, been invited to Steph's wedding, and had memorable interactions with nearly everyone who walked into the bar. The immediate standouts were a tall guy named Bert who was missing an entire ear due to it having been bitten off in a fight, and another guy whose heavily bandaged head made him look like he'd arrived straight from the set of *The Mummy*. The poor guy was a mess, couldn't stop shaking. He told me how he'd just got out of hospital after being electrocuted while working at the docks. According to the doctors he was lucky to be alive, let alone down at the pub.

But it wasn't all shock and maim. Drew, a youngish dead ringer for local actor Peter Postlethwaite, waxed lyrical about the game of football – not a remarkable thing in a place like Liverpool, apart from the fact that Drew didn't like watching it. What he found fascinating was the symbolism of the ball as sphere and how it spoke volumes about the human condition when people were so obsessed with controlling and propelling this mini-sized world with, not their hands - no no, that would be too obvious - but with their feet. Their feet! For proof that human existence is truly absurd, look no further than football, he said.

Steph and Sue rolled their eyes. For them, football, from any angle, was boring. A life permeated by the game was enough to put them off for many lives to come. It was now snowing outside – not the thick, heavy kind of snow that turns everything into a winter wonderland; more the light wispy kind that becomes instant slush on impact with the ground. It prompted the girls to state that what they found absurd was that I had spent my money travelling to Liverpool when I could have been somewhere sunny.

'I came for this,' I said. They looked confused. 'I came for the Birkey. This place is great – this is what I've been looking for. It's like a big extended family, young and old alike. You don't get this back home – not like this.' They rolled their eyes once again and laughed.

'Problem is,' said Steph, 'you take a shit in Crosby – everyone wants a smell.'

It took a while, but they reluctantly agreed that they wouldn't swap The Birkey for anything, except for somewhere warm. Steph admitted that, thanks to the Birkey, she'd saved on wedding invitations, knowing that everyone here would turn up anyway.

Barry said this is why he'd chosen to stay this side of the bar. He said the other side was too straight-laced; this was the side that knew how to have a good time. However, he added, not so long ago a number of scallies (Scouse for bogans) had decided that the left half of the Birkey was their idea of a good time as well. Barry said it was up to him and the lads to expel the rough element – with silliness rather than force. This involved spending a whole afternoon pretending to be excitable little girls, ordering cheap and nasty cocktails in high pitched voices from the bewildered staff, and dancing the night away to the likes of Abba and the soundtrack to Dirty Dancing. According to Barry, every scallie present headed for the door and never came back.

It was a shame for me that after a few more pints, more banter, and more spontaneous sing-alongs, thanks to Drew's excellent selection on the juke box, it was all starting to feel like too much of a good thing. Barry had been surprised earlier in the day by the amount of alcohol I was putting away, to which I shrugged, as if to say 'this is the norm.' In truth my fast consumption was just a desperate attempt to keep up and, if I'm brutally honest, seem more interesting. Some five hours later I needed a moment to collect my thoughts before they drowned in an amber sea. For respite, I went outside for a smoke in the small, partially sheltered concrete courtyard. I leaned next to a sign that said: *This is a designated smoking area. You must smoke or you will be requested to leave. Thank you for smoking. P.S. Shhh...!*

For a minute or so it was just me and a wizened-faced gent in his sixties. He stood with minimal motion, enjoying a cigarette in the relative silence. He seemed more akin to the men of his generation I knew back home – neatly trimmed and attired, and laconic like he'd only call a spade a spade.

Little did I know he was picking his moment.

His target came in the form of a huge guy in his twenties who emerged from the bar. A bit like humpty dumpty teetering on the wall, the lad swayed and hopped from one foot to the other.

'What's wrong?' I said.

'I've just been to the toilet.'

'So?'

'I've got drops,' he replied.

'Did you say drops?'

'Yeah. Drops on the insides of me legs.'

'To stop the drops,' announced the laconic man, 'you need to take one hair from your head to put into the end of your penis.'

'What will that do?'

'The penis will snort, and that will be the end of your drops.'

'What if it sneezes?'

'Sneezes? I can't help a sneezing penis, lad. Just be sure to keep it away from me.'

So much for collecting my thoughts.

Still, I wasn't complaining. I'd laughed more in one session at the Birkey than I had the entire year. They may not have been the most athletic-looking bunch, but, if banter was an Olympic sport, the patrons of the Birkey (left half) would win gold every time. True to form they would accept their gold with a piss-taking grin and sell it for another round – straight back into training.

Their style of banter was akin to an exciting passage of football – a verbal pass and go where one-liners would be exchanged until a cross was delivered from left field to be finished off with the glorious goal of a punch line, sending everyone into stitches. It was a game where the women were just as good – if not better – than the men.

Most of the time I was happy just listening. Normally, if I'm quiet around a group of people, it's because I'm uncomfortable. Maybe someone's getting on my wick or maybe the conversation is just boring my mind elsewhere. I didn't say a lot at the Birkey for the reason that I didn't want to interrupt the performers' flow. High praise considering I was struggling to decipher every other word.

So why is the gift of the gab so strong here on Merseyside? Is it a survival skill developed over generations of hardship? Or was it because there was nothing else to do? Too cold to go for a run, too many puddles for tennis?

According to local author Alan Edge, it comes down to football fervour – a long time preoccupation of passionately contesting the Red and Blue issues of the day: '…the first question to greet a stranger arriving at anyone's door would be to enquire whether they were Liverpudlian or Evertonian and extract their views on the latest football gossip. This would often be even prior to it being established who they were and for what they had come and the crazy thing was that a football debate, perhaps lasting as long as an hour or so, might ensue before the purpose of the stranger's visit was established, at which point, it might be found they had, in fact, knocked at the wrong house…'

Considering the football fervour that still exists today it was inevitable that, despite the convivial atmosphere at the Birkey, talk would soon turn to tomorrow's game between Manchester United and Liverpool. It was talk with serious overtones, as everyone was far too aware that Liverpool was yet to win against Manchester since Benitez had become manager. But the consensus was one of quiet confidence that the reds, based on their strong form of recent weeks, were ready to break the hoodoo. It was going to be tough; luck would no doubt play a part, but Fernando Torres' form would surely tip the balance in Liverpool's favour. It had to, I was relying on it. I'd already paid for my ticket. And when you're a haggling halfwit buying from Tony the Tout, these things don't come cheap.

10. Man U v Liverpool

When Chris had driven me past Old Trafford the previous Sunday, I feigned hunger, pretending to have mistaken the stadium for the largest McDonald's restaurant I'd ever seen. The glass exterior of the East Stand entrance and the modern grey and brown façade made it look like a suburban style McDonald's, just a thousand times bigger.

A conversion would be easy. First, pull down everything Man U-related. Second, erect the golden arches. Third, replace the Old Trafford turf with that spongy playground surface, add a few swings and slides and the kiddies would come from far and wide.

In no time the second largest stadium in Britain would be the largest McDonald's in the world. After a few years we could all pretend that Manchester United never even existed. Judging by what Roy Keane and Sir Alex Ferguson said about their fans, all you'd need is a McPrawn burger on the menu and they'd barely notice the difference.

You can't tell me that Malcolm Glazer hasn't thought about it. Who knows, it might entice him to visit more often.

Alas, the night before my return to Old Trafford that marvelous vision of McManchester came back to haunt me. I dreamt that I was in the stadium, trying to watch the actual game while growing terribly frustrated by a series of rotating circular playgrounds. Big mechanical arms moved the rotating playgrounds from left to right in front of the stands. Even worse was the discovery that each playground was packed with Malcolm Glazer clones, red bearded fatties wearing head bands and netball skirts -swinging, sliding, jumping up and down – even shooting hoops. Just when one playground was out of the way, another would take its place, obstructing the view of the pitch. I took to scampering up and down the aisles to catch a glimpse of the football but I was chased by faceless ground staff into dark tunnels filled with rats.

It seemed that no one had a problem with the lunatic setup but me and before the game had even finished – God knows who was even winning – I had to flee from the so-called Theatre of Dreams out of fear for my mental well-being. I did so with a full body jolt and a cerebral *whack* back into consciousness. At first, I wasn't fazed. Just a little nightmare, I thought, staring into the darkness. But when it became apparent that getting back to sleep wasn't possible unless I actually re entered the dream, I realised I had a problem. Cue several hours of nodding off and waking up seconds later – considerably more bamboozled every time.

The sluggish, dreary, sense of foreboding I felt when it was time to get up was hardly surprising. I showered, dressed and ate breakfast on autopilot before finding my way to Lime Street station.

On board the train it seemed the other Liverpool fans were in a similar state. For a moment I wondered whether we'd shared the same dream – a kind of Jungian collective unconscious something-or-other where archetypes and symbols pertain to a cosmic tribal mythology. But instead of asking the guy sitting across from me if Malcolm Glazer in a netball skirt meant anything to him, I said, 'You going to the game, mate?'

'Yeah. Bloody nervous like.'

'Yeah, me too.' And that was it.

We returned to our butterflied stomachs, knowing that the only possible way for this experience to be anything but utterly demoralising was if Liverpool beat Manchester United. Nothing less would do. There would be no 'football was the winner on the day', no 'hard luck, fellas - better luck next time' consolations. It was all very black and white; today we experience one of two things: football hell or football heaven.

Because there were no trains to the ground itself it was necessary to catch a tram from one of the Manchester stations, inevitably jam-packed with United fans. I'd been warned that displaying Liverpool colours would only lead to unwanted attention. It was too cold just to be strolling around in a shirt anyway, but the same excuse wouldn't suffice when it came to wearing my scarf. Scarves, unless you're something of a fashionista dandy, are predominantly worn to help keep the body warm. I'd barely stopped wearing the thing since my arrival – reluctant to take it off for a shower.

But in addition to its practical use, Shankly once anointed the Liverpool scarf as having a purpose more profound. The story goes that, on one of his last days as Liverpool manager, Shankly spotted a policeman step on a reds' scarf that had been thrown from the Kop. The Scotsman promptly picked it up, wrapped it around his neck and told the policeman: *This scarf is someone's life.*

Hence the Liverpool scarf is no ordinary scarf. Mine had been good to me. It was frayed and threadbare yet, unlike some, had not unraveled when I needed it most. How could I betray its integrity by not wearing it to a game against the biggest rivals? So, with Shankly in mind, I decided it should be with me, around my neck where all good scarves belong. It would've been easy enough to keep it hidden beneath the bulk of my coat but no, that wouldn't do either. This was a question of dignity – I was determined to have it visible.

Standing between the tram door and me was a guy in his late forties who looked at me as though I represented everything he hated in life. To my side a young brick shithouse bore the flared nostrils and icy stare of a boxer about to enter the ring. Did I, at this intense juncture, wedged between the dark forces of aged bitterness and aggressive youth, reconsider my decision? Was I tempted to redefine the scarf a silly inanimate object that I owed absolutely nothing? Of course I was, but I wore it anyway. I stood tall with the most disinterested look I could muster. And when the tension got to a point of suffocation I did what dumb Americans do – I asked a really obvious question. 'Does this take us to Old Trafford?' The forty-something-year-old scowled; the brick shithouse grunted. In the minutes that passed, the brick shithouse retained his silent focus while the scowler went on scowling, no doubt incensed at having to breathe the same air as some Liverpool-loving foreigner.

Everyone avoided eye contact, and when the doors finally opened, we poured onto the platform. From the tram stop to the stadium I managed to separate myself from the Mancs to merge with Liverpudlians. The walk was a brisk affair. The only interaction with the other side happening when some grot with a pendulum Manc swagger announced that we looked like we were off to a funeral. Ironic.

The closer we got to the ground the more outnumbered we became until we were separated from the red devil masses and directed between two lines of horse-mounted police. I caught a glimpse of the 'Munich tunnel', built to commemorate the eleven United team members and staff who died when their plane crashed after trying to take off from Munich Airport in 1958. Apparently, there's an exhibition on the team, the 'Busby Babes' (after manager Matt Busby), inside the tunnel. But the police and their horses were too nervous to let us deviate from the cordon, and we were swiftly ushered to the appropriate turnstiles.

In the bowels of Old Trafford the Scousers were in good voice. The sound of the familiar songs momentarily settled the butterflies. But they were back the moment I ascended the stairs that opened out into the arena.

Stadia are often referred to as cauldrons yet with Old Trafford this seems like an understatement. It was immense – a sheer bloody brute of a place where aesthetic aspirations wilt in favour of uniform mass. From my relatively low position, some fifty odd rows up from the field, you could barely see the people in the upper tiers looking back at us. It was so dark and distant up there it seemed incredible they should be here to watch the same game. Even as people were slowly finding their seats, the sheer size of the stands gave it the kind of latent menace you might ascribe to the shaded side of a looming mountain, or a front of turbulent cloud muscling its way across the sky.

First impressions suggest visiting teams don't stand a chance.

But coming from a place like Anfield where the pulling together of fans feels so integral to the team's success, it was a welcome sight when, within minutes of being unfurled, a gigantic banner that was supposed to cover a large section of the United fans became twisted and tangled and eventually discarded as a useless cause. *What the- fuck- is, what the- fuck- is, what the- fuck- is- that?! What the fuck is that!* we chanted, pointing with glee. I felt a fleeting hope that their bumbling show of strength through unity was a sign of things to come. Was this the day United would put on a display as deplorable as the majority of their fans?

No such luck.

A few minutes and they were one up. Here, unification wasn't required. They were a different monster altogether. Only when Pepe Reina took a swing and a miss at a crossed ball to see it bounce off the shoulder of Nemanja Vidic and into the Liverpool goal did Old Trafford roar en masse. All together they let us know, in no uncertain terms, that they were champions and that we were shite. Scouser shite, to be exact. When 80,000 people direct a collective outburst of vitriol your way, even hard line atheists could be forgiven for mistaking the boom and clamour as the howling wrath of a deranged god. With a rebellious verve we reacted by singing even louder than before, trying to catapult Liverpool free of their nervy shell. Just when it seemed as though the tide was slowly turning, our optimism was dealt a bitter blow by thirty seconds of chaos.

This is what happened.

While battling brilliantly for the ball, Fernando Torres was hacked not once, but twice, from behind by the terrible twosome of Rio Ferdinand and Paul Scholes. When the referee decided to foul Fernando Torres for being hacked from behind, Torres, as is his wont, turned to the ref to say something along the lines of 'What's up?' only to be shown the yellow card.

Being Argentinean and therefore knowing an injustice when he sees one, the Liverpool midfielder Javier Mascherano ran over to dispute the decision only to receive the same treatment. Because he'd already received a yellow card for a tackle (that was in no way malicious), the second yellow meant his ejection from the game. It was a truly unfair turn of events, a mockery of massive proportions. Mascherano duly flipped out and had to be led from the field. At the sight of the implosion the Manchester crowd jeered and chastised; never before had I seen such an injustice applauded so vehemently.

From across the cordoned divide of a twenty-metre gangway, fans made eye contact with opposing fans of equal hostility and proceeded to give them the fingers, make vigorous wanking signs, and yell the word 'gobshite' as loudly and frequently as possible. After thirty-three years of not knowing the word 'Gobshite' even existed, I would hear it several dozen times within a matter of seconds. Expressions such as *Shut your bleedin' gobshite!* and *You fucken' gobshite twat!* sprayed back and forth like machine gun fire. Once that line of verbal attack was exhausted those who wanted to prove that they really meant business tried to make arrangements for post match punch-ups outside the ground. But, as it turns out, trying to enunciate phone numbers and establish meeting points via hand signals to a person twenty-odd metres away while trying to remain ferocious isn't easy. The sight of thugly males pausing their mutual hostility in order to actually communicate before reverting back to mutual hostility made me feel embarrassed on their behalf. This was not an occasion that brought out the best in people.

As the players took to the field again, we all knew in our heart of hearts that, as bad as it had been, things could easily get worse.

The fact that United's supporters still didn't feel the need to sing only reemphasized their smug disposition, so we chanted: *Fergie's right, your fans are shite! Fergie's right, your fans are shite!* They reacted by chanting something about Hillsborough, to which Liverpool fans responded with chants of *Mu-nich! Mu-nich! Mu-nich!* Ouch. 'This feels like it could blow!' said a guy behind me. Just when the mutual hatred seemed beyond containment, United scored again. Not long after, they made it three. If the scoreline wasn't bad enough, what really rubbed it in was that the only time their fans seemed to band together was when they tried to sing over the top of You'll Never Walk Alone with their own version: You'll Never Get a Job. What a pack of arseholes. The final whistle couldn't come soon enough, although a policy of letting the respective fans out of the stadium at different times delayed our exit.

With the police forming cordons along the gangways of the Liverpool section, we watched the stadium empty around us, forced to listen to Mancs hurling their final insults before leaving the ground. For up to an hour we were kept behind like naughty schoolchildren on detention. This was the last place we wanted to be – the very spot where team and fans alike had taken a pounding. To keep our spirits up we sang the Fernando Torres song. Although the compulsory bouncing that goes with the song's crescendo was vital for keeping warm, the repetition soon became tedious. With the adrenalin produced by the spectacle of the match worn off, the mixture of tiredness, cold and frustration had me feeling that maybe these policemen were extending their authority a bit far. Maybe they looked down on Scousers and maybe their holding us back for so bloody long was less to do with our own security and more about sprinkling a little salt on the proverbial wound. Were they treating us with a degree of derision, exerting a little power over the lowly Liverpool supporters to show who was boss? Surely three quarters of an hour inside an empty stadium was enough time to get things orderly on the street.

I began to imagine how easy it would be for a few thousand recalcitrant fans to simply push a few hundred police out of their way. The longer they kept us, the more it seemed we had every right to. Their stern looks suggested the police knew it as well; they couldn't keep us here forever – something had to give.

But instead of threatening to do something as extreme as rushing a line of cops, the Scousers had a different way. As if to test their true intent, they changed the prelude of the Torres song from *We're gonner bounce in a minute* to: *We're gonner bounce with the bizzies* - 'bizzies' being Scouse for police. It took a couple of choruses and a great deal of encouragement from the fans but the police eventually dropped their stonewall professionalism to get into the spirit of things by jumping in unison with the Liverpool crowd. There was resounding applause for their efforts; they genuinely looked to be enjoying themselves. There was still a while to wait, but now we could do so without the tension. The bizzies had responded well.

When we were finally let out, light-hearted moments were soon forgotten. From behind a makeshift barrier, hundreds of United fans vied for a place from which they could ogle and yell through their rotten lemon peel lips the kind of insults you'd expect to hear leveled at a pedophile leaving a courtroom. But apart from the odd pissed-up Manc out to provoke, the road leading to the station was relatively easygoing. The thirty-metre queues for the tram were not. Within minutes of waiting in line I saw a fat drunken Manc charge at a father and his seven-year-old son who were dressed head to toe in Liverpool colours. He was intercepted and dragged away before his raised fists could connect but, just when we thought we'd seen the end of him, he was back yelling, "I fucken' hate Scousers! I fucken' hate the Scouser cunts.' Once again his acquaintances managed to get a grip on his flailing arms and the folds of his jacket to pull him back.

If I'd doubted it before, I now knew it to be true – you really do stand to have the shit kicked out of you just for wearing rival colours. In broad daylight, and even when you're with your seven-year-old son ... maybe even if you *are* a seven-year-old son.

The fat bastard Manc turned out to be the first of the failed bullies. After a short tram ride I walked to Deansgate station where I hoped the train to Liverpool wasn't too far away. Being one of those days, it was. With a large group of Scousers and a cordon of policemen who stood guard at the top of the stairs leading to the platform, I waited for over half an hour for the train to arrive. For half that time we were entertained by a bunch of Mancs shouting lame insults while pacing the platform on the other side of the tracks. With a dozen police gathered at the top of the stairs on our side, they were unable to come any closer. They threatened to cross the tracks and beat the living daylights out of us but everyone present knew that wasn't going to happen. And when they kept repeating their bad-assed intentions ad nauseum, it all got a bit tired, a bit boring, a bit sad. The Mancs were like coke-addled zombies, their grey matter too riddled and rotten to come up with a decent plan, let alone a decent comeback.

A beanie wearer and his hooded mate made noises that, police or no police, they were coming to get us. They separated from the rest of the group and disappeared down the stairs only to pop up again some forty metres away, embarrassingly enough, back on the same platform. Their mean-eyed faces flickered with confusion.

'If it isn't tweedle dum and tweedle dee,' shouted a Scouser, shaking his head.

The Mancs seethed.

When the train finally arrived we hastily jumped on board. As we moved towards Merseyside and the howling mobs of Manchester receded, I couldn't help but feel that, even though Liverpool had taken a thrashing, it was the Mancs who'd emerged the biggest losers.

As tempting as it is to just leave this chapter with the image of the pitiable United fan stomping on the platform of his own misery, we must remember that even degenerates such as these deserve a fair go. Yes, the temptation to cast them off as humanity's malignant sores, devoid of reason and kindly deeds, is a strong one.

I'd love to chalk it up as simply Liverpool: *good*; Manchester; *bad*, and try to leave this passion play by way of the high horse. But moral victories are as good as worthless and, having read the confessions of two Scousers, Messrs Reade and Edge, it's difficult to sum the situation up so easily. Yes, United are bad but it's not simply because they're United. Prejudice should only be used in the spirit of fun and never taken seriously. Hubris is the crux of the problem. In Greek tragedy, any character displaying hubris would often be struck down by the gods. I would've welcomed wrathful punishment on every insolent Manc present that day but the sticky knowledge is that, during their pomp, Liverpool succumbed to hubris as well.

For Brian Reade, a pivotal moment of his Liverpool fandom came after the shock defeat to Wimbledon in the 1988 FA Cup Final : 'We were an arrogant shower of pricks who'd got carried away with all the hype and flattery surrounding the side. We'd believed in our own publicity and forgotten the very basis of the Liverpool Way. We insulted Shankly's mantra about football being a simple game made complicated by fools. And we deserved to get our conceited arses spanked.'

Likewise, Alan Edge recalls the inability to cope with Liverpool's decline in the nineties as the moment he realised what the success had done to them: 'For us, to be starved of exaltation, was to deny a junkie his regular fix...Of course, nobody had any sympathy for us. Every other supporter knew the score – we were spoilt rotten, elitist, arrogant, pompous, condescending, patronizing, conceited prima donnas who deserved everything that came our way (just like Man United fans now).'

In light of this, all we can do is *will* United to lose, *will* Liverpool to win and, when the cycle turns in our favour, recall our recent history and know not to let success go to our heads. That way, it might never go away.

If only noble intentions weren't so unrealistic. And dull.

11. Cynicism, Again

One of the good things about being a lover of English football in New Zealand is that when your team suffers defeat, you can almost get away with pretending it didn't happen.

Turn off your phone, jump in the car, head into the great outdoors. Simple. Nothing like a nature buzz to exorcise the demons. If the weather's bad you can head to a rugby-obsessed bar where football could be just a figment of your imagination. Here, among posters of All Blacks and beer, rugby rules the world. If you include Wales, it's a world of about four and a half countries.

Unsurprisingly, a Sunday on Merseyside after losing to Man United is a dreary place indeed.

I was back at the Sefton flat watching mindless TV from the leopard-skinned couch, when who should pay a visit? Micky. Micky Manc. He came right up to me singing *We're not Brazil we're Man United!* and thrusting his hips as though rogering a rabbit that only had seconds to live. He unfolded the Daily

Star and gleefully read the headlines: *Three and Easy, Mad Masch, No Stopping United as Liverpool Kop a real good hiding, It's Mas stupidity*, and so on. Naturally, Mick agreed with every word these hacks had written. What surprised me was that Graeme agreed as well. The bastard! I took umbrage with their bird-brained views and silently questioned Graeme's authenticity as a red's supporter. What a let down, I thought. Nicest guy on the planet; pity about the misinformed treachery. Knowing that anger was probably an overreaction, I settled into a good, stern grump.

The basis of their argument against Mascherano was the new prerogative of the FA, a movement to clamp down on players' bad behaviour towards referees. The so-called 'respect campaign' had been on the tip of media tongues all week, prompted by the standover tactics employed by the Chelsea team the previous Saturday.

At one point the blues' defender Ashley Cole had abused the referee to the point of intimidation before turning his back on him like a spoilt little brat. After that, the FA made it known that such behaviour would no longer be tolerated by the game's authorities. It was time to clamp down. Therefore, a week ago, Mascherano's run towards the referee for an explanation why Torres had been yellow carded would almost certainly have gone unpunished. But in light of the campaign, consensus was that Mascherano's questioning of the referee was 'stupid' and 'pathetic'. One article displayed the headline 'Liverpool Show Their True Colours,' completely ignoring the reds' disciplinary record, one of the best in the league.

The incident had everyone talking. You could easily dismiss it all as an example of football's over-inflated self-importance - grabbing headlines over truly serious matters, stories of oppression in all its different guises.

But if you're trying to justify a football obsession like me, you could see the Mascherano ordeal as a metaphor for society's perennial failings, the kind of behaviour which reflects why the world is so prone to oppression in the first place.

One of the great things about football is that, more so than rugby or any other code, players have the right to question a referee. If the player is insulting or in any way disrespectful he should be punished. If there's a culture of disrespect, such as that shown by Chelsea, then a unified stand needs to be made. But that doesn't mean a player should lose his right to pose the question just because others have behaved badly. An authority figure should strive to differentiate between those who are being objective and those who are being unruly, in any given situation.

If he or she doesn't bother, and simply opts to punish the objective as he would the unruly, it all gets a bit fascist. That's right, *fascist* – I've said it. It may sound extreme but isn't the whole Mascherano affair a classic example? All the ingredients are there. You have the authoritarian (the ref), the perceived scourge (coined 'the culture of dissent'), the propaganda machine (the Man U-ligned media), and the scapegoat (Liverpool's Mascherano).

William Goldsmith and George Orwell wrote great works of literature showing us how easily society can descend into savagery. In this particular story was Mascherano not the football equivalent of a 'Napoleon,' or a 'Piggy'? Doesn't brandishing him as 'stupid' and 'pathetic' render things a tad simplistic? And by agreeing with such a simplistic take, are we not revealing the same susceptibility as those throughout history who have succumbed to the hollow rhetoric and misinformation of dictatorships?

With Micky it came as no surprise – he consciously backs the evil empire. But Graeme? Liverpool fans are supposed to be able to see through this bullshit!

Feeling a dubious mood worsen, I pushed up off the couch. I wasn't afraid of calling Graeme and Micky Nazis; I was afraid of meaning it.

'I need a walk,' I said.

And off I went, along the puddled paths of the slippery green bog otherwise known as Sefton Park. Within minutes I passed two underdressed women smoking cigarettes beside a pram. I grumbled, shook my head, and continued walking until I came upon a wide basin of dark sludge - an empty pond that looked as though its plug had been pulled for no other reason than to piss-me-off. For one lousy moment I needed a world without fallibility. I tucked my chin inside the collar of my coat and reduced existence to a mere two metres in front. I wondered why the world had to be so thick, why it is that I'm so much smarter than everyone else, and what kind of dumb deluded prick thinks he's so much smarter than everyone else.

I came across a large domed glasshouse.

It reminded me of one of my last days with Erin, walking through Auckland's domain to the winter garden where our love for each other had never felt so real and impossible. Ours was the fiery fraught kind that comes with two righteous people who won't give in until they've succeeded in telling the other person exactly why they're wrong. Our fights would last for days. Only emotional exhaustion could ever win. And when we were too exhausted to start again, the truth eventually surfaced. We were incompatible. As we wandered through the winter garden breathing in the warm musk of exotic plants, it felt as if we'd come to the same conclusion. We didn't stand a chance.

It was the first thing we'd agreed upon in ages.

And now, months later, sentiment had grown exponentially and swung like a wrecking ball beyond that logical conclusion. Now we thought we'd be okay.

Was I really such a fool to think my move to Australia would change anything? Six months in, would it not be more of the same, but to a backdrop of okka trash, cackling kookaburras and looming bush fires?

I had no idea. No answers. Nothing even close. I couldn't even find a way into the domed glasshouse; the spiked iron fence encircling it was firmly padlocked.

I tried to get angry but couldn't even muster that. There was a sign on the fence that said the park was being restored. That explained why the pond was currently sludge and the glasshouse, with its odd broken window and its peeling white framework, was closed.

So with nowhere else to go, the grump turned in on itself. I questioned everything I thought I knew. I became acutely aware of being consistently wrong about everything – I had no right to put forward any opinions on any subject whatsoever. The notion was like an abyss, a whirlpool that swallows you whole but leaves you standing where you are. Doesn't have the decency to make you disappear. Everything I thought I knew was wrong. All the predictable people – everyone who stated the bleeding obvious, everyone who backed the status quo, did and said what was expected of them and ignored the bullshit rising to their armpits – they were all right. Go autopilot, go complacency, go unquestioning. Go with mediocrity and delusion. Isn't that what we're here to do, find our delusion, the delusion we've secretly been yearning for all along? Happiness isn't for fools. Honesty is. Great fiery barbs of honesty. Erin and I flung them at each other from the couch, down the hallway and onto the back lawn of our personal predicament. We couldn't help ourselves.

When I got back I sensed some unease in the flat.

You get that when you're an irritable prick.

People pick up on it.

My avoidance of Kate and Graeme over the next few days was indicative of the depths of my prickdom. You'd think that, having realised I was a prick, I could just stop being one but, no, I couldn't even trust myself to do that.

On Monday I caught a bus into town. I went to the Tate Modern where a series of paintings by a famous French artist provided some respite. Her bright, bulging caricatures seemed to prove that life with an imagination can be as boundless and fun as you want it to be. Then she broadsided me with a twisted film pastiche featuring the artist herself and an actress playing her daughter. It was a sexually graphic affair: simulated orgasms (without the simulation) and repetitive dialogue consisting of 'Mummy I want to fuck you,' and, 'No you have to fuck Daddy,' and, '...Mummy I want to fuck you,' and then, 'Go fuck Daddy and pretend you're fucking me.' It was ultra-contrived, arty-farty shock nonsense on overdrive, designed to help women realise they deserve better and men to feel like creeps whose sexual impulses are just a pretext to abuse.

She got me on the creep aspect. Watching the film, I began to lift off. Thankfully, it was nothing a sheepish exit from the gallery and into the chastening wind couldn't fix.

I stayed on in town to see the powerful *There Will Be Blood*, which reminded me of my floundering connection with my old man – another failed relationship, another righteous stand off, another confounding repair job.

Figuring a shift from my morbid disposition was going to need more effort, on Wednesday I took off a hundred k's south to the town of Chester where I walked its Roman walls, snooped around its jumbled bookshops, and made light banter with the locals. But an otherwise pleasant stay came to an end with an argument with a bunch of lawyers outside the aptly named restaurant, *Fat Cats*. One of them had noted my accent when asking for a light. He exhaled deeply and flapped his glossy overbite in my direction: 'What brings you here?'

'The greatest football club in England,' I said.

'United?'

'Liverpool.'

'Shows how much you know about football,' the toff scoffed. As usual, the derogatory tone felt like a kind of affront.

He wore cuff links and braces and looked at me like I was some heathen from the colonies, a right old peculiarity he couldn't get his head around. He had the rotund shape of a well-fed swine and skin that looked glazed with a honey-based marinade. Pop an apple in his mouth and he was fit for the banquet. I licked my lips and reminded him that Liverpool were still the most successful club in England and, as far as I was concerned, always will be. He scoffed in unison with his fellow toffs. They smirked at each other for reassurance. 'That was a real football display at Old Trafford, wouldn't you say?'

'What? Coercing the ref and then winning against ten men?'

'Oh come on – Liverpool got their comeuppance.'

'I don't know about that.'

They looked aghast. 'Now, you seem like a relatively intelligent chap – how could you come away from that match thinking Mascherano was anything but an animal? He ran thirty yards towards the referee!'

'He's a footballer. Footballers run. It's a habit. Besides, why should Mascherano have to pay for the sins of Ashley Cole? Ferguson's more disrespectful to referees – and he's a manager. Mascherano is the FA's sacrificial lamb. Lawyers – of all people – should respect the right to question authority, right?'

No response. I guess they weren't *that kind of lawyer*. Then, with a good amount of wine down my gullet, I foolishly fancied they were taking a moment to acknowledge my point. I tweaked my ears for a 'by Jove, you're right,' or a 'splendid – this chap's really onto something!'

Instead: 'Football should be more like rugby. You don't see *them* complaining,' said the pig in need of a spit.

It would take less than a week before games played with utterly polite players wishing to avoid the Mascherano treatment were declared 'damp squids'. Even the hacks who'd lambasted Mascherano agreed, and within weeks everything would be back to normal – players acting in the same way as Mascherano, without the overt punishment. Everyone welcomed back the drama and those who had criticised Mascherano probably didn't give their opinions of two weeks ago another thought. Just moved on to the next thing. Nothing learned.

12. Canal

On Thursday I got a call from Eddie. He invited me back to Crosby, specifically for a boat ride along the canals with Joyce and Barry. I couldn't get there quick enough. I left Chester on an early morning train and made it to Eddie's at around 9 a.m.

As happy as I was to be back, there was trepidation in knowing that my irritable prickdom might well taint what had thus far been a positive experience in Crosby. I hoped I wouldn't ruin it.

As far as the canal boat was concerned, Eddie and Joyce had been offered a free day trip so their 'hub of Crosby' status would lead to ongoing business. We loaded up a taxi with several boxes of beer and drove to our meeting point, a small country pub beside the canal. We waited in a light drizzle until the boat master and several other passengers arrived to welcome us aboard. The canal boat was a long, low, red and green wooden barge. Simple, well kept, and a worthy source of pride for its owner.

Chugging along, it was soon obvious that we weren't in a hurry to get there. We didn't even know where 'there' was. Droning languidly, the motor propelled us with a placid momentum. If we didn't have beer we could've served cups of tea in the time it took to pass the handful of walkers along the banks. Joggers left us for dead. Feeling a little more relaxed, I sank into my seat and appreciated life aboard a motorised vessel that can be easily overtaken by a sprightly person on two legs.

Up on the deck we smelt the good, honest blend of fresh air, diesel smoke, and damp earth. We contemplated the undersides of stone bridges and bore down on ducks who avoided us with nonchalant strokes of their webbed feet. Canal boat owners travelling in the opposite direction grinned with a mutual trust, as if to say 'we couldn't want for anything more,' as though the grace of sailing, the thrill of jet boating, or the luxury of a launch was nothing to aspire to. Their world was free of pretension, the watery slow road: no potential strife, no high speed crashes, and most importantly, no jumped-up wankers. Don't get me wrong; when it comes to boating, there's nothing better than the wide open seas, but if you want some time away from the flash, screech and bang of modern life, you'd be hard-pressed to find a better route than the narrow waterway of the Liverpool-Leeds canal.

Eddie was in his element. The barge was perfectly in line with his sensibilities. He described how luxurious modes of living held little appeal, how affluence suppressed personalities and turned people bland. In contrast, life aboard a canal boat represented a life of endless possibilities. Every patch of sighted land secluded by a bunch of trees was perfect for a plot of 'do-dah'. And every time Barry pointed out another, Eddie turned to Joyce to say, 'Oh, I'm made up with this, luv.'

Joyce smiled, her arms locked against the biting breeze, one sorely exposed, trembling purple hand cradling a cigarette: 'Big dreams these two – big dreams,' she said.

Our destination along the canal was a pub offering a hearty breakfast before the soft yellow flames of an open hearth.

As we washed our meals down with local ales, a stooped geriatric staggered in spruiking homegrown veges at homegrown prices. Joyce's eyes lit up. She was so taken by the wizened old bugger she demanded Eddie buy everything he had to offer. His ears must've pricked, for the instant he'd sold Eddie three heads of cauliflower he was out the door and back again with fistfuls of garlic. Once the obligatory purchase was made, the old man became the wrinkled embodiment of eternal gratitude. Again, he headed from the pub. Minutes passed and he was back with freshly dug carrots. Joyce gave Eddie an expectant look.

'Every time he walks through that door I lose two quid!' he protested, handing over the money. The old fella wasn't fazed, and soon reappeared with onions. This time he didn't want the money. He handed the onions to the loving Joyce and declared her smile was all the payment he needed. Eddie took a long, wry sip of dark beer.

We boarded the barge with anchored stomachs and more veges than a farmers' market.

Sheltered from the now torrential rain in the low cabin we were well on track to polishing off the boxes of beer when, out of politeness, Barry asked the boat master if he'd like a puff on the do-dah he'd rolled for the trip home.

'Oh no, yer can't be smoking that in here,' said the boat master. In the spirit of joyful anarchy, Barry sparked it up all the same. The boat master shifted in his seat and harrumphed, but his fleeting stand was no match for the collective charm of Crosby's finest. Despite the illegal activity aboard his vessel, the boat master seemed so appreciative of our company that the joint became something of a white elephant, then it just became smoke, then it disappeared all together, making way for barrels of laughter. The boat master enjoyed every minute of it. Spotting our eagerness for his story he scratched beneath his captain's hat. He looked at his boots and rubbed them self-consciously on the carpeted floor.

'I spend a lot of time by me-self,' he said in a sombre tone that caught us all off guard.

'You don't have a wife?' said Joyce.

'No. She's passed on.'

'What about your family and friends?'

'They're at the funeral.'

So many jokes followed. And while some of the punch lines were better than others, the delivery itself was always worth a laugh.

13. Scouse Only Day

After the canal boat ride I stayed the night with Eddie and Joyce. I stayed the 3 nights following as well - they'd have trouble getting rid of me.

A normal day at Harvey Rd involved being woken at around 4 or 5a.m. to the sound of Eddie coughing like old Joe Camel before he set off to work.

I would fall back to sleep until late morning when it was Joyce's turn to unearth some tar before fixing Eddie a late breakfast on his return.

With Eddie buggered from his early start, and the bump and haul of his brother's furniture moving business taking an extra toll, I'd come downstairs to find them on the couch watching episodes of Shameless or Coro St from the night before. Apart from the northern accents on TV, the house would be quiet until the afternoon when the day's first beer would help ease things back. The music would go on, and life would return.

After breakfast I'd head down Liverpool Road to pay my respects to the iron men. Without fail, the combination of exercise, iron and salty air had an almost magical affect on me. My moulded mash of brain acquired a whirr of anticipation – rather than fretting, I was positive, actually looking forward to a new life with Erin. A failed relationship is one of the most humbling experiences a person can have. When you're coming off half a dozen or so over the course of adult life, it can send you to the point of cluelessness. Thus, the positivity that came from my iron men walks was welcome. It even felt honest.

After studying their unassuming faces and understanding their awe-struck silence, I just really wanted to be silly again. It was something worth aspiring to. And because the silliness you share with the person you love is the best kind of silliness there is, I started to feel incredibly lucky: Erin's capacity for silliness was vast.

Much as the Kop makes up new words to popular tunes, Erin had a similar knack. Or so she thought. The songs she liked to hijack ranged from Mellow Yellow to something from the Sound of Music, with a bit of freestyle rap thrown in for (what I hesitate to call) good measure. Her performances were impromptu, her lyrics poorly thought out. Sometimes she would take an eternity to think up the next line – and when it arrived it hardly ever made sense. With a bizarre mix of anguish and glee, she'd jolt, shake, and eventually break out into a full body crunk. Once the spasms subsided, she'd dance like Alexei Sayle. I'll admit, when I first saw my sexy brown-haired girl dancing like a big bald white guy I felt a little cheated. I wished I'd been aware of this earlier in the relationship. When I pleaded for her to stop, my protests were futile – she'd just keep on dancing until I gave in with a smile. Only then would she relax.

This is how it would be, I thought, facing the ocean. With anguish and glee we were bound to each other, helpless to end even if we wanted to. It's the stuff the schmaltzy types might call 'destiny'. They can call it what they like.

On the Saturday morning – while Ed and Joyce were with their grandson Reece – I took off to Crosby beach once again. Today was different from the rest, as the weather wasn't quite so oppressive. It wasn't exactly balmy on Merseyside but it wasn't freezing either. I wouldn't venture to call it sunny, but the pale morning light was enough to remind me that the sun still existed. Never has an overcast sky felt so reassuring. Adding to this pleasant shift from bleakness were fragments of Gerry Marsden's *You'll Never Walk Alone* – the song emitting from the occasional car seen coasting the Crosby streets, windows down due to the nearly fine weather. This was no mere coincidence. There was cause for anticipation, for today was derby day.

At 12.45p.m. Liverpool were to kick off against Everton at Anfield for the 202nd time since 1894. It was the longest-standing derby in the land, and despite my attempts, no amount of pleading worthiness or pounds sterling would be enough to get me a ticket to the game. This was strictly a Scouse only affair: Liverpudlian v Evertonian, Mighty Red v Royal Blue.

Back in the eighties, when the teams were on a more even keel, the fixture was known as the 'the friendly derby.' Reds and blues (sometimes from the same family) would sit side-by-side chanting 'Merseyside, Merseyside' and 'Are you watching, Manchester?' as their respective teams battled for titles and cups on a regular basis.

In the days following the Hillsborough disaster, the solidarity between the supporters was symbolised by a mile-long chain of red and blue scarves that stretched between Anfield and Everton's ground, Goodison Park. A month later they mourned the disaster by singing YNWA together before another FA Cup Final at Wembley.

Despite reports of an increasing degree of animosity between the fans over the last decade, my experience thus far had revealed nothing of the sort. Naturally, when blues fans found out I was a reds supporter the common response was a cringe and shrug, and a promise not to hold it against me. The biggest problem they seemed to have with reds fans was that we wouldn't shut up about our success, in particular a certain final in 2005. And when I said I'd more or less been accused of the same thing in New Zealand, they didn't look surprised. Yet despite their doubts over the moral fibre of Liverpool players (curiously Steven Gerrard in particular), one Liverpool icon who always drew their admiration was Bill Shankly.

Indeed, the Scot enjoyed good relations with the blue half of Merseyside, describing how much more warmly he'd been received by Everton than he had by Liverpool in the years following his retirement. The claim was directed at the Liverpool hierarchy, whom Shankly believed had ostracized him and whom many believed should have offered him a position on the board of directors, in view of his virtual making of the club. Aside from that, I sensed Evertonians almost felt privileged that some of Shankly's best insults came at their expense. None better than when he spoke at the funeral of the legendary blue, Dixie Dean: 'Now while this is a sad occasion,' said Shankly, 'I think Dixie would have been amazed to know that even in death he could draw a bigger crowd than Everton on a Saturday afternoon.' He also quipped that if Everton were ever playing at the bottom of his garden, he'd draw the curtains. Frank, a blues fan I met at Cad's bar, told me of the time he was coaxed by mates into going to a reds game at the Leicester City ground. Frank had to blink when they spotted Shankly beneath an archway in the stands. 'With the sun behind him, he looked like the messiah,' said Frank. 'I remember thinking: if that man fell down a toilet, he'd come up clean. Oh, we loved to hate him – but you can't compete with that.'

If Shankly was indeed the red messiah, history books suggest that John Houlding, the man who founded the Liverpool Football Club (for the sole purpose of pissing Everton off), was somewhat less divine.

John Houlding was not only a successful brewer with his own bar on Anfield road, he was also a councillor for the ward of Everton (of which he eventually became Lord Mayor). Before he created the Reds, however, Houlding had been a prominent figure in the creation of Everton FC in 1878, making it Merseyside's first professional football club. Thanks to his polarising actions, Liverpool came into existence in 1892, much to the distaste of the locals. At the centre of the kafuffle was Anfield which, back then – it's so very hard to believe – was Everton's original ground.

As Anfield's owner, Houlding built stands for the Everton supporters and in doing so created a platform from which the club became well off financially. Everton's successful style of 'scientific football' attracted good crowds, and, with the coffers almost full, all should have been well for the blues. Yet eyebrows were raised when Houlding (now known as 'King John of Everton') increased the interest rate on his initial loan to the club. When he increased the rent at Anfield as well, the muck started to fly. With what were seen as blatant attempts to make a personal profit, Houlding was accused of tyranny and employing 'the policy of Shylock'.

Outraged, Houlding threatened to boot Everton out of Anfield altogether, thus setting the stage for a meaty stand-off.

1891, The Liverpool Post: 'Murmurings of discontent grew to thunder as 'the King' began to assert his power; his subjects broke out in open rebellion. Very soon it became a war to the knife. On one side were the King, the sinews of war, and a small and chosen band; on the other side were a big army of malcontents. Fighting, armistices, and stratagems, first on the part of the King and then on the part of the rebels, followed alternately. Finally, the King has been 'kicked', and the victorious host have elected to migrate to a fresh field and pastures new, where a heavy rental will cease from troubling and the footballers be at rest.'

As the article suggests, the press of the day relished the spectacle.

Indeed, the club meeting in which 'the King was kicked' could not have come better scripted. When it seemed that John Houlding would not be attending the meeting, it was reported that the leader of the revolt, George Mahon, felt obliged to take the chair in his absence. When Houlding eventually turned up, Mahon offered him the chair out of courtesy. But before a packed and hushed audience and with the impeccable timing of an aging thespian, Houlding replied: 'I am here on trial. And a criminal never takes the chair; he stops in the dock.' Mock cries of sympathy rang out. 'Best place for him!' someone shouted. If it was ever in doubt, the democratic process that followed confirmed Houlding's unpopularity. Of the 500 present that day, only 18 chose to stay with him. The majority moved less than a kilometre away from Anfield to a piece of land now known as Everton FC's very own Goodison Park.

Six days later, it was reported that George Mahon had come to the meeting willing to compromise. Whether this is true or not is anyone's guess. According to Percy M Young, who penned the 1963 book *Football on Merseyside,* it wouldn't have mattered. Houlding would not have obliged, for it was 'the King's' sense of entitlement along with his many other foibles that let him down: 'What he lacked was finesse, and Houlding's brusque approach and patent egoism brought him to disaster.'

As you'd expect, Houlding didn't take defeat well. Seeing his downfall as more the result of a sinister plot than any fault of his own, he made life difficult for the Everton members as they tried to remove their club's items from the Anfield ground. On one occasion he fought them over a length of hosepipe; on another, a challenge shield from Everton's trophy cabinet. Later, he would even try to steal their name. Not surprisingly, considering he was a councillor at the time, Houlding was heavily criticised by the press for putting football matters before his duties as a politician. And considering his appetite for destruction, Houlding's dramatic fall from grace was relatively short lived.

If the beer baron chose to drown his sorrows in his own product in a dark corner of his Sandon pub, it would make for one of the most productive self-sympathy drinking sessions in football history. In less than a year the hangover was gone, and Merseyside was the home of a second professional football club, *Liverpool F.C.*

Houlding employed a dynamic Irishman known as 'Honest John McKenna' to be the club's first manager. McKenna assembled a team drawn from the

Scottish ranks, and Liverpool FC won the Lancashire League in their very first season. The following season, they toppled the second division unbeaten; by 1901 they were First Division champions.

For Percy M Young, the creation of the new club was a 'brave, even foolhardy gesture.' Its early success, however, made Houlding 'the perfect example of the Aristotelian figure of tragedy, brought down by unseen agents which inverted his qualities so that they become defects; but, beyond that was a neat reversal of fortune which quickly saw Houlding re-established, and once more at least a local hero.'

Houlding died in 1902, yet despite the famous falling out, his funeral saw members of both Everton and Liverpool bear the weight of his coffin.

As far as football games go, the latest Merseyside derby wasn't great. A single goal gave Liverpool the win when Fernando Torres slotted home early in the game. After that, Everton couldn't muster anything even close to a comeback and the only real excitement came from a couple of long range pot shots by Stevie G.

When it came to competing banners, the Liverpool crowd displayed a declaration that the *The City is Ours!* The Evertonians more than matched it with a dig at reds support being less than local: *Everton would like to welcome all Liverpool fans to Merseyside.* Cheeky buggers.

We stayed at the Birkey well after the game and when Barry went home relatively early in the piece (he and Eddie rarely lasted beyond 7p.m.), I stayed on with the rest of the Birkey regulars. I'd agreed to accompany Joyce to Stamps at some point, but at around 11p.m., I was bundled into a car heading for the suburb of Bootle.

A guy called Tony was in the back seat beside me; his mate Tosh was behind the wheel. In the passenger's seat was Tomo who, an hour earlier, had shown a particular interest in what I was doing here on Merseyside. Whatever I told him must've sounded good, for he responded by pulling off his Liverpool shirt and pushing it into my hands. His mate Tony slapped me on the back. 'I've never seen him do that before!' He looked as taken aback as I was. 'Do you know how much that shirt means to him? That's an official shirt. That's the first time I've seen him take it off, let alone give it to someone!' 'Are you sure about this, Tomo?' I asked. He patted me on the arm for reassurance while Tony looked on the point of collapse.

'You owe him, mate,' said Tony, shaking his head.

'No you don't,' corrected Tomo, gently reprimanding his friend. I promptly shook Tomo's hand, held the shirt up admiringly, and thanked him with a beer.

When they insisted I come to Bootle with them I politely declined. When I offered the excuse that I was meeting up with Joyce, Tony looked offended. 'Tosh is coming to pick us up,' he explained. 'It won't cost a thing. And besides,' he said, 'you can't do Liverpool without going to Bootle'.

Again, I hesitated. I couldn't remember whether someone had warned me not to go there or if it was just the sound of the place that didn't sit well: *Bootle. Boot-hill. Boot-ill. Boot-all. Boot-hole...Bootle.* Doesn't have much of a ring to it, does it? Maybe it was Joyce who said not to go there (she'd warned me of a few dodgy neighbourhoods), or maybe it was my first impression of Tony that made me unsure. He was one of those guys whose sense of humour was a touch heavy on the side of mockery. His nervy intensity made it difficult to tell whether he was trying to make fun or a fool of you. At one point he nearly came to blows with the highly likeable Ian when a quip about Ian's portly shape didn't hit the mark. The verdict on whether Tony was actually egging for a fight, or if Ian had just got the wrong end of the stick, remained inconclusive. Tomo, big brother-like, stepped in to calm things down.

Tony's blabbering mouth and the thin line of clear snot below his right nostril suggested the balance of optimum coke intake had been tipped some hours ago. With every good-humoured salutation from Tomo came an ill-humoured stipulation from Tony. Despite these reservations, I put up little to no resistance when they bundled me into the car. In the back seat Tony reiterated how privileged I was that Tomo had given me his Liverpool shirt, which I now had on. He repeated: 'You ride with us, you ride for free.' Again the ambiguous tone, the hint of proviso. One look at these boys was enough to know they weren't made of money, and it seemed I was about to learn what this was really about as we pulled into a poorly lit street without explanation.

What's going on?

Hopping out of the car, Tomo said that he'd be back in a second. He ran across the road and up the front stairs of a terraced house.

Tony watched until he disappeared, then looked back at me with a glint in his eye. 'He doesn't normally do this. What do you think he's up to?' he said, imploring me for the impossible answer.

I slumped into the seat and wondered if I was too drunk to fight all three of them. Probably. I blinked and tried to focus on the slick of wet street before us and thought, bugger it, whatever happens, happens. I was too drunk to care.

'So,' said Tony, changing tack. 'Been poundin' some puss since you been here?'

'Nah. Got a girlfriend.'

'Come on, mate. That accent of yours – I would be.'

'Well, I've got a girlfriend so I'm not.'

'I'd be pounding as much puss as possible,' said Tony, shaking his head.

'It's a crime. Guy like you should be making the most of it – I would be. I would be, wouldn't I, Tosh?'

Tosh shrugged.

'No girlfriend, Tony?' I asked.

He shifted his bony arse and looked sullen. He explained that since he'd been out of jail – a matter of just a few weeks – most females had avoided him. Aside from the stigma of prison, the issue was what he'd actually done to be put away. Two years ago, Tony had caught his girlfriend having it off with another guy. As a man is inclined to do in such a situation, Tony dealt the guy a severe beating.

'So you went to jail for two years for beating up the guy who was having it off with your girlfriend? Sounds a bit harsh,' I said.

'I beat up my girlfriend as well.'

'Oh. Well, yeah – no, you can't go doing that.' Tony looked at me – with less ambiguity.

Finally, there was movement across the road. Tomo's broad frame emerged from the terrace and came bounding towards us. There was an added bulge in the front pocket of his hoodie. He climbed into the car, pulled out whatever it was, and tossed it into the back seat. In the half light I could only discern that the article was very yellow and very polyester. Then, the crest appeared from the folds of the material - a Liverpool away top, circa '93.

'You didn't think that was coming, did you, lad?' said Tony.

'It took a while but I managed to convince me brother it was for a good cause,' said Tomo. My *thank yous'* seemed meek in return.

True to form, Tony was quick to suggest that I was indebted to his friend. The good news was that it would only take a pack of beers to right the ledger. When we pulled up at Tomo's Bootle flat, Tony and I walked a couple of blocks to a pokey little bottle store. Before Liverpool, I'd never been in a bottle store where you couldn't just grab your preferred poison and stroll on up to the counter. Here you had to point at whatever you wanted from the other side of the bullet-proof wall-to-wall Perspex that sealed you off from the alcohol – a sad state of affairs which didn't seem to bother the Indian man behind the counter one bit. He almost fell over when he heard my accent wasn't Scouse. Eyes as wide as japatis, he pushed the beers through the slot and thanked me for my custom.

Back at the flat I briefly met Tomo's pregnant partner before she went to bed. Tosh disappeared as well. That left the serious business of watching *Liverpool FC* DVDs to me, Tomo and Tony. Sadly, due to my growing difficulty in understanding Tomo's *worra lorra corra* dialect, the finer points of his football commentary will forever be lost. Judging by the confused looks he was giving me, my *wotta lotta cotta* was likewise beyond him. Still, despite the language barrier, the tone was congenial. It must have been, or else I wouldn't have been on the receiving end of yet another grand act of generosity.

I was admiring a framed birds-eye-view drawing of Anfield hanging from a badly peeling wall when Tomo strolled right up, wrenched it from its hook, and plonked it into my arms. I even understood what he said straight afterwards - that as long as I manage to make at least one New Zealander a Liverpool fan, it will all be worth it. Don't worry, I said, I intend to convert them by the thousands. We grinned at each other. He nodded, then tipped his head slightly forward and to the side. *Yer wha?*

When Tony said that when you ride with the Bootle boys you ride for free, he was good to his word. At some point in the wee hours his Dad picked us up. Tomo insisted – as if the two Liverpool tops and the picture of Anfield weren't enough – that I should take the leftover beers as well. I did so reluctantly and when I tried to push them onto Tony and his Dad they took one each out of politeness.

They dropped me off at Harvey Rd where I fancied I could make it inside without making a racket. I felt fiendish, like a thief in the night.

14. A Lot of Mither

The next morning I scrambled downstairs to apologise for last night's commotion. I could vaguely remember entering the house and being so bloody careful not to make a noise I virtually banged the place to pieces. But compared to the noise I made with the kitchen tap, the clonk and bump of stumbling between rooms was nothing. The tap was unforgiving.

A problem with the plumbing meant that if you tried turning it on without one eye closed, one foot off the ground, and your tongue extended to touch the back of your neck, there'd be trouble. It would cough, splutter, and spew forth a raging torrent that splashed from the basin with the force of a decent punch.

The violence of the tap started a chain reaction. The walls came alive as every pipe in the house clanged and shuddered in revolt. The tap loved its freedom, and turning it off required squeezing it into submission and waiting out the three-count before the win was assured.

The prize was a chance to dry out. But on this particular night there was something extra: a tasty prawn curry left out for me on the stove. Joyce found it impossible to cook small meals and would glare as though you'd spat on her mother's grave if you didn't go back for more. She was the queen of comfort food – and the reason Mike had returned to New Zealand the size of a small house. I was currently the size of a single garage, but I was gaining on him. Knowing Joyce would expect me to polish off the prawn curry, I scoffed with bulging eyes and drunken greed. Not wishing to go another round with the tap, I left the pan out to clean up in the morning.

When I made it downstairs around midday everything was spick and span. To her credit, Joyce kept an exceptionally clean house. It wasn't the sterile kind of clean you find in homes of sterile minds; more a house-proud clean where you can feel perfectly at ease just as long as you practice the basic etiquette. Leaving the dirty pan to fester was poor form and although she played it down, Joyce wasn't happy about waking up to a stink of curry.

I apologised, and described my problem with the kitchen tap.

Joyce smiled and shot a glance at the hovering Eddie. He told me that when the kitchen tap goes into spasm the network of pipes go crazy and somehow trigger the bathroom tap upstairs to do the same. At about 4a.m., Eddie had got up to deal with it on my behalf. He said not to worry. It was a bastard of a thing, especially after a night on the lash.

'Then why don't you get someone to fix it, Eddie?!' pounced Joyce. Eddie acquired his trademark pose: cigarette in hand, gazing over the fence to the calming green expanse of the adjacent park.

'And the bloody radiator's playing up, as well! It's freezin' in 'ere, Eddie!' she added.

Eddie, still gazing, tipped his head to one side, and, with an exasperated 'Yeahhhhh,' somehow managed to encapsulate the quandary of every man who has ever felt that life is too short to be thinking about – let alone paying for – broken taps and bloody radiators.

'Didn't Barry say he was going to fix it?' I said.

'Oh, we've tried that one before,' said Eddie. He explained that that was how the two of them met, down at the pub. Barry, who had only just arrived back in Liverpool, mentioned in passing that he was a bit of a handyman. Eddie told him to finish his beer and promptly marched him home to sort out the taps – Joyce's famous home cooking the payment for his troubles. But a couple of years later and Barry had proven that he was a better friend than fixer-of-things. And while the problem of the taps remained, so did Barry – albeit a welcome regular at the dinner table. Joyce looked at me and shrugged the shrug of a woman bound to a life of useless but adorable men.

'What about the landlord?' I said.

'Thing is we don't pay much rent. Sometimes he likes to use the house to meet up with people,' said Joyce with a you-know-what-I-mean kind of look.

'We leave him to it,' said Eddie.

'Right.' I took a moment to think. 'Keeping things clean, is he?'

'Somethin' like that, Glenn.'

Eddie's phone rang. While he spoke, I shot a look at the papers. Much of the news concerned the acrimony of yesterday's derby. There were claims that Everton's captain, Phil Neville, had been punched in the back by reds fans while he was leaning into the crowd before taking a throw-in. Punching a player in the back is not on, but the incident was easy to dismiss.

First, Everton's captain is Phil Neville. The same Phil Neville who once played for Manchester United with his brother Gary, a hater of Scousers who once said: 'I can't stand Liverpool, I can't stand the people, I can't stand anything to do with them.'

Secondly, it just so happened that, in the process of taking the throw-in, Neville was leaning back into a section of reds supporters standing against the barrier. Pushing the back of his sweaty blue shirt unnecessarily into opposing fans is more or less an act of provocation. He *wanted* a reaction. According to the papers, he got one.

Yet the so-called punch didn't have any noticeable impact. Neville took the throw-in without any sign of injury or complaint. So if it really was a punch, it must've been a very soft one. Sometimes a very soft punch is nothing more than a tap. And a tap is nearly always just a tap. It was probably a tap.

For me, the real acrimony came from the vitriol towards Stevie G.

Everton were full of songs and chants about the Liverpool captain's wife having slept with a Bootle drug dealer, the consequence being that Stevie G isn't the biological father of his eldest daughter.

I remember being disgusted at Mike for singing *The baby's not yours, the baby's not yours, Oh Steven Gerrard – the baby's not yours* around his Auckland flat upon his return from England. I remember thinking that such bad taste could only come from the mouths of some pretty low-life forms. (The fact that Mike seemed to think the chants were funny proved a point of contention, and he was lucky to escape that day without a fierce tap on the back.)

The claim was part of a wider conspiracy propagated by blues supporters that the world of Stevie G is a particularly sordid one. Nearly every blue nose I'd met had done his bit to add fuel to the fire – stories about how he was once rude to a mate of theirs, how he doesn't tip anyone even though he's impossibly rich, and that he doesn't talk to taxi drivers – just like he never talks to his team mates. All in all, too big for his boots, they said. Every thing I heard seemed flimsy at best and therefore easy to rebuke. For example, no manager on the planet would employ a captain who doesn't talk to his team. And so what if he occasionally comes across as being rude? Some people deserve rudeness in return for being idiots. We can't just let the idiots of this world go on being idiots without reprisal. If you've never slammed the door on a fool, hung up on a harasser, or scowled at a scumbag, then you're not really living. Being rude has its place.

And when it comes to not talking to taxi drivers you'd have to be the patron saint of endless chitchat to converse with every cabbie you've ever come across. Sometimes I don't talk to cabbies because they don't want to talk to me, and sometimes I just don't want to talk because I've either got something, or nothing, on my mind. Maybe I've just had an argument with Erin, maybe I'm wondering how to deal with a tricky situation, or maybe – as is the case with Steven Gerrard – I'm sick to death with half the city thinking the father of my child is a Bootle bloody drug dealer! (Blue nose taxi driver included.)

And as far as the accusation of not tipping despite being filthy rich goes, well, let's face it; sometimes the service just isn't worth it. It doesn't matter whether there's two pennies or two hundred pounds in your pocket, if the delivery's no good - fuck 'em!

Or maybe Steven Gerrard doesn't tip because, beneath it all, he's still very much the lad from the Huyton council estate who – millionaire or not – still values the price of money: that is, he's just not accustomed to giving the stuff away.

And besides, if you were Steven Gerrard, you'd have every right to be wary of the people around you. If you were once the target of an extortionist thug, you would be too.

In 2001, with his career already hitting the heights, Stevie G had a problem. The problem was a man known in gang circles as *The Psycho*. The misery that The Psycho inflicted on the young footballer included chasing him while he was driving home, smashing his car up, and ambushing him outside his Southport flat. When Gerrard refused to hand over any of his footballer's salary, The Psycho threatened to shoot Gerrard in the legs. Knowing that police involvement would be futile, Gerrard's father had no other choice but to employ the services of John Kinsella, an underworld enforcer.

Only when Kinsella went to The Psycho to 'sort him out,' did the reign of terror end. Exactly what *sorting him out* entailed is down to your imagination. Fact is, ol' Psycho don't bother Stevie no more.

I put the paper down and voiced my disgust at the Everton chants. Joyce, to my surprise, completely disagreed. 'That's the way we are,' she said. 'That's the way it is with everyone. Everyone knows everything about everyone. We all have each other on – if there's nuthin' against your name, you're not a bloody scouser. Why should he be any different from the rest of us?'

Of course, Joyce was right. Me being upset by the taunting of Stevie G didn't matter a jot. It didn't seem to matter all that much to Stevie G, either. The one thing they couldn't accuse him of was succumbing to slings and arrows: his performance in the derby earned him Man of the Match, once again.

After an animated conversation with his brother and co-worker Phil, Eddie held his phone lifelessly in front of him. As usual, he'd have to be up at 4a.m. the next day. The job was to deliver a large cabinet to a house in Edinburgh. The cabinet was so heavy it had already been decided they'd need skates to shift it from the back of the truck to the house. But the skates Phil had procured for the job weren't the factory ones Eddie had hoped for. Phil reckoned a couple of skate boards - the kind better suited to the half-pipe - would be fine. To make things worse, Phil had organised for their nephew to help out on the job. The news had Joyce in stitches. She recalled the time when the same nephew came over to fix the circuit board in their house. Several minutes into the job he electrocuted himself, having forgotten to turn off the mains switch.

'I'm terrible with things like that,' she chuckled. 'Me and Eddie heard this bang and found him at the bottom of the stairs, pale as a ghost with his hair sticking up. I couldn't stop laughing at him. I just fall apart when I see things like that. Even I know you have to turn off the power. He was fresh from a course and all – we were going to pay him and everythin'!' Joyce was almost in tears. '...And then he thought he was going to be sick so Eddie had to take him home!'

The pleasure derived from retelling the nephew's misfortune opened the way for tales of folly galore. It seemed everyone they knew had some hilarious blunder in their past – like their friend Jackie who was the same age as Joyce yet wore the kind of fat-soled trainers 'you couldn't burn on a bonfire.' Jackie's infamy was complete the day Eddie and Joyce turned up to her house and walked into a kitchen covered in pea and ham soup. They found Jackie sitting in the living room completely unaware that the sauce pan had overflowed. Asked why she hadn't smelt it she replied that she had, but thought it was just the smell of her skin after an extended session that day on the sun bed. When she saw the mess, she turned bright orange.

Then there was the time Joyce's daughter and her partner (grandson Reece's dad) decided it would be boss! to drive their car onto the sand bar of a Spanish beach. When the sound of water lapping against the car doors signaled they were stuck, the couple waded to shore. Anticipating certain trouble, they caught a cab and promptly abandoned the car. 'They just left it there! A bloody BMW!' cried Joyce. 'That's bluddy drugs for yer.' She gave me a cautionary look. 'I'll have no cocaine in my house! They're my only two rules – no cocaine and you can't leave a mess.'

'When our Michael was here he tried to hide it from me. But I knew he was takin' it. He changed,' she said, slowly shaking her head,' – it was written all over his *kipper*.'

'Written all over his kipper?'

'His kipper – his face. You haven't heard that one?'

'Joyce knows plenty of sayings,' said Eddie. 'She's got a unique way of putting things –you see things differently to everyone else, don't yer, luv?'

Joyce sat back. 'Alright then,' she said.

Eddie continued: 'Like the time when we were walkin' in New Zealand and Joyce stopped and looked around and said *Aye, we're in the bewilderness now, Eddie.* And there was the time she came out of this pub toilet and instead of saying to the barman that the light bulb needed replacing, she said *Your lights are in darkness.* When we all worked out what she was meaning, it seemed to make perfect sense. Sometimes you just have to kind of decode it, you know what I'm saying?'

'Your lights are in darkness – it's poetic,' I said.

'He has me on all the time about many things, many things,' said Joyce.

'I know I do, luv, but that's why I love yer,' said Ed. He then tested the waters by asking if he could tell me about 'the pole-vaulting'. Joyce feigned embarrassment with a smile. Eddie went right ahead: 'We were watching the Olympic pole-vaulting on the telly one day when Joyce turned to me and said: "I used to do that". I looked at her. You used to pole-vault? I said. Yeah, at school, she said. I couldn't believe it – we've been together for twenty-odd years and that was the first time I'd ever heard about pole-vaulting. Then I thought about it. I know the school she went to and I had a pretty good idea it wasn't the kind of school that did pole-vaulting. But she said it so confidently I thought, alright, and left it there. But over the next few days I got to talking to some people who went to her school. When I came back and said to Joyce that her school only did high jumpin' she looked at me like I'd lost my mind: "It's the same thing, Eddie," she said. "Just without the pole."'

Joyce shrugged.

'You see what I mean, Glenn,' said Ed, 'it's just a matter of adjusting to Joyce's wavelength. We were camping once and we saw a guy going down the river in a kayak. You know, Joyce had been kayaking too, just without the kayak.'

'Wading?' I said.

'No, Glenn. Kayaking without the kayak – different mindset altogether.'

Not to be left out, there were tales of folly for Eddie too.

Having grown up on Scotland Rd, a life in the armed services was almost expected. Eddie tried the air force first (helicopter pilot) but was deemed too short. Likewise, the fire service. So he settled for the royal engineers. In 1982 he was in jail for brawling with a pilot, only to be released the day the UK invaded the Falkland Islands, where his services in bomb disposal were much needed.

After the Falklands, Eddie worked as a hard man for one of Liverpool's gangs, simultaneously accruing gambling debts ('I would've bet on two flies') he couldn't repay. He fled to New Zealand where, thanks to having a New Zealand passport (on account of his father coming to New Zealand as a two pound pom), he could live beyond the reach of those he owed money. Meanwhile Joyce, whom Eddie had to leave behind, organised with his brother Phil for the debts to be repaid. She then flew to New Zealand and found Eddie with the news he was debt-free and no longer in danger. After a spell running a pub on the Kapiti coast, they found their way back to Merseyside together.

When Barry turned up that afternoon he did so bearing gifts – a block of do-dah for Ed and a black leather pouch for me. Barry had purchased the pouch after he'd seen me admire his own on the canal boat. He'd managed to track down the old fella he'd purchased it from and convince him to give up the last pouch he had (and was also currently using) for his kiwi friend who'd be sure to appreciate it.

Appreciate it I did. The leather felt as soft as dough and the immaculate stitching ensured it would last as long as I could keep from losing it. Rubber lining and a domed flap kept the tobacco fresh. It even came with a decent clump still inside – a dark, sticky blend that smoked like an effigy of the Marlborough man. It was all class; if you're going to have a nasty habit, have it in style. As the saying goes, *I was made up*, once again. I pointed out the shirts from Tomo which I'd displayed on a chair next to the picture of Anfield.

Then, like a bad joke, I remembered the Scouser stereotype.

15. Reputation Precedes

Whether it's a joke: *Why does the Mersey run through Liverpool? Because if it walked it would get mugged.*

Or a Manchester chant [to the tune of You are My Sunshine]: *You are a Scouser/ A dirty Scouser/ You're only happy on Giro day/ Your mum's out thieving/ Your dad's drug dealing/ Please don't take my hubcaps away...*the association with thieving – among other things – is well-ingrained in the UK's stereotype of Merseyside. But the stereotype has spread.

Before I left New Zealand a friend of my brother's told me to leave my valuables at home. He also said to budget an extra donkey to buy a hand gun and a gold sovereign pinky ring. So take from that what you will.

Then there was the woman I spoke to on a flight within New Zealand (about a month before I'd departed for Liverpool) who described the time she was drinking with a friend in a Liverpool pub. They'd been laughing and playing pool with two locals, but when it was time to leave they walked outside to find the very same Scousers in the process of nicking their bikes.

'They'll make you laugh and be friendly - but as soon as you turn your back they'll try and steal from you!' she said. I asked what else had happened for her to form such a strong opinion, but she only had the one example.

Perhaps Herman Melville got the bad reputation ball rolling.

This is his narrator's depiction of Liverpool in his 1845 debut novel, *Redburn*: '...of all the seaports in the world, Liverpool, perhaps, most abounds in the variety of land-sharks, land-rats, and other vermin, which makes the hapless mariner their prey. In the shape of landlords, bar-keepers, clothiers, and boarding-house loungers, the land-sharks devour him, limb by limb; while the land-rats and mice constantly nibble at his purse.'

'And yet,' he added, 'sailors love this Liverpool; and upon long voyages to distant parts of the globe, will be continually dilating upon its charms and attractions, and extolling it above all the other seaports in the world.'

More recently, the 'thieving Scouser' stereotype was no doubt bolstered by hugely popular television series such as *Bread*, and Boys from the Black Stuff. Both were written by Liverpudlians and featured characters who weren't opposed to (and often relied upon) stealing to get by.

In Boys from the Black Stuff it was factory closures and the decline of Liverpool's port that led to the harrowing existence of its characters.

In Bread, it was Thatcher's public spending cuts and tax increases that underpinned the Merseysiders struggle.

Very recently, a spate of burglaries of footballers' homes hasn't helped the cause. In a little over two years, Lucas Leiva would become the eighth Liverpool player to be burgled while he was playing for the club. While the pundits aren't short of opinions on such things, I was keen to know what the locals thought of their bad reputation.

On Tuesday, I popped into Cad's where I found some familiar faces. Drew, Mick, and a few of their friends dominated the small bar. They were *all in* on a gambling scheme that didn't seem to be working. Regardless, they ogled the betting channel and spoke feverishly of their next move. Amidst the giddy excitement of pursuing a lost cause, I asked Drew about criminal activity on Merseyside.

Drew was the man to talk to. While not a *known* criminal, he was actually writing his thesis on that very subject. Much of his research involved interviewing the old gangsters he'd met through Eddie and Joyce.

He admitted it hadn't been easy. Many of the old timers were prone to long-winded tangents and had memories that were either severely failing, or uncannily selective.

Nevertheless, he confirmed that the thieving reputation of decades ago is warranted. In the 1960s/70s you could 'grease someone down with a few quid' and receive cartons of cigarettes and whiskey for your troubles. And, on top of the safe cracking, armed robberies, and cargo theft, Drew was convinced there wasn't a scam invented elsewhere that hadn't already been thrashed in Liverpool.

For unlawful ingenuity you barely had to look beyond the home.

Drew explained that when houses were fitted with coin meters for gas and electricity in the 80s, it was familiar practice to feed them with washers that had been filed down to the weight of a penny. And just so the meter man wouldn't find out, occupants would rip their meter from the wall right before he was due a visit.

'People would steal their own meters?'

Drew nodded. 'In the eighties it was about the only thing they could steal.'

'Churches were looted as well,' said Frank, sitting at the next table. He explained how the rot set in with 'too much religion' and a 'rubbish school system'.

'The Catholic Church had too much power,' he said. 'Priests and nuns ruled the curriculum. We were brought up on religion – it was inverted bigotry –

they encouraged closed minds. We were made to be factory fodder – it was sinful.' Then the factories closed.

Warranted the reputation may be, but, if you trust recent crime statistics, then Liverpool is generally falling behind in the burglary stakes.

While still nothing to be proud of, Home Office statistics show that the rate of stealing on Merseyside is well below that of other areas. Even better are the comparative rates for Violence Against Person, which have also dropped since 2001.

The numbers suggest that the idea of Scousers being the leading thieving bastards of England is now wrong. And anyone who accuses them of such, especially if they're from London or Manchester, where the rates are significantly higher, is plain hypocritical and probably quite nasty.

Despite this apparent shift, Frank maintained that, when it comes to their well-being, he and his fellow Scousers are often their own worst enemies. His criticism was in line with what I'd heard from others as well. Although proud of their identity, Scousers are honest about living in a crime-ridden city; honest about how it came to be. They often refer to certain areas and local elements with caution and suspicion. Nevertheless, it's their ability to criticise themselves which represents a crucial omission from the stereotype.

In 2004, Boris Johnson wrote about Liverpudlians in his column for the Daily Times: 'Part of their flawed psychological state is that they cannot accept that they might have made any contribution to their own misfortunes, but seek rather to blame someone else for it, thereby deepening their sense of shared tribal grievance against the rest of society.'

Unlike Johnson, I'd now spent a few weeks here. The idea of apportioning blame seemed redundant. While things weren't exactly booming, Liverpool was definitely enjoying life out of the doldrums. If the city was harbouring 'a shared tribal grievance,' it was cunningly hidden beneath layers of banter and generosity.

Of course, Derek Hatton's council in the eighties did indeed blame big business and the government for its predicament. Opinions on whether the stand was the right thing to do often come down to a person's political leanings – but surely even the most pompous of pug-faced Tories would have to admit that Thatcher's reforms could've been done with much less pain. But as always, the blame game is never a one-sided affair. And without question, Merseysiders have been on the receiving end of more outright blame than any society deserves. Liverpool fans in particular.

At the 1985 European Cup Final between Liverpool and Juventus, thirty-nine spectators lost their lives. The venue for the final was the Heysel Stadium in Belgium. The dilapidated state of Heysel was, sadly, not uncommon at the time. Back then, the safety of spectators was a low priority, even in the aftermath of the 1971 Ibrox disaster in which sixty-six Ranger's fans were crushed, and the 1982 stadium disaster in Moscow where 340 people succumbed to a similar fate.

Just a few months before Heysel, fire engulfed Bradford's football stadium (starting when the buildup of rubbish under the wooden stands caught alight) taking fifty-six lives and injuring over 200 others. And just eighteen days prior, a wall collapsed at St Andrews stadium, killing a fourteen-year-old boy after police pushed into fans.

But a run down stadium wasn't the only factor which made going to the football unsafe. 'Hooligan firms' were at their peak. Nearly every 1st or 2nd division club had a small minority of so-called supporters whose objective was to fight, throw missiles, and invade the pitch whenever they felt hard done by – which was often.

Before the Heysel disaster, the firms of Chelsea, Leeds, Millwall, and Manchester United were arguably the most notorious – their 'deplorable and menacing behaviour', which included attacking players, police and stewards, led to the introduction of caged pens in order to contain the hooligan element.

After Heysel, however, the dubious mantle of 'most notorious' belonged to Liverpool.

In the lead up to the disaster, Liverpool's club secretary, Peter Robinson, officially warned UEFA and the Belgian authorities that the crumbling Heysel Stadium wasn't fit for the final. With 50,000 fans expected, he also expressed deep concerns about the level of security and policing. Yet his pleas were ignored.

Sure enough, just before kickoff, taunting between poorly segregated fans boiled over. The only thing separating the opposing groups was a chicken wire fence which Liverpool hooligans pushed through to get at the Italians. When the Juventus supporters retreated, the build up of pressure caused a concrete retaining wall to collapse. In addition to the thirty-nine deceased, 600 or so were injured, the vast majority of whom were Italians.

UEFA wasted little time in laying the blame solely on Liverpool. Less than a week later UEFA representative Gunter Schneider claimed, 'Only the English fans were responsible. Of that there is no doubt.' A five- year ban was imposed on English clubs competing in Europe, with an extended period of three years placed on LFC (eventually shortened to one extra year).

Some said the charge towards the Juventus fans was an act of retaliation after being spat on and pelted by lumps of terrace concrete. But regardless of who sparked the violence, the fact remains that, if Liverpool fans hadn't charged, there would be no fatalities.

In a move that showed she fully backed Schneider's statement, Prime Minister Thatcher introduced an ID card system for all football spectators. It inferred that the problem could be solved by broadly treating all football fans as though they were all potential hooligans. Never mind that the hooligans were the minority, and never mind the antiquated stadiums, the failed safety checks or the inadequate policing and security. A comprehensive rethink was avoided simply by blaming the fans.

Many voiced their disapproval. Fans and players from both the Liverpool and Juventus clubs challenged the idea that there was just one culpable party at Heysel; a lack of awareness of the potential problems and a lack of police numbers were cited as contributing factors. The consensus was that, if authorities had heeded Robinson's advice, the tragedy would have been prevented.

After an eighteen-month investigation, Belgian judge, Marina Coppieters, concluded that the blame should indeed be shared by the Belgian police and football authorities. As a result of her findings, several officials were incriminated, the police captain responsible for security charged with involuntary manslaughter.

But it would take a six-year campaign by Otello Lorentini (founder and president of the Heysel Association for Families of the Victims) before UEFA's negligence was acknowledged and duly punished. A Juventus fan who was at Heysel, and who sadly lost his son Roberto in the tragedy, Lorentini fought 'a long and hard battle' for justice which culminated in a historic sentence. Finally, from 1992, UEFA would be legally responsible for every event it organised. Since then, UEFA games have not seen the horrors of the Heysel disaster repeated. This is no mere coincidence. Tellingly, the Heysel stadium was never used as a football venue again.

It would take a disaster on home soil for spectator safety in Britain to be taken as seriously. The Hillsborough stadium disaster took place on the 15th April 1989, four years after Heysel. This time there was no hooligan element to blame, no reprehensible behaviour by fans.

The Taylor Report, published in 1990, cited the main causes of the tragedy to be poor crowd control by police and a stadium that did not conform to safety requirements.

The Hillsborough disaster took the lives of ninety-six Liverpool supporters – a devastating toll to mark the catalyst for major redevelopments to English stadiums. Terraces and their ten- foot high caged pens would become a thing of the past; all-seater stadiums the norm. With the image of English football in tatters, the FA then launched the English Premiere League to replace the first division.

Yet before the Taylor Report was published, and only days after the disaster happened, Liverpool fans copped outright blame once again. As if the unbearable grief over so many deaths wasn't bad enough, Liverpool fans were soon subjected to a litany of blame shifting lies and vicious accusations. The Sun newspaper claimed that they'd urinated on and picked the pockets of victims; that they'd attacked and urinated on police, firemen and an ambulance crew; that they'd acted, all in all, 'just like animals.'

Liverpool journalist, Brian Reade, was in the crowd that day. He has strived to deny the allegations of the 'myth-making media' ever since. Published in the Daily Mirror, this is Reade's account of what happened:

'The morning could not have been more perfect. A cobalt blue sky, blood orange sun and a warm air filled with birdsong and blossom. Spring's optimism flooded Liverpudlian hearts.

It was the second year running we'd been drawn to play Nottingham Forest in an FA Cup semi-final at Hillsborough and those of us in that red procession which snaked along the M62 to Sheffield had few worries about reaching Wembley again.

But different kinds of doubts were creeping in. Major road works, an accident and persistent police checks were causing delays, and fears spread that the kick-off might be missed.

On reaching Hillsborough those fears were realised. At 2.30pm, Leppings Lane, the entry point for all Liverpool fans, was human gridlock.

No police or stewards were on hand to filter the thousands of fans into queues.

The only visible authority was half-a-dozen forlorn figures in blue on horseback and a few on the ground, screaming at the swaying crowd to back away from the turnstiles. For the second year running, and despite protests,

Liverpool were given 4,000 fewer tickets and the smaller end of the ground – despite having a much bigger following than Forest.

Geographically it made the police job of getting fans in and out of Sheffield easier.

Ensuring safety is how they termed it. It meant all 24,000 Liverpool ticket-holders, whether in Leppings Lane or the West and North stands, had to pass through 23 turnstiles, most so old they constantly jammed.

At the much newer Kop end, Forest had 60 modern turnstiles. As the ground erupted with expectation at the entry of the teams, outside in Leppings Lane, there was pandemonium.

Fans, angry at the lack of movement and organisation, berated the police, some of whom were screaming into their radios for assistance. Many of us moved away from the turnstiles and looked on from a distance, convinced the kick-off would be put back while they sorted out the chaos.

Instead, at 2.52pm a huge blue exit gate opened and 2,000 of us poured in. At the back of the Leppings Lane terrace, stewards who were supposed to be dispersing the supporters evenly into five pens had vanished. Consequently the bulk of fans ignored the lesser populated pens at the sides of the terrace and headed into the two central ones behind the goal, already over-crowded. Those at the front became packed tighter and tighter. The game was now under way and fans at the back, ignorant of the crush, concentrated on trying to get a view of the pitch.

They weren't to know that ahead of them on this shallow-sloping concrete there was panic, fear, hyper-ventilating, fainting, hair drenched in sweat and vomit matting on the metal fencing.

And death. Survivors speak of faces pushed against them that were wide-eyed and blue, of their bodies going numb and limp, and their minds suffering near death experiences. Eddie Spearritt, whose 14-year-old son Adam died in the crush, lost consciousness. He said: "They've said it was a surge but it wasn't. It was a slow, constant build-up of pressure, like a vice getting tighter and tighter until you couldn't breathe."

Fans screamed at passing police to open the perimeter gates but they walked on by. Some who tried to climb over the fence were battered back down. Others crawled on all fours above heads towards the back of the terrace and were hoisted to safety by fans in the stand above.

Despite the obvious density of the crowd, the screams, and the pain etched on the faces of the suffering – and despite CCTV cameras feeding these images back to the police control room – the perimeter gates remained locked.'

It became apparent that the police were treating the crush as an attempted pitch invasion rather than a death trap for the terrified souls inside the central pens. Even goalkeeper Bruce Grobbelaar could see what was happening. When he remonstrated with a policewoman to open the perimeter gates, she replied that she was unable to do anything until she'd received a command from the control room. The consequences of the delay were dire. The sheer pressure of the crush caused some to perish while they were still standing up, while others were trampled when a crash barrier gave way. When the police finally opened the perimeter gates, fans spilled out and collapsed onto the grass. Many of the 96 victims might have been saved if ambulances, stretchers and oxygen had been in place. As it was, only a few St John's Ambulance volunteers were on hand to aid the casualties, prompting able fans to do what they could. Some performed CPR while others retrieved advertising hoardings to carry the victims clear of the carnage. It would be half an hour after the players had been led from the pitch before a lone ambulance made it to the Leppings Lane end. There had been dozens of ambulances waiting outside the ground yet the police, still treating the scene as that of a mass hooligan brawl, prevented the ambulances from entering. The only reason one got through was because the driver, paramedic Tony Edwards, defied police orders. Once inside, Edwards did not witness any fighting. (Nor has a single fight scene been found among the hundreds of photos and hours of footage taken that day.) Nevertheless, the Hillsborough ground must have resembled a battlefield. Edwards was inundated with desperate survivors trying to hoist the bodies of their loved ones onto his ambulance. Amidst the chaos, and without the help of police or medical staff, fans had to prioritise who should go first and who could hold on. Critically, no more ambulances made it inside. Only fourteen of the almost one hundred victims made it to hospital.

The police wasted little time in trying to cover their mistakes. When the man in charge, Chief Superintendent David Duckenfield, was asked how it happened, he claimed a hooligan mob had stormed the stadium and killed their own. Duckenfield had been responsible for opening the blue exit gate beside the turnstiles to alleviate the initial crush outside the ground. With the exit gate open the crowd had no choice but to enter a tunnel that lead directly to the central pens where the tragedy would take place. But according to Duckenfield, the fans had turned up late and drunk, kicked the gate in, and stormed the terrace on their own accord.

Following Duckenfield's lie, the slurs against Scousers came thick and fast. The UEFA President, Conservative politicians, and the South Yorkshire police all backed claims of a drunk, ticketless mob. Desperate to prove their theory, police grilled survivors about heavy drinking and whether or not their fellow fans had arrived with tickets to the ground. The police even took surreptitious blood samples from the corpses in a failed attempt to reveal excessive levels of alcohol.

Then, four days after the disaster, the Sun editor Kelvin Mackenzie published the aforementioned article with the front page headlines: 'THE TRUTH • Some fans picked pockets of victims • Some fans urinated on the brave cops • Some fans beat up PC giving kiss of life.' The article even went so far as to quote an 'unnamed policeman's' claim that Liverpool fans had tried to instigate the sexual abuse of a female whom the policeman was trying to revive.

With its overt allegations and dubious sources, journalists working for the Sun at the time have since revealed that they knew it was a 'classic smear'. However, they chose not to challenge Mackenzie, stating that the only person who could've mitigated the editor's mindset was the Sun's owner, Rupert Murdoch. It seems Murdoch was oblivious to Mackenzie's intentions, and immediately after 'The Truth' issue was published, Murdoch attempted to quell the angry response from Merseyside by forcing Mackenzie to make a cursory apology.

It was all too little, too late. Most of Merseyside chose to boycott the Sun immediately –that is, after existing copies were burned in the streets. All this while the city was trying to cope with its grief. Brian Reade:

'The club's chief executive Peter Robinson opened the ground and the Kop and its goalmouth, became a shrine to the dead.

Within days, a third of the pitch would be blanketed with flowers, scarves of all colours from followers of different clubs and heart- felt messages of support from around the world.

The players became social workers, sometimes attending half-a-dozen funerals a day... As spring turned to summer there was little to extinguish the pain and anger among Liverpudlians. Until August 4, when the late Lord Justice Taylor published his interim report into the disaster and finally the truth was heard.

And it was the complete opposite of the lies being peddled by certain people in Yorkshire and Wapping.

He ruled that drunkenness, late arrivals and fans turning up without tickets were red herrings. That there was no evidence of any kind of hooliganism and that fans were not to blame for the crush. He even described their role in trying to save the dying as "magnificent".

Instead, Lord Taylor laid the blame squarely at the door of the police.

He highlighted their planning failure which allowed "dangerous congestion at the turnstiles" and ruled that " the immediate cause of the disaster was gross overcrowding, namely the failure, when the exit gate was opened, to cut off access to the central pens which were already overfull.

"They were overfull because no safe maximum capacities had been laid down, no attempt was made to control entry to individual pens numerically and there was no effective visual monitoring of crowd density."

He hit out at the police's "sluggish reaction and response when the crush occurred" and claimed that the total number of fans who entered the Leppings Lane terrace " did not exceed the capacity of the standing area".

So much for the thousands of ticketless fans theory.

And he lambasted Chief Supt Duckenfield who he said "froze" after ordering the exit gate to be opened.

"A blunder of the first magnitude," he called it.

Taylor's report not only vindicated the fans but gave hope to the bereaved families that they would receive justice. That the people into whose care they had entrusted their loved ones would face up to their responsibilities for allowing a wholly avoidable disaster to happen. But their hope was short lived.'

The accountability that the families sought would not be eventuate. An inquest in 1990 and an investigation in 1997 proved controversial when crucial evidence was deemed inadmissible. Both purported that any evidence after a 3.15pm cutoff time was irrelevant, as all the victims were already dead, or brain dead, from traumatic asphyxia. Painstaking research undertaken by family members and friends of the victims has revealed that many of their loved ones could have been saved with a supply of oxygen after 3.15pm. There were victims whose injuries were not consistent with traumatic asphysixia. They had the evidence, but the cutoff time effectively let police and emergency services off the hook. Further calls for the appropriate scrutiny would go unheard, and the persistence of those it affected most would be met with scorn.

16. The Arsenal Trilogy.

Part 1. Birkey Embarassment

It was the final week in March 2008 when the Champions League draw pitted Liverpool against Arsenal in the competition's quarter finals. The first game would take place at Arsenal's Emirates Stadium on the 1st of April with the return leg a week later at Anfield. Slotted in between these two games was the preordained Premiership match (again at the Emirates), which meant these two magnificent teams would have to play each other three times in the space of a week.

It was dubbed *the Arsenal Trilogy*. As far as trilogies go, it was incredible. It wasn't one of those trilogies that peter out, tricking you into liking it more than you actually did in order to justify your emotional investment. There was no soft redemption for its villains, no unrealistic late minute plot developments, no farcical characters introduced to prop up tired themes or to distract you from the inevitable conclusion. In short, there were no Ewoks.

The first two instalments provided just the right amounts of intrigue and suspense to suggest that it would all come to a head in an explosive finale – no script required.

The styles of the two sides differed greatly. Arsenal, under the enduring reign of their French manager, Arsene Wenger (a.k.a 'The Professor'), were a team capable of bedazzling the pants off any follower of football. Athletic and skilful, they could out pass, out pace, and therefore out play any team in the world on their day. But Wenger's team of pretty young things had a tendency of becoming overly precious when they didn't get their way. Once hustled off their stride, the line between precocious and prima donna is a thin one. Seeing Arsenal lose their shit is like watching eleven Veruca Salt's have a go at Willie Wonka – the transformation from golden to bad eggs as rank as it is riveting. It would be up to Liverpool's men of steel to deny the pretty young things their starlet aspirations.

I watched the first game at the Birkey. It was the first night that I became aware of the drink getting the better of me. I've always prided myself on being able to drink with the best of them and remember, for better or worse, what happened the next day. But the morning after the first game in the trilogy I was only able to recall one thing. It was the goal Stevie G had set up for Dutiful Dirk that made the game 1-1.

When Barry came over to fill in the gaps he was in high spirits. Under his arm was the Anfield picture I'd taken to the Birkey for everyone to sign, but had forgotten to bring home. Barry said the staff had found it at the end of the night in a corner of the bar before putting it somewhere safe. There were 12 or so signatures on the back yet I was buggered if I could actually remember anyone signing it. But that wasn't all.

Aside from the good result for Liverpool, Barry stated the highlight of his night had been my drunken attempts at getting the Birkey crowd to sing *We love you Liverpool,* not once, not twice, but thrice! With a wave of embarrassment, fragments of best forgotten memory filtered back. I recalled that my first attempt had partially worked, with six or so sympathetic Scousers singing along. But on my second and third attempts I was left hanging. My singing tone flat, my timing non-existent – everyone just looked and laughed.

'It just doesn't sound right in kiwi,' said Barry, chuckling away. He consoled me with a pat on the back. He was right – my singing voice is best left unheard – you'd think I'd have learnt my lesson. Whenever I'd tried to sing You'll Never Walk Alone back in New Zealand I'd been told to stop. The first time I wasn't even leading. I was at a restaurant with my brother Lyndon, a work mate of his, an old NZ rocker and his wife. The rocker's name was Graham Brazier, and when I told him in the course of conversation that I hoped to visit Merseyside one day, he announced that his family was from Liverpool. He then swung into a rendition of YNWA, right there in the restaurant. It was a special moment that was nearly ruined when I was hushed by his wife for trying to sing along. So while everyone else listened with their special moment smiles sellotaped across their faces, I sat there incensed, desperately wanting to join in on the chorus. How could she cut me down like that? I'd barely cleared my throat!

The second time was at my own book launch. We were down to the last dozen or so people when I sang a couple of lines and tried to get everyone to join in. But before anyone had a chance a Russian woman no one really knew announced that I couldn't sing to save myself. She said it in a really abrupt Russian way – as though I'd mortally offended her by even trying – as though me singing was worthy of the tone someone might use if the KGB was trying to poison them, or if they'd just found out the Gulag had booked their next holiday.

Of course, Erin – who doesn't suffer fools – didn't suffer my singing right from the start. 'That's *terrrrible,*' she'd say, barely giving me time to reach the chorus.

'But I listen to your songs – they're terrible too.'

'My voice is wonderful. You don't know what you're talking about.' And off she'd go – into that disturbing realm of almost lyrics and spasmodic dance, beautiful girl/big bald man.

My point is, having been degraded so many times, I should've known better. The Birkey incident completed my humiliation – I'd been denied by the Scousers, the only people who might understand, might appreciate that it's more about where it comes from (deep within my soul!) than the actual sound. After all, I was singing their songs - I should at least get marks for flattery.

Then again, many a less tolerant bunch would have told me to 'shut the fuck up' – it was the least I deserved. There was no denying it; the drink was taking its toll.

Pub singing. Who would've thought? Next it'll be face paint and a flag around my shoulders. Anyone would think I was Australian. The irony absorbed easily into my hangover.

Part 2

Red Requirement

On Thursday night I scored two tickets from Tony the tout to the second instalment of the trilogy. On Friday I was on the midday train to London.

Richard, my friend on a working visa from New Zealand, offered to put me up, and, despite being a Chelsea supporter, humoured me by coming along to the Emirates stadium for a gander. To his surprise, he came away thoroughly smitten. The morning after the game (another tense one-all draw) he woke me with the sound of the Liverpool crowd singing from his laptop via You Tube. Before his 90 minutes with the Scousers, Richard had dismissed football crowd singing as inconsequential noise, such was his experience at Chelsea's home ground of Stamford Bridge. And despite Richard's initial refusal to get too excited on Liverpool's behalf, the away section's vibrancy proved contagious.

The reds' goal scorer that day was the 6 ft 7" Peter Crouch.

With his gaunt, crooked face, 'Crouchy' was heroin chic on stilts. Skinny as a catwalk waif he was probably the most unlikely striker on the planet, and therefore one of the most likable. Think back to the gangliest kid in school and you'll probably agree that anyone who clocks in at such a height looks more inclined to bump his head against the moon than possess the coordination to kick a ball. Head the ball yes, but no player has ever succeeded in the top flight of football just because he was taller than everyone else.

After his goal, the only thing taller than Peter Crouch was The Emirates stadium itself. Poised above the trees and terraces of Highbury – The Emirates is a steel, space age bowl with a contoured upper tier which gives the impression that the whole circular structure could take off into the stratosphere at the push of a button. It was all very nice and comfortable.

Having watched so much football with Richard back in Auckland, it felt good to be with him, experiencing that which we'd only seen on a screen. There was even a song he joined in on: *Pe-ter Crouch, Pe-ter Crouch: He's big! He's red! His feet stick out the bed! Pe-ter Crouch, Pe-ter Crouch.*

He was getting into the spirit of things and I wondered if this was the moment he finally agreed that there was some truth to the pro-Liverpool spruiking he and our friends had endured from me back in Auckland. I fancied he might even surreptitiously drop them a line over the next few days to say that it's true, *Liverpool is special!*

But when he looked up at me from his laptop the next morning and said that he might be converted – as in *goodbye blues, hello reds* - I wasn't overjoyed. It sounded too easy, too clean cut. Richard said that he'd just emailed an ex-work mate and reds fan back in Auckland to say he was on the verge of changing clubs. For a moment there, I could've sworn that all he was waiting for was my blessing, some kind of Road to Damascus speech sprinkled with poignant Bill Shankly quotes to pull him over the line. And even though Tomo had given me his picture of Anfield on the condition I start converting, I just couldn't do it.

Richard had chosen Chelsea for their new spending power back in 2004. Except, if you actually asked him, he'd try and bullshit you into believing he's been a fan since childhood just because it sounded better. Before 2004, however, there'd been no mention of any preference for any premiership team, even though we watched the competition religiously from the same couch, week in, week out. The truth was that Richard became a Chelsea supporter when the billionaire Roman Abramovich decided to spend more money than anyone else. In doing so, Chelsea suddenly had themselves a star-studded team with a charismatic Portuguese manager who referred to himself as 'the special one'.

The idea of simply buying success was right up Richard's alley because Richard was nouve riche personified. Of all my financially-fixated Auckland friends, it was Richard who led the way. He spent so much money on wine and shoes he deserved a role in Sex in the City. He only ever drove expensive European cars and believed that $100,000 a year was the minimum you needed for a decent lifestyle. Forget appreciating what you have, forget inner enrichment; how you were doing was more about what you've got. $100,000 a year gets you a lot. Anything short of that was unfortunate. Anything well short of that was unseemly.

Just the previous night I'd had words with him about the disrespect he'd shown to a beggar. Richard just couldn't get his head around the idea that people often become desperate because of the shitty hand life has dealt them, couldn't comprehend what a huge advantage it is in this world to be white and middle class and born somewhere like New Zealand. With my Auckland friends it sometimes felt as though this privilege was something they'd shifted from feeling lucky about to something they felt entitled to; and that people on the street or the people who struggled to feed their families were paying the price for their own recklessness, for not trying hard enough, for not fitting in.

Now, no one – let alone a Liverpool fan not from Liverpool – has the right to say who should and who shouldn't be a Liverpool fan. Perhaps Richard could've made a very good Liverpool fan. But surely with Liverpool's history, there has to be a minimum requirement. Surely that requirement is at least something of a social conscience.

Shankly made the club great because of his social solidarity, his recognition of what it means to those who grind away at their poorly-paid, demoralising jobs to have their club recognise them as being just as important as the players and management. He was renowned for organising free tickets for the disadvantaged. He even took phone calls from fans after the games and spoke at length with them about the progress of the team. And if any of that culture was lost when Shankly passed on then surely the emotional links with the community were never stronger than in the aftermath of Hillsborough, the Liverpool players making their concerted effort to meet with the victims' families and attend as many of the victims' funerals as they could. Kenny Dalglish attended ninety funerals all up, and paid for it when emotional trauma forced him to resign as Liverpool's manager in 1991. Even after the Taylor Report brought about the necessary shift to new all-seater stadiums, Dalglish wrote of his concern that the financial burden to the clubs would be passed on, resulting in working class families being priced out of the game. 'Poorer fans should not be discouraged…We should never forget the wee boy in the street whose father cannot afford to take him. One has to be mindful of the fans of the future.'

And today the notion of community club is echoed by players such as Jamie Carragher and Steven Gerrard, the latter's cousin a Hillsborough victim who Gerrard recognises as his inspiration for doing the best by the fans. It's the spirit born from such extremes of triumph and tragedy that makes Liverpool so unique and gives such resonance to YNWA, so much so that, when they sing it as though their very lives depend on it, they can spark their team towards winning the greatest trophy any club can win. That's what Liverpool's about, and no matter how much money the billionaire Abramovich pumps into Chelsea that is something he'll never be able to buy.

Richard swapped his laptop for a Sunday paper, and opened to a photo of a very dapper looking Stevie G and a two-page article on the impressive investments he was putting back into Liverpool. 'He looks quite good in that photo,' said Richard.

'Of course he does,' I said. 'He's a good-looking man… Has been all along. Even before he was making big investments.'

'What?'

'You can't become a Liverpool fan, Richard. I need you the way you are.'

'I was never going to.'

'Sure you weren't. You're Chelsea through and through.'

'And you're Liverpool through and through,' he said.

'That's right,' I said. 'Best club in the world.'

'But not the best team,' he countered.

I shrugged. 'That's debatable.' But instead of using the miracle of Istanbul to illustrate why – with the greatest club you don't necessarily need the greatest team – I took a step back, and sauntered down the hallway.

In truth, I just really wanted a shower. The air mattress Richard had set up for me the night before had pretty much deflated the moment I lay down. While I was asleep a ghostly hand had reached up through the floor boards and clung with an icy grip to my lower spine. I knew it wouldn't let go until I could scald it free with a torrent of hot water.

So I took a nice long shower, knowing that Richard probably wouldn't convert after all. Instead of feeling ambivalent about discouraging my friend from swapping hollow blue success for priceless red glory, I felt just fine – as though a slight crease in the fabric of our friendship had been neatly ironed out. No conversion, no problem.

Part 3

Priceless Glory.

Before I made the call to Tony the Tout about the likelihood of two tickets to Anfield for Wednesday night's game, I took the time to rehearse what I needed to say.

Talking to Tony took a similar courage to calling a beautiful girl. One little crack in my ever-so-casual veneer would reveal my desperate need and put the whole exercise in mortal danger. A single stutter and the beautiful girl might realise she could do better. With Tony, it was pretty much the same; he might realise he could do better – up to fifty pounds better, if I wasn't careful.

But what I liked about Tony was his grace in sparing me the obvious salesman tactics of pretending that I was asking the impossible. Instead, he employed the slightly less obvious tactic of sounding like he really cared, that getting me these tickets meant the world to him, the least he could do for an old friend. 'No worries, mate. Look, I'll see what I can do for yer. I'll have a word, mate; we'll work somethin' out. Leave it with me, don't you worry.'

'Thanks, Tony,' I said. 'Thanks, man, really appreciate it. Will you call me or should I call you?'

'I'll call you back, mate.'

'Okay. Later tonight?'

'Yer. Don't worry. I'll call you back soon like.'

'Sweet, sweet. So, about an hour?'

'Yer. Give me an hour or so – I'll talk to some friends.'

'Great, great. It's just that my battery's getting low so—'

'I'll call you back in an hour – no worries, mate.'

'Sweet. Thanks Tony – big game eh, be bloody great to be there.'

We ended the conversation with the shared knowledge that I was about to be fleeced once again. But, as gracious as he was, when Tony called back, he kindly went to the effort of sounding genuinely sorry as he named the exorbitant amount it was going to cost me.

Of course, it was as low as he could go. Yes, he'd played me like a fiddle, but what a sweet song it was. I said I'd have to think about it and would call him back soon.

I lowered my phone then raised it again to bash against my head. I had my heart set on shouting Barry a ticket but, boy, it was going to cost me. I took a moment to weigh my emotional want against actual reality. The latter didn't stand a chance. Joyce had mentioned a number of times how Barry was the biggest Liverpool fan around but had sadly never been to a game. He couldn't afford it, she said. And as a child his Seventh Day Adventist parents condemned football due to its negative spiritual influence.

Yet an indication of just how much of a fan Barry was could be gleaned from his eternal hope. On the night I arrived in Crosby, Mick mentioned how he'd found Barry enthusiastically pouring over the Premiership table and coming fixtures that day. Somehow he'd managed to calculate that as long as the impending games played out in Liverpool's favour, the reds could still clinch it by being level with United on points, but ahead on goal difference. Barry was buoyed by the reckoning that as long as United dropped a highly improbable amount of points with just a handful of games to go, the title was ours. Around the same time even Jamie Carragher had conceded that all title hopes were dashed. He said the focus was now on securing fourth place instead, proving Barry's quixotic optimism was the kind you could only get from a hopelessly nutty fan. Just the kind of fan I'd been looking for.

It seemed a little misguided – not to mention fiscally irresponsible – to be spending 150 pounds (250 NZ dollars!) on someone I only met a few weeks before, but the thrill in Barry's voice when I rang to ask if he'd like to go to Anfield convinced me I was doing the right thing.

'I'm buzzing already!' he said. 'I finish work at 1p.m.'

'I'll meet you at the Birkey around then. Actually, it could be a bit later.'

'I will meet you anywhere, anytime you like, my friend!'

I did some sums in my head hoping this show of generosity wasn't going to leave me selling the Standard Issue in order to feed myself. Of course, the generosity of people like Kate and Graeme and Eddie and Joyce meant it would never come to that. Without question, the worst thing that could happen now was for Liverpool to lose. Arsenal were always dangerous and had a history of raining on Liverpool's parade – most famously the goal that stole the league from the reds in 1989, documented in the book *Fever Pitch* by that sadly obsessive Arsenal fan, Nick Hornby. How horrible it would be for Barry's only time at Anfield to be a demoralizing loss. Stevie G, you better come out to play. These thoughts, accompanied by a million or so others kept me up, tossing and turning in twisted sheets of turmoil the night before the game. Even more so than against United, I needed Liverpool to win.

We met at the Birkey where Drew, Mick, Ian and a guy called Johnno were braving a cold but dry afternoon around a picnic table in the courtyard. I was in the middle of batting off the probing questions about how much I'd paid for the tickets when Ian brought up an issue that needed to be resolved. Ian, the one-eared Evertonian, wasn't happy. His issue was with Johnno, whom he claimed was making lewd gestures at his wife's breasts on the dance floor the previous night. There was a moment of high tension when Johnno tentatively challenged Ian's perception of what really happened – and just when he seemed perilously close to questioning Ian's wife's integrity, Johnno did the honorable thing and apologised. He even backed it up with a conciliatory beer which Ian graciously accepted, the issue dealt with and discarded. The mood eased with the focus shifting to someone everybody was shitty with.

In January, Ringo Starr had opened the Capital of Culture celebrations with an outdoor concert from the rooftop of St George's Hall. Every Scouser to a man had condemned the performance as *bloddy terrible*, although their criticism might have been tainted by what Ringo had said afterwards. When asked on live TV what he missed most about Liverpool, Ringo replied: 'Nuthin'. The very next day the hedge that was sculpted to look like the fab four at John Lennon Airport was conspicuously missing the head of its drummer.

Johnno mentioned that he had the shits with Paul McCartney as well, even though his comments about Liverpool were generally positive. 'If he likes it so much, why doesn't he live here?'

I glanced at the sky – its pallor that of a shark's underbelly – and held my tongue.

We were joined by a couple of lads in their early twenties, one of whom had taken over Barry's mantle as the Birkey's champion pinball player and who Barry only referred to as 'Nemesis.' Nemesis and several of his mates were going to the game as well, prompting the inevitable question of how much *he'd* paid for *his* tickets. He gave his answer without hesitation: 'The guy said he wanted a hundred. I said "fork orf" and got them for seventy.'

So that's how you do it, I thought. The attention swung back my way.

'Come on, Glenn, how much?' said Mick.

'69.95,' I said.

'Bollocks. How much really?'

'I'm not telling.'

'He fucked you up the arse, didn't he, lad,' said Johnno.

'I think I might've been slightly fucked.'

'How much did he fuck you, lad?'

'I think he fucked me quite a bit.'

'How much?'

'I'm not gonna say. I'm new here – I was desperate.'

'Who is he? We'll get your money back.'

'No, it's done. Don't worry – doesn't matter.'

'How much doesn't matter?' said Drew.

I knew the interrogation would only stop once I said the amount. It was like knowing someone you want to impress is seconds away from detecting your fart. I was just about to reveal the mystery amount when I was saved by a true freak of nature: a bumble bee.

A few weeks earlier Kate and Graeme had reacted to a bumble bee flying into their apartment as though it was a deadly escapee from Jurrasic Park. I told them it was harmless but their terror didn't subside until I ushered the bee back out the window. The reaction at the Birkey was the same. To the cries of *Bee! Bee! Bee!* five grown men scattered to the four corners of the courtyard. Amid the clamour, Barry suggested we seize the moment and, with that, we were off.

On the way to Ed and Joyce's, Barry said he'd pay me for his ticket by the time I had to leave. I waved the matter away. The last thing I wanted was for Barry to feel indebted. He seemed a little downcast anyway, and, as we walked, I couldn't help but think that for a 'red or dead' kind of guy about to visit Anfield for the first time, he was being a bit grumpy. I soon found out that it had nothing to do with me, but everything to do with the massive hole in his front teeth.

I'd noticed it the second I'd arrived at the Birkey. With no front teeth, Barry's big top lip drooped at a sombre angle, and, despite his jockey sized frame and swept back salt and pepper hair, he almost looked tough.

He was angry all right, but only at himself. This was the second time he'd lost his dentures in the space of two years. His first set went missing after he'd decided to put a wooly jumper away until the end of summer. When the weather was cold enough again for the jumper, he put it back on only to be stopped in the street by someone who kindly pointed out the teeth hanging from his back. According to Barry, they were nothing but a bloody pain. Barry preferred his original teeth, despite their sizable gap in the upper row. Importantly, the gap proved a valuable source of laughs down at the pub. 'One night there was this lass who reckoned she had a bigger gap than mine,' he said. 'We had a competition to see whose gap could fit the most coins. I beat her with one pound 72 p. I didn't mind me gap but when I was working on this building site a board went "fork off" and smacked me in the gob.' Barry showed me the scar where a tooth had actually pierced his lip. 'Dentist said the board had widened me gap – if it had hit the other way, it would've straightened them. That's when I had to get the plate. Now I can't do without it.' Over the past few days Barry had not been able to eat anything more substantial than mushie peas. Sick to death of mushie peas, he was grumpy.

We arrived at Harvey Rd where Joyce made the point that, despite his eating problems, Baz should be happy, for tonight was the night he was finally off to Anfield.

'What do you mean finally off to Anfield? I was there two seasons ago!' said Barry. 'I've been a reds' fan all me life, Joyce! Of course I've been to Anfield – I been goin' since I was five years old!' Barry looked at me: 'No matter how many times I tell her, she won't listen.' He looked imploringly at an unconvinced-looking Joyce. So did I.

'Joyce, when are going to believe me?' said Barry. If Joyce was listening, you wouldn't have guessed it. The story of Barry never having been to Anfield was entirely her creation. It had usurped the truth simply because she preferred it.

She folded her arms and set us in stone with a circumspect gaze. Me, with my pre-match nerves and realisation that Barry's trip to Anfield tonight wasn't quite the ground-breaking event I thought it would be; and Barry, with his sallow cheeks, gappy gob, and toothless exasperation. Defiant as ever, Joyce shook her head. *Football should be for entertainment and entertainment only and anything more means football is more trouble than it's worth!* She couldn't understand what we saw in it, and didn't really want to. As far as entertainment goes, *football was rubbish.*

She went for a swig of beer but before the bottle could complete the upwards journey to her mouth, there was a delay. 'As long as you two have a larf!' she said. 'Promise me you'll have yourselves a larf!!'

Poor Joyce, she simply didn't understand. We were off to see a thriller, not a comedy. Unless Arsenal succumbed to a clown-like capitulation, there would be no laughing. Barry knew this; I knew this. All the same, we promised Joyce we'd have a larf.

Half an hour later at the bus stop on Liverpool Road, Barry chirped up no end. We'd just bumped into one of his ex-girlfriends. This wasn't the first time, and it only served to verify my suspicion that old Bazza was something of a Lothario. The encounter was a friendly one and, once on board the bus, Barry was soon back to his optimistic self. He spoke once again of his great friendship with Ed and Joyce, pointed out the bar they used to run as we went through Bootle, and took to calming my nerves on a regular basis by assuring me Liverpool were going to win. We got off at Derby Street, parallel to the city's northern dockyards, and headed inland, up a slight rise through the darkening neighborhoods, preternaturally quiet as though this really was the calm before the storm. When the bulk of Anfield's main stand could be seen, we found ourselves walking with fellow fans – the streets now moving with the hastened gait and excitable chatter of the happy Anfield bound. Barry bought a couple of beers at the packed King Harry pub and had a quick whinge about having to pay €3 per bottle as we joined the overflow of bodies on Blessington Rd. We then continued our way through cobbled laneways of a 'renewal zone,' where the windows of derelict terraces are either broken or boarded up and barbed wire coils stretch the length of mildewed walls. We passed a group of kids playing a manic game of street football, oblivious to the adult migration around them. I caught sight of a brilliant header by a girl of barely eleven wearing an Everton tracksuit top. It smacked against a section of brick wall for a goal – as good an Everton goal as you're ever likely to see. Before entering the stadium, Barry was still the prince of positivity, in stark contrast to my creature of unease. No matter how much I tried to rationalise and put into perspective the possibility of a loss, my body was unwilling to undertake anything close to a sense of calm. Prior knowledge of what I was about to experience wouldn't have changed a thing.

We got in without fuss, and, as we made our way up the main stand, we took a moment to admire the mosaics, flags and banners concentrated on the Kop. Barry described how one of his most vivid memories as a lad was being right up the back of the famous stand in the days before Hillsborough made seating compulsory.

Barry said he and a mate had been on the verge of tears at not being able to see the field when a couple of men hoisted the boys on top of the crowd and a sea of hands passed them swiftly down to a raised platform near the front. Despite their new vantage point almost on top of the game, Barry and his mate had so much fun crowd surfing down the 45-degree human slope they decided to sneak all the way back up to do it again.

Without doubt, Barry's formative experience of the Kop coupled with his unmitigated belief in his team, meant he was truly one of Shankly's originals – just the kind of fan the famed manager had envisaged and done so much to nurture. The cost of the ticket flittered away and I was proud to have thrown common sense to the wind.

We sang YNWA (the 40,000 strong choir masking my vocal inadequacies) and within ten minutes another ten Kop classics had been sung with barely a second separating each one. The big game synergy was electric. It ripped through the stands and melded us together into a mass of spiritually-charged maniacs. I caught my breath – this atmosphere, fuckin' hell, *THIS IS ANFIELD!* The sheer adrenaline heightened our senses to near supernatural levels and every movement, every gesture, every kick, slide and tackle we responded to together.

The only hitch to our rowdy omniscience was an Arsenal goal in the twelfth minute. *Shit!* After a spell of typically intricate passing, Abu Diaby finished the move by slamming the ball past Pepe Reina, in front of the Kop. It was almost disrespectful.

Still, Anfield bounced back straight away by singing *We Love You Liverpool!* to reassure both ourselves and the players that it was nothing more than just a slight inconvenience, a minor disruption that would, if anything, spark the team into action. But unlike the crowd, the players didn't bounce back. They lost their composure and stopped putting pressure on the ball, chasing an Arsenal game that was smooth and slick and threatening. Our singing continued but, without the appropriate response from the players, the volume went down. The Arsenal fans pounced: *Where's Your Special, Where's Your Special, Where's Your Special Atmosphere? Where's Your Special Atmosphere!*

The Kop was quick to counter: *Where's Your Europe, Where's Your Europe, Where's Your European Cup? Where's Your European Cup!*

But as we sang our reminder of their club's failure to win what we'd won five times, we did so with one eye on our floundering players, hoping like hell they'd show something to suggest they were up for another. The moment that would finally swing momentum our way came in the thirtieth minute when Sami Hyypia escaped his marker from a corner kick and scored with a bullet header that ricocheted in from the left post. Anfield roared. Everyone swung their scarves wildly above their heads turning the crowd into a sloping delirium of red woolen rotor blades. With that, the team took off, now dominating a game that just seconds before they were barely a part of. They won every tackle, passed with confidence, and very nearly took the lead twice, while Arsenal stood back, dumbstruck by the sudden turn of events.

Apart from a few minor hiccups, Liverpool kept their stolen thunder for the next half hour until the frantic pace of the game stalled under the strain. The noise level remained as loud as ever but, as is often the case, the lull suggested the game was heading into a new phase where just a little bit of luck either way could well determine the winner. It was in the sixty-eighth minute when Arsenal's Adebayor came dangerously close to beating the offside trap which would have seen him clear and bearing down on goal. It gave me a fright that seemed to stun my rational mind while something I can only describe as a sheer primal scream spewed forth. More than animal aggression, heightened euphoria, or anything in between, the scream was all encompassing, indecipherable, and, in the eyes of an onlooker, probably not very pretty. It must have been a spontaneous confluence of symbols, sound and emotion which caused everything at once to take flight, my self set free before a visual impairment of sudden darkness and crackling stars returned me downward and dazed. Slumped back in my seat I had the soul of a new believer fresh from the cosmic dunk and the glimpse of the almighty. What a feeling – a divine swirl of self-loss that I'll forever be grateful for. Having since viewed a replay of the game I have timed it at around twenty seconds, remembering that I regained my bearings to pop up just in time to see Fernando Torres smack a brilliant goal.

Liverpool ahead: 2-1.

The searing voltage of another Anfield eruption had me jumping into the embrace of the two screaming Indians to my left. Meanwhile, Barry was lifted clean off the ground, his legs cycling in mid-air due to the exuberant bear hug of the portly middle-aged Scouser to his right.

There are very few occasions in life where strangers (men especially) will randomly embrace each other in a spontaneous manner, jump up and down and cheer. You would think the rare nature of such behaviour would lead to an onset of embarrassment once the euphoria died down, but it wasn't that way at all. We just grinned and laughed at each other and didn't give a fuck about anything but the great goal we'd just seen, marveling at what blessed fools we were to have witnessed such a thing.

Yet despite Arsenal's consternation, they had one last weapon to unleash. When Arsene Wenger brought on the talented whippersnapper Theo Walcott, his fresh legs and frightening pace soon had him gathering the ball and slaloming the length of the pitch past desperate red defenders. A short pass into Adebayor directly in front of goal meant the Togolese striker couldn't miss. 2-2. *Noooooooo* – a Bruce Lee one-inch punch to the sternum could not have felt any worse. Anfield fell silent with the knowledge that this second away goal was enough to put Arsenal through to the semi-finals, thus ejecting the mighty reds from the tournament. The Arsenal fans went berserk. We looked down to our left to see the jubilant Londoners reel back in ecstasy, a painful mirror of ourselves just a short time ago.

'That's where the party's at now,' grumbled Barry.

Never fear. If our euphoria had been rudely cut short then theirs was about to be extinguished in the cruelest fashion. Exactly a minute after the Walcott-crafted goal, Liverpool's own fresh pair of legs in the form of Ryan Babel surged towards Arsenal's penalty area only to be grappled to the ground by a desperate defense. Barry, who'd picked the wrong time to sit down and roll a cigarette, shot bottle rocket-like from his chair. "I missed it! I missed it!"

'Definite penalty! Definite penalty!' I yelled, pointing at the scene of the crime.

A week ago, in the closing minutes of the trilogy's first instalment, Arsenal had had a legitimate penalty claim denied when Dirk Kuyt pulled down Alexander Hleb. If the referee had chosen to deny Ryan Babel on this occasion even the staunchest Liverpool fan could not cry foul the balance of an even ledger. Hard to swallow, but fair. So when the referee pointed to the spot and awarded Liverpool a penalty, a little injustice took place. And it may or may not surprise you that, if it were in my power to turn back time and alter the referee's decision in the name of fair play, I most certainly wouldn't. I know that's a less than virtuous position to take, but honesty is a virtue too, you know. And with only five minutes of normal time to go, it could easily be Liverpool's last opportunity to win. If the penalty kick went wide or was saved, the anguish would surely suck dry the marrow of the team's spirit and thus serve to strengthen Arsenal's resolve to see out the game. One sure kick would mean glory. One mis-kick would mean all the highs, lows and hard work it took to make it to this penultimate juncture would be in vain. A season in tatters, right in front of the Kop? It was enough to make any mere mortal shiver in his boots and go running to Mummy. Who could take on such pressure? Who could bear such responsibility? What if you slipped, what if you just remembered saying something that might've offended someone earlier, what if you were overcome with existential angst and suddenly didn't give a shit either way? So many variables!

Thank God for Steven Gerrard – Liverpool's own, the man most determined, the man most capable to further his club's cause. There was no sign of nerves as he approached the ball and no hint upon contact that it was going anywhere but the back of the net. He didn't go ballistic after scoring; he just ran towards his team mates along the sideline and lit up Anfield with a smile of equal parts relief and utter joy.

The goal ensured there were no more twists in the tale. There was, however, a generous spread of icing on the cake as an exhausted Arsenal pushed forward for one last attack only to be caught on the counter as Ryan Babel ran onto the path of a clearance kick, fended off the incoming challenge of Cesc Fabregas, and slotted the ball past Almunia to bring an emphatic end to the trilogy. A thriller, without doubt. We all cheered and emphasised the Scouse defiance with *We Shall Not, We Shall Not be Moved!* closely followed by an intensely proud *You'll Never Walk Alone.* The Arsenal fans showed grace in defeat and directed their clapping towards the Liverpool crowd, thanking Anfield for the spectacle. It was a mark of respect returned in kind.

17. The Hero

With less than a week before I was due to fly back to the southern seas, and with my head still in the clouds after Tuesday night's game, it was time for some good old-fashioned voyeurism. I'd read somewhere that the best place around for football star gazing was Jamie Carragher's Sports Bar on Stanley St in the city. I arrived under the guise of someone innocently looking for lunch.

Much like a well-marshaled defensive line, JC's restaurant was well set out and organised with staff who knew their jobs and executed their duties without hesitation.

There was a long polished bar, leather booths, and a plethora of screens featuring non-stop footage of Liverpool glory.

I glanced around the place, hoping to spot the thin determined features of the man himself. No luck.

Patience I thought, and opted for a table beside the street window, looking back at the restaurant. I ordered a pint of lager and a Thai chicken salad from a menu that promised fresh produce cooked on the spot without any excessive fat. At first it seemed a welcome departure from the slimy stodge and brown sauce served everywhere else, but when the salad came with just four strips of chicken on top, the notion of portion control seemed less like a heart 'tick for life' and more an act of cruelty. Accustomed as I was to Joyce's grand servings, this would never do. There was a more pleasant surprise, however, when my waiter turned out to be from New Zealand.

Since leaving home the only evidence I'd had that New Zealand still existed was news footage of our cricket team, a newspaper article about a dolphin who'd saved someone from drowning near Gisborne, and the unsettling story of a man who was having a baby. The pregnant man (who turned out to be a 'guy in a girl's body') received the most attention of the three, which sadly made him/her the most newsworthy item to come out of my country in the five weeks I'd been away.

Hamish, my kiwi waiter, was in Liverpool because studying here was cheaper than London. I congratulated him on his job.

'Pays the bills,' he shrugged.

'Yeah, but must be pretty good working for Jamie Carragher.'

'I didn't even know who he was before I came here,' he said. 'Apparently he's a bit of a legend. Apparently the rest of the team comes in all the time, but I don't know who the fuck they are.' I was about to slap a strip of chicken across his ungrateful arse of a face when he quickly redeemed himself. 'He's here today,' said Hamish.

'Who, Jamie Carragher?'

'Been doing an interview downstairs. There's another one in the corner over there as well, some Spanish guy.' Suddenly, four strips of chicken for €9 seemed like the best deal in town. I looked in the direction my fine fellow countryman had nodded and lo and behold, there he was – El Nino, the boy from sunny Spain, Liverpool's no. 9 - *Fernando Jose Torres*. He was sitting at a table next to an attractive female I assumed was his girlfriend. A male friend of similar age sat opposite. Their conversation was animated, but not in that look-at-me-I'm-so-vivacious-and-glamorous-yet-can-still-laugh-just-like-the-commoners kind of way. He looked happy. So nice to see him happy. The soft light above his table brought out the golden flecks of his blonde hair. His aura was 24 Carats of vibrancy and calm. He sat below a screen showing the 2005 Champions League triumph as though he was destined for red glory on par with the greatest victory of all.

I shook Hamish's hand and rushed the conversation so I could sit back and revel in the moment. Me and Fernando, sitting in the same restaurant. I recalled how Chris had proudly claimed to have been in the same café as Manchester United's Dutch goalkeeper, and gave him a call. "I'll see your Edwin Van der Sar with a Fernando Torres and, wait – ' I paused as the restaurant's owner walked past to sign his autograph at a nearby table. 'And raise you a Jamie Carragher!'

'What are you talking about?' he said. I boasted like a booger-faced brat and hung up before he could say anything to ruin it. There were two Scousers sitting at a table adjacent to mine who'd seen Jamie Carragher walk past and, in their excitement, failed to spot Fernando. I leaned across. 'Look. Over there.' They looked in the direction I was pointing from under the table. Their faces lit up. They thanked me profusely for the tip off and then poked fun at me for being a stalker. 'You've been here since breakfast, haven't you, lad?'
I played along but, as the laughter at my expense petered out, the possibility crossed my mind. Could I be... is it possible that.... maybe this is.... Am I a bit sad?

Is a thirty-four-year-old heterosexual man inwardly giggling over a guy ten years his junior sad? Surely there's nothing wrong with a little admiration? I admired Torres for his ability, his adherence to the Liverpool way, his apparent lack of ego. As a journalist for The Daily Telegraph had noted, the

Spaniard really did have the air of someone who genuinely doesn't know what all the fuss is about. Yet here I am, sneaking furtive glances, struggling to maintain an expression of blatant disinterest to the point where I may well appear to have given up on life. Like I wasn't even a Liverpool fan, and this just happened to be a restaurant I'd stumbled into for one last meal before I committed the unmentionable.

I suppose I've answered my own question. Thankfully, I have a tenet – that as long as my admiration stops short of hero worship, I'm okay. Hero worship's for the kids. Kids and, apparently, fashion designers. A week earlier, I read an article about Giorgio Armani designing the Chelsea team's 'off-field ensembles'. He seemed determined to have them looking like even bigger dandies than they already are, and was even quoted as stating that footballers are 'genuinely heroic.' He went on: 'I like working with footballers because it means I get the chance to dress heroes: men at the very height of their powers, physically and mentally.'

As I said, admire a player for his skill, his cool head under pressure, his discipline and determination to excel. Develop a little man crush even; it's okay, football allows that. If the player has succeeded despite an impoverished background then maybe he really is heroic. But only if there's a cause, only if he exudes mana and doesn't squander his elevated status by being a dick. As a rule, footballers, as gifted with almost superhuman powers as they are, are not heroes. The heroes of this world perform selfless tasks for the good of others, sometimes to their own detriment. They are also the ones who have endured cruelty and suffering yet still have the courage to recognise the good in others and thus maintain a faith in humanity, something humanity doesn't often deserve. To uphold a sense of compassion and kindness in a world that has shown you very little, that's heroism.

Before going to Jamie Carragher's restaurant, I had visited a museum on Albert Dock which refreshed my perspective on such things.

Opened in 2007, Liverpool's International Slavery Museum is the physical manifestation of a solemn admission. Much as the burden of current prosperity is the profit gained from sweat shop labour, polluting water sources, and stripping sacred lands of their minerals, the burden of Liverpool's prosperity in the late 18th and early 19th century was the trade of African slaves. Liverpool was the European port most involved in the trade during this period, right through to its abolition in 1807. Even though England was far from the main exploiter of actual slave labour on its own land, it nevertheless reaped the benefits from exploiting the trade itself.

I already knew of Liverpool's involvement in the slave trade on account of it being Europe's connection between Africa and the Americas. Stepping into the International Slavery Museum at the Albert Docks provided a better understanding of the forces at play. Just metres away from a wall display of inspirational black people and an exhibit of African life before its hellish disruption, there was a letter displayed in a cabinet that had been written and signed with utterly dubious – if not evil - intent.

It was entitled 'Petition of Liverpool to the House of Commons', 14 February 1788. The goal of the 'humble petition' was to 'humbly pray' that Parliament would do an about turn on its hitherto sanctioning of other petitions that wanted the African Slave Trade abolished. The Liverpool petition emphasised how important the slave trade was to the commerce of Liverpool and how terrible it would be if 'this source of wealth', which 'in effect gives strength and energy to the whole' (i.e. the rest of England) were to end. It was signed by the town's Mayor, several MP's (also investors in the trade) and, of course, the ones who profited directly; the slave merchants themselves.

One name in particular stood out from the rest. It was James Penny, the man Liverpool's own 'Penny lane' was named after, and subsequently made famous by the Beatles.

Although Liverpool had an underground of those who backed abolition, there's anecdotal evidence that it wasn't just greedy politicians and merchants that were hell bent on keeping the trade going. Thomas Clarkson, founding member of the Society for Effecting the Abolition of the Slave Trade, recalls a visit to Liverpool where nearly everyone he encountered justified the slave trades' existence and thought the idea of stopping it was mad. Clarkson received death threats and even claimed to have narrowly escaped a mob of men on the pier head - but 'not without blows amidst their imprecations and abuse.'

In Linda Grant's novel *Still Here*, set in Liverpool during the 1990s, an American entrepreneur suggests that the city's then desolate state might be a kind of punishment for the sins of its past, including 'the various iniquities of the slave trade'.

It's a poorly informed viewpoint to have, especially if you're American.

As racism is a product of ignorance, so too is pointing the finger and saying shame on Liverpool for doing what it did. Shame on the world, more like it. After all, it was the Americans who were using the slaves to pick the cotton which was taken to the mills of Manchester. Slave labour in the Americas was also used to produce sugar, coffee, tobacco, and rice which also ended up back in Europe - Portugal, Spain, France, the Netherlands, Denmark and Sweden all heavily involved in the trade. As far as England is concerned, while Liverpool was the biggest slaving port (with a total of 5300 voyages), London and Bristol also played a significant part with 3100 and 2200 voyages respectively. And as it was a trade, England did well from producing what West Africa wanted in return: textiles from Lancashire and Yorkshire; copper and brass goods from Warrington, North Cheshire and Staffordshire; guns and ammunition from Birmingham.

Yet out of all the guilty parties involved, it was Liverpool, in 1999, who issued its first official apology for its involvement. London did so in 2007, while at the time of writing Bristol is still holding out. There was talk that Liverpool's apology would need something to back it up, so in 2004, a transatlantic slave trade gallery was installed as part of the Maritime Museum. Then, in conjunction with the University of Liverpool, came the Centre for the Study of International Slavery followed by the International Slavery Museum in 2007 – apparently, the only one of its kind in the world.

Included in the museum is a learning facility named the Anthony Walker Education Centre, built for the study and understanding of the slave trade's legacy of racial intolerance and discrimination. The centre's importance is in the name itself.

Anthony Walker was a black A level student who was murdered in an unprovoked attack with an ice axe in the Merseyside area of Huyton in 2005. The killers (two cousins aged 20 and 18 years) were found guilty of racially-motivated murder. Upon sentencing, the judge said the pair had carried out a 'terrifying ambush', a 'racist attack of a type poisonous to any civilized society.'

As you'd expect, the murder of Anthony Walker – as he accompanied his white girlfriend to a bus stop – was received with widespread shock and disgust. Around 3000 people held a candlelight vigil at the park where he was murdered, and just as many attended his funeral a few days later.

This horrific reminder of the foul attitudes which still exist in modern society prompted LFC to commission a film against racism set in Liverpool and directed by Lenny Henry.

Steven Gerrard, pained that the murder took place in the neighbourhood he grew up in, delivered a speech at the film's opening. He spoke for many when he paid special tribute to Anthony's mum, Gee Walker. Gerrard cited her as true inspiration in light of her dignity – her willingness to forgive Anthony's killers. If there is ever a sight that has the potential to poison the mind with hate, it's surely seeing your child dead with an axe lodged in his or her skull. Not only was Anthony taken from her in an act of pure horror, Gee Walker was also denied the opportunity to be with Anthony in his final moments. However, in an impromptu speech on the night of the vigil, she expressed her wish for the people gathered to not let her son die in vain. Ever since, she has maintained her line, always stressing the importance of forgiving Anthony's killers. It was the only way she could prevent the hate which controlled them, from controlling her.

She went on to start the Anthony Walker Foundation which is proactive in promoting racial harmony through sport, music and education, providing outreach and opportunity to, not only the victims, but also to the offenders of hate crime.

She travels to schools and talks openly to children about what happened to Anthony and why. She says she often talks to Anthony to see if she's doing okay. She has every reason to be bitter and resentful of everyone and everything, yet she has emerged truly heroic.

When asked how she was doing on the BBC's North West Tonight programme some six years after Anthony's death, she said, 'If you can picture the sharp edge of the knife which cuts deep, that sharp edge is gone but the pain's still there.'

Do you think Liverpool is now a better place, that there's less hate, less chance of what happened to Anthony happening to anyone else?

'I know Liverpool gets a lot of stick but I believe they're such unique people, such big hearts. Scousers are like the water in the desert, the blanket when you're cold, they're just a unique set of people and I wouldn't want to live anywhere else.'

If Gee Walker can keep her faith, there's hope for us all.

18. Back to Reality.

Telling the good people of Harvey Rd that I'd had lunch just metres away from Torres and Carragher was a mistake.

'What do you mean you didn't go up to them?' said Barry.

'I thought it might be out of place,' I said.

'Out of place? Out of place?! You help pay their wages! You've got every right to go up to them!'

'Eddie! Eddie! Come hear this!' Joyce called into the kitchen. As it was my second to last night in Crosby, Eddie was cooking up his trademark dish of fish fillets with tomato and cheese. He came into the living room looking resplendent in a blue apron that nearly touched the ground.

'What's wrong luv?' he said, greasy spatula in hand.

There was a moment when the conversation could've switched to the unlikely sight of Eddie in an apron but Joyce stayed on track: 'Glenn was sitting beside his football heroes in a restaurant; he didn't even say hello.'

'Yer wha?' said Eddie. 'You come all the way from New Zealand and you don't get their autographs?'

'I didn't want to be the one to push him over the edge, you know, with all the pressure and that. Besides – they're not actually my heroes. Heroes are those who have endured — '

'Rubbish!' said Barry. 'When you're on that kind of money, you can afford to write an autograph for a guy who's come the length of the earth for yer.'

Their outrage was such I feared that if I didn't come up with a better explanation I might be out on the street. So I pulled out some crap about the ideological risks of 'meeting your hero' which rang a bit hollow considering, well, you know.

Barry said that everyone who has ever met Jamie Carragher says that he's a great guy. 'And what about that one you met, Eddie?' said Joyce.

'Oh yer, the captain,' said Eddie.

'Steven Gerrard?'

'That's the one.'

'You met Steven Gerrard? Why haven't I heard about this! What was he like?'

'He was a good lad. I picked him up when I was a taxi driver and started chattin' to him like he was an ordinary bloke. We were chattin' away and then he said to me, "do you know who I am?" He didn't do it in a snooty way or nothing and I told him I had no idea. He couldn't believe it. He mentioned he was a footballer for Liverpool. I told him I'm not really competitive so I don't really follow it – but when I'm away I always stick up for Everton. He liked that – he tipped me €20.'

So there you have it, I thought.

Eddie turned towards the kitchen, looking worried. He said that he always felt a little guilty frying fish because of the goldfish they kept on the bench right next to the stove. They'd kept their previous fish there until someone said they shouldn't be so close to the splatter and heat. But when they moved the bowl, the fish promptly died. Eddie said that although he can appreciate the apparent danger, the current lot had survived right next to the stove for over two years. 'I only worry when I'm cookin' fish – they tend to get a bit jumpy,' he said, disappearing into the kitchen.

My last day in Crosby was always meant to end with a fine farewell at the Birkey. All I wanted was to share a long drink with the Tomo's, the Mick's, the Drew's and Sue's and everyone else who'd made me feel so welcome from the start. What I didn't expect was to be accused of being disrespectful before being led to the front door, ejected onto the foot path, and told not to show my face here again. Banned from the Birkey? Disrespect? Shame.

To think the day had been going so well. As you know, I came to Liverpool seeking the generosity of spirit I'd seen from afar. The day's proceedings had only served to exemplify that notion – first at lunch with Barry, his partner Jo, and Barry's employer, Mr Vintage.

'Dougie' as Barry knew him, was an ex-captain of industry, an engineer who'd laid train tracks in countries far and wide and lived a rich and full life in defiance of the polio he'd contracted as a child. At the age of eighty-four, his mind was still good, yet he was constricted to a wheelchair and wholly dependent upon Barry in retaining a quality of life. According to Barry, Dougie's family was just waiting for their widowed father to die. They'd more than once expressed their disapproval of Barry's involvement, seeing him as more lower class scoundrel than saviour. Yet Barry had been caring for Dougie for fifteen years. In that time they'd travelled to different parts of Europe and even as far as America together, forming a strong, if unlikely, bond. Barry had given his word to Dougie that he'd be there for him till the end. And just the previous night he'd openly stated that he worshipped the man, and could hardly bear the thought of life without him. I had no reason to doubt Barry on any of this, and seeing the forbearance and respect he afforded the old man only boosted my appreciation of what a genuinely good soul he was. As Jo and I waited in the back seat of Dougie's old BMW, Barry wheeled him alongside the passengers' door where he attached a purpose made board from the chair to the seat of the car. Dougie was carrying a bit of extra weight, so it took a decent heave from Barry to lift and slide him into position. Much practice and preparation ensured the transition was swift and safe. Yet despite Dougie's condition, theirs was very much a co-dependent relationship.

After Eddie's excellent fish dinner, Barry told me what he'd been doing before he became Dougie's carer. He began with his 12 years living in 'the sticks' – a remote Welsh valley with enough land for a decent plot of do-dah. During summer, when he was tending to the plants, he would often strip off his clothes due to the heat, wearing just a black balaclava to keep the blowflies (that were attracted to the plants) off his face. When the police arrived to surprise him, he was naked (bar the balaclava) and standing in the middle of his crop with clippers in hand. Barry knew no amount of excuses was going to save him. Amiably, he went about helping the police pull out the plants. He even assisted them with the ones they found drying from the rafters in the attic. The haul came to twenty-three kilos, yet while they were busy chatting away to the genial Barry, they missed the twenty-two ounces he had wrapped in newspapers and piled up in a corner of the attic. After an eleven-month stint in jail, they were a welcome sight for Barry to come home to.

Unfortunately, any respite from the harshness of prison life was short-lived. In the small conservative village close to where he lived, Barry's reputation as a convicted cultivator of marijuana preceded him.

It wasn't long after he'd been let out on probation that Barry found himself in trouble again, yet this time it was trouble of a far more serious nature.

One night down at the pub, Barry was playing pool with a couple of local girls when a member of the village rugby team, on a post-game piss-up, accused him of selling drugs to school kids. The man had apparently been tipped off about who Barry was by other members in his team, a couple of policemen well aware of the Scouser's ignominy.

When Barry denied the rugby player's accusation the situation became hostile. Admitting he'd never won a fight in his life, Barry left the pub hoping to avoid any further confrontation. His accuser, however, followed him to the car park and made a lunge for Barry by reaching into his car window as he looked to speed away. As Barry tried to flee, the man clung to the window frame only to lose his grip as the car accelerated, his heavy landing on the car park's gravel causing serious injury.

Barry returned home, much shaken but physically unscathed. That night however, he woke to the sound of breaking windows – the mob was out to get him.

Barry jumped out a window but was captured and beaten. He was arrested the next day over the car park incident and charged with attempted murder. The 'victim' claimed Barry had wound up his window, jammed his hand, and sped off with the intention of killing him. He even had witnesses. The two girls Barry had earlier been playing pool with had apparently seen Barry do just as the victim claimed. According to their testimony, they watched Barry purposefully jam the man's hand in the window from their vantage point of an adjacent parked car. But when it came to saying this in court, the girls' stories differed – one said she viewed the incident out the front window, the other out the back. Maintaining his innocence throughout, Barry figured the only explanation for the girls to be testifying against him in the first place was that they'd been pressured to do so by members of the rugby team. It was the small town mindset of the community, wishing to expel the bad egg Scouser from their midst.

To Barry's relief, the judge wasn't having a bar of it. The likelihood of a hand being 'jammed' in a car window, unable to be pulled or wrenched free in the face of mortal danger seemed far from plausible. The nervous and confused demeanor of the girls, along with the revelation that the so-called victim had drunk around thirteen pints leading up to the altercation was enough to throw the case out.

Barry may have dodged a somewhat speculative bullet yet the whole ordeal was too much for his girlfriend. She soon left, and, with her gone, Barry was forced to return to Liverpool, under parole to his Mum. I imagine she must've imagined a prodigal son type scenario where Barry would live with her, repent his sins and become a driving force behind the Liverpool chapter of the Jehovah's Witnesses. Not bloody likely.

They say bad things come in threes so there was an inevitable feel to it when after a week back on Merseyside, Barry was caught with a joint on Crosby beach. This time, however, the police were more lenient. They took him away all right, but, once they'd retrieved the information on all the crap he'd been through, they decided to let him off with a warning. Barry stayed out of the big house and was allowed to remain on probation.

It was through a government 'Job-search' scheme that he found employment tending to the garden of a large property on one of the plusher streets in Crosby.

He did maintenance jobs as well, and got along so well with the owner that, sixteen years later, he was still there. The man who'd been busted, beaten, incarcerated and conspired against with the kind of torment normally reserved for ogres, found himself caring for a polio-stricken old man that nobody else has time for.

After lunch we dropped Dougie back at his big two-story house near the beach. Barry made sure he was well set up for the weekend. I sat chatting with Dougie about his impressive book collection as Barry fussed over any potential obstacles blocking the hallway, double checking that everything he needed was within reach.

Dougie was currently reading Richard Dawkins and although he admitted it was ' a bit heavy going' I thought it impressive that a man of his age - very much staring into the blank face of his own mortality – was reading a treatise on atheism rather than falling for the uncertain promises of scripture.

Walking back along Liverpool Rd towards the village, Barry was pleased with our excursion. It had left Dougie in good spirits. He knew the old man would be housebound without visitors until Barry's return Monday morning. It was a sad thought that contained an even sadder truth: that the worst kind of loneliness is that which looms late in life. It was also a timely reminder to those still able to get out while you can!

We stopped in at Cads and caught up with Georgie James – seven lemons in to a vodka tonic – a little red-eyed yet undefeated.

At the Birkey we were joined by Eddie and Joyce and many of my favourite regulars – the laughter and anecdotes on a par with the high revelry I associated with the Birkey at its best.

When we found that day's edition of The Sun sitting unread in the courtyard (planted there, we surmised, by a deviant of the angry Manc or bitter blue persuasion), Barry encouraged me to set it alight. I felt privileged at being invited to take part in such a time-honoured tradition. Nearly twenty years on from Hillsborough, the spiteful claims cannot be forgiven. Yet this particular burning was more for the fun of it.

Barry held the paper up while I applied the lighter. It burned more slowly than expected, and as the smoke filled the courtyard we all became a little self-conscious. Barry might have been doing the sensible thing by putting it out, although his method – peeing on it – showed the rebellious streak was not to be denied.

We rushed indoors like a pack of naughty schoolchildren where I enjoyed a rampant run on the pool table only to be beaten by Tomo in a game that went on forever. The grog I'd needed to endure it had me suddenly very drunk and seeing double. A quick fix presented itself back out in the courtyard. I was standing around a table with several others when it became my turn to make a tiny cup out of my right thumb and index finger. I'm by no means a fan of the white powder poured onto my thumb nail, but at the time I was too drunk to care. If a quick snort was the best chance I had at remaining upright, I was always going to take it. As I raised my thumb there was a tap on my shoulder which I ignored, only to turn around after a quick snort to the angry face of the bouncer. I *ummed* and *arghed* for an explanation. To be caught out on my first time partaking in this ubiquitous drug seemed so unlucky it was comical, yet the narrow eyes of security didn't agree. 'You're disrespecting this place and everyone in it – get out now!' he demanded.

'Shit, sorry.' He shook his head and looked accusingly at those around the table.

'Look,' I said, 'it was nothing to do with them. I'm new here – just trying to impress everyone – make a few friends—'

'Leave now!' He took me by the arm in the direction of the car park.

'I need my coat from inside,' I said.

'Go on – be quick.'

As the bouncer lingered to reprimand the others I sauntered inside. He'd spoken with such vehemence that for a moment I actually believed the issue was every bit as serious as he made it out to be. Had I really offended everyone? I unashamedly wanted the Birkey regulars to like me – they were funny, welcoming, and caring. They were far from boring. If they liked me, then maybe I was too – you are the company you keep, after all. Drew spotted me putting on my coat and demanded to know where I was going.

'I've gotta go,' I said.

'Bollocks!' he said, 'I'm buying you a drink.'

'I've been kicked out.'

'Who says?'

'The bouncer.'

'No fuckin' way. Where is he – I'll get the boys.'

'Look, it's my fault – I got busted having a snort. Haven't got a leg to stand on,' I slurred.

Drew looked me over and laughed: 'You're legless all right – you're fucked!'

We shared a farewell hug until I felt the unwelcome tug of the narrow-eyed terrier pulling me towards the door. 'I'm going, I'm going!' I shook my arm free from his clasp in the haughty time-honoured manner of every drunk person who has ever been kicked out of a bar.

I didn't know where the hell Barry and Eddie were and couldn't believe it was all about to end under such graceless circumstances. The Birkey had given me so much. They'd accepted me without reservations. And now this, the walk of shame?

I can't recall the music that was playing as we reached the door but I can recall the clapping. I turned around. To my surprise everyone was standing in applause. Within seconds my guilt over my act of recklessness had turned into feeling more like a badge of honour. The bouncer gave me one last moment of respite as I waved goodbye. He then sent me out to a chorus of cheers into the harsh yet ineffectual cold of night. Mick burst out onto the street to state emphatically that there's always room for a kiwi at Anfield.

He handed me my notebook which, unbeknownst to me, had been lifted from my person and passed around the bar. At first I was just thankful that the notes I'd scrawled hadn't caused offense. It wasn't until the following morning that I regained the faculty to read what was inside. There were plenty of best wishes and *we'll miss you* sentiments and plenty of Shankly quotes too. There was a message from Tony stating *If you're reading this it means your(sic) home and bored so go have a pint borin ass. Tony.* But there were those who recognised that about now another pint was the last thing I needed.

A combined message from Sue and Drew read: *Dear Glenn, I will allow Susan to continue this message because as you can see my hand writing is akin to a seven-legged spider dipped in ink and forced to scurry at great speed across the page. Thus Susan's elegant hand shall continue...*

Glenn, it was lovely meeting you. Shame you have to go so soon but as our old Dad's said 'When it's brown it's cooked, when it's burnt it's fucked.' See you soon mate xx Sue and Drew.

Barry and Eddie exited the Birkey all smiles and we stumbled our way back to Harvey Rd where we drank as much as we could before it was time for Barry to bid farewell. Before doing so he told me how, when he was a child, it had always been his family's intention to move to New Zealand. Barry could vividly remember his mum actually packing all their belongings in preparation for their departure on board a liner. But due to a last minute problem his father had in procuring passports, the move never eventuated.

In light of this, and in light of meeting Eddie (with his kiwi connections), then Mike and now me, Barry believed it was divine destiny that he would one day live in the land of the long white cloud.

In keeping with the bonhomie, Barry gestured towards the painting of Anfield, still propped up against a chair in the living room. He vowed to get it signed by the Liverpool squad. I told him that wasn't necessary. I wondered out loud how he could even organise such a thing but was told in no uncertain terms that that's what was going to happen. As soon as the signatures of Gerrard, Torres et al had been scribbled alongside those of the Birkey regulars, he would mail it my way.

As we shared one last hug Eddie made the comment, 'Like family, you two.'

It was true that Barry and I had made an important bond. He was estranged from his children (one being a son of my age) while I was estranged from my dad. Through meeting and spending time together we'd initiated a father/son relationship by proxy – a brief assuage to the failure that festers in the mind of a man, young or old, who's missing such a vital connection to himself.

Once he was gone Eddie took me to Stamps where Kate and Graeme had travelled from Sefton Park to meet us. I downed my final Stamp's drink at the end of the bar before we all headed back to Harvey Rd where I swiftly crashed onto my bed fully clothed.

19. Farewell

My final night at the Birkey was also my final night with Eddie and Joyce, as they were off the next day to see family in Ireland. Kate and Graeme stayed at Harvey Rd as well, and initially the plan had been to get out early so the landlord could hold one of his 'meetings'. However, the meeting was called off at the last minute, meaning we were free to hang around as long as we liked after Eddie and Joyce had left for the airport.

When it was time to bid them farewell, no amount of gratitude seemed worthy. They had been utterly generous in every way. I felt so much better than I did when I arrived, which was strange considering that, after all the beers, smokes, curries, bacon ribs and Scouse stews, I had no right to feel anything but terrible. Physically, I was in the worst shape of my life: my leg muscles had wandered somewhere else, I lacked the strength to suck my stomach in, and my face felt lifeless – an old rubber mask in a box of discarded toys. Conversely, it all came with a sense of achievement. And as we hugged and said goodbye I realised why.

Eddie, Joyce and Barry had cured me of my prickdom – my snaring, duplicitous prickdom. Of course, a relapse was just a matter of time. But for now I harboured no ill-feeling for anyone in the room – nothing negative at all. I just felt incredibly thankful for knowing them. Normally, saying goodbye couldn't have come quick enough. How do you hang out with the same people for this amount of time without every final last second feeling like a minute, and every minute a conviction? You don't, do you?

Yet here I was, missing them already.

Saying as much was out of the question. So when they left for their flight to Ireland I set to work. The house was a bombshell from the night before, and while Joyce had said not to worry about it, I was determined to have it looking immaculate for their return.

I wanted them to walk in and say *Our Glenn – what a good'un* he turned out to be, or something along those lines. It was amazing – I really cared what they thought of me.

With the house all spic and span, we went to the beach so I could bid farewell to the noble iron men. I thanked them for being the most thoughtful and comforting inanimate objects I have known. True to form their faces remained levelled at the sea, their eyes unflinching towards another incoming tide. They contained their emotions very well.

In less than a week I'd be passing through Sydney to see Erin. In a quest for vitality I tried turning over a new leaf with wholesome activities such as taking the ferry 'cross the Mersey, nosing around more art galleries and cathedrals, and feeding squirrels in Sefton Park. If there's an activity more wholesome than feeding squirrels in a park, I don't want to know about it. I did it all alcohol free. It lasted two days. As long as I was in Liverpool I was destined to be liquored. The Scousers had conspired it from the start. Fittingly, it was up to one of Liverpool's ever-compelling cabbies to finish me off.

Seconds after jumping into his black cab, Lez voiced his dismay at the news that I was Liverpool supporter - a red shite and not a blue nose.

But when he learnt that I'd written a novel, he shared a story about a friend of his father who'd recently passed away. Upon hearing the prognosis, the friend dedicated the time he had left to writing poetry. Lez offered to meet up again so he could bring the poems for me to read.

So, two weeks and two sober days later, I met Lez, his brother Norman, and several of their friends at Liverpool's oldest pub, *Ye Hole in Ye Wall*; juicing up Scousers since 1726. This was the old man's pub to end old man's pubs. Oozing between wooden partitions a small, heavily Brylcreemed man sang distant era schmaltz into a big bulbous microphone. The joyous middle-aged patrons waltzed the carpeted floors, indulging in the sweet illusion that they were sexy once again. Everyone – including the bar staff – was drunk.

It wasn't long before Lez announced he'd forgotten the poems. When pressed he looked flummoxed as to how he'd obtain them. But any disappointment was short-lived as the brothers plied me with more beer than sense. To top it off, they had musical talent to burn. Lez, balding and moustachioed, was the family's guitarist. Norman, big haired and charismatic, was the singer. Within minutes of taking the microphone from the Brylcreemed man, Norman's crooning had the ladies swooning.

'What a voice!' said Lez, leaning against the bar. 'Did he tell you he's got a wife half his age?'

'He sure did,' I said.

'Amazing,' said Lez, shaking his head. 'What a voice.'

The brothers took me on a tour of their regular clubs where they were greeted as old friends. Miraculously, a free bowl of bacon ribs appeared at every bar. We ended up at *The Liverpool* where we listened to the silky voice of a man who'd once performed with Little Richard, and where a stranger came up to me and kissed the Liver bird on my scarf. Incidentally, he was the third person to do so that night.

When it was time to go, Lez and Norman walked me out, nudging the doorman on the way to tell him I was from New Zealand. 'He's got a long way home then,' said the doorman, hailing me a taxi.

I stumbled into Kate and Graeme's flat, flopped onto the couch and announced that Liverpool is the greatest city in the world. Naturally, they humoured me.

With time ticking towards take-off, I had two Anfield visits to go.

The first was for the Liverpool v Blackburn game. Thankfully I wouldn't have to pay Tony the Tout any more money on account of my friend Greg purchasing two match tickets online. Greg was an old Christchurch friend I hadn't seen since he'd moved to London, and then Brighton three years ago. Football match aside, any positive aspects of my personality he thought warranted driving the six hours from Brighton were surely missing upon his arrival. By now, my poorly state had gone holistic, my shabby appearance an accurate reflection of my mind.

To his credit, Greg hid his disappointment well. As I rubbed some life into my face and mumbled my mindless jabber he was good enough to pretend he understood. He even engaged in conversation and happily spent the night on Kate and Graeme's living room floor. All he asked in return for the €36 ticket was that I buy him breakfast in the morning. Agreed, I said. It was the least I could do.

As it turned out, it was the least I didn't do. After another late night, and another late start, we made it to Anfield just moments before kick off. I tried to make up for breakfast by buying Greg a scarf from a stall. The gesture doubled as a last chance for me to man up, grow a pair, and prove myself capable of wheelin' a deal.

'How much for the scarves?' I said, full of confidence.

'5 quid each,' said the teenage seller.

'8 quid for two?' I proposed.

'Five times two equals ten,' he countered. The kid was deadpan. I hesitated – I hadn't seen deadpan coming. Bugger, I thought, handing him a tenner. 'Sorry mate,' I said. 'Just really bad at maths.'

The kid smiled and handed me two scarves and two quid in change. I handed Greg a scarf and made sure he caught sight of the two pounds. I could barely restrain my glee.

Compared with Tuesday night, the atmosphere was subdued. The game was won comfortably enough with another inspired performance by Stevie G that saw him score the first goal after nutmegging a defender. He then set up Torres for the second.

(It should be noted that the captain of the Blackburn team was Ryan Nelsen, the only person from Christchurch to have played in the English Premiere League. I remembered an interview with Nelsen in which he mentioned his father's reaction to his ascendancy into the top league in the world. Because it wasn't rugby, his father didn't know what all the fuss was about. *Talk to me when you're an All-Black, son.* And even though today's game against Liverpool wasn't one Nelsen would want to remember, he was one to admire all the same: a sissy soccer player come good.)

Even without the crowd intensity, I was glad to be experiencing yet another side to Anfield's personality. In addition to edgy, excitable, defiant, and euphoric (with bursts of self-loss lunacy), today Anfield exuded a comfortable din of relative calm. The people around us still watched with intent yet there was more casual humour and an overall sense that everyone was just happy to be here. This potent, storied yet unassuming stadium felt as solid as a good home. Here we were, one big family, all gathered and utterly secure in our red allegiance.

To think Shankly himself once described this place as looking like a slum. With the wind rattling the flimsy corrugated iron roofs; and pieces of brick, stone and broken glass littering the Melwood training grounds, Shankly's first task as manager was to clean the place up. He walked the fields with his back room staff (including future managers Bob Paisley and Joe Fagan) and removed every foreign object by hand. It took days, yet Shankly wasn't happy until the Liverpool pitches resembled virtual bowling greens of 'professional grass.' Now, with the stands only rattling when there's a goal, and the pitch looking as perfect as any patch of grass you'll ever see, you'd have to say the soul of Bill Shankly is in a good place.

Greg drove me into the city. Before he tackled the long haul back to Brighton, we caught a Blackburn supporter complaining about Liverpool on a local radio station.

The Blackburn supporter was a father of four. Unemployed, he'd brought his children to see the game, but declared it a waste of time: 'The game was rubbish and the atmosphere was rubbish!' For good measure, he said the city was rubbish too.

'Maybe he could get a job here cleaning up all the rubbish?' said Greg. The Blackburn supporter finished his diatribe by stating he'd never be coming back. The broadcaster thanked him for calling, cleared his throat, and moved on.

I hopped out of Greg's car on Lime St near St George's Hall and thanked him once again for the effort. We had one of those bloody awkward moments you get when you're saying goodbye to someone you won't be seeing for a long time. I tried to say something witty but it came out a little half-baked, so we left it there.

As his car merged with the southbound traffic I hoped he wasn't secretly disappointed with his trip to Anfield. Surely, a clued up fan such as Greg would understand why, at least, the atmosphere had been like it was. Firstly, having already secured 4th place and therefore inclusion into next season's Champions' League, there was little at stake for the reds, and therefore less crowd intensity than Tuesday night. After the exhilaration of that particular game, there was always going to be a comedown. But what influenced the general mood even more was the tragedy that took place nineteen years before, nearly to the day. It would take an uncharacteristic degree of apathy for it not to.

The purpose of my final visit to Anfield was to pay my respects at the 19th Hillsborough Memorial Service. On Monday I caught the bus down Ullitt Rd and took a cab from the city to the stadium. When we halted for a red light, the cabbie asked me why I was attending the service. I told him why I thought it was important, how Hillsborough was one of the things that set Liverpool apart from the other clubs. The cab driver then revealed he was actually at Hillsborough, and that he and his son were lucky enough to be positioned away from the main crush. Slight and softly spoken, he said that, although he'd since been to Anfield to watch a few games, he hadn't attended any of the services. He didn't know why.

I nearly said that he should take the time one year as it could be a good way of coming to grips with what happened, but I'm glad I didn't. What the hell would I know? The disaster was worse than any of its kind. Its fallout – a disaster on top of a disaster – is unique to Liverpudlians.

Earlier, you may have detected the problem I have of feeling aggrieved and holding grudges against those I deem to have let me down. I can't begin to imagine how I'd react if I lost a loved one to gross negligence, only to have the source of that negligence deflect the blame back onto the innocent, and continue to do so even after an inquiry proved otherwise.

To offer advice on how to deal with a tragedy you haven't experienced yourself is one thing. People have actually had the gall to criticise the way Liverpudlians dealt with not only Hillsborough, but other tragedies as well. They were condemned for their outpourings of grief and outrage after the murder of young James Bulger in 1993, and of the civic engineer Kenneth Bigley, beheaded in Iraq in 2004.

'Intimidatory self-pity', 'self pity capital of the world'; 'nursing resentments' and having a 'propensity to linger over every misfortune' were the charges from the south.

It's true that Liverpool deals with death in a different way. One look at the obituaries in the Liverpool Echo and you'll see what I mean. Instead of the bare minimum of tastefully chosen words, you'll see heartfelt tributes which actually give you a sense of how much the deceased actually meant to his or her community. Maybe Hillsborough was the catalyst for Liverpool expressing the kind of emotion that makes much of England feel uneasy.

But there were no signs of intimidatory self-pity from my taxi driver. Nor from the withdrawn man I'd met at the Birkey who had also been at Hillsborough. There was nothing of the sort at the memorial service either. The overriding theme of the day was simply to remember.

The full playing squad was there, and I recognised many faces I'd seen at various games – including the young guys at Deans Gate station after the match at Old Trafford.

There was a children's choir from a local church and a moving speech by Phil Hammond, who lost his fourteen-year-old son to the crush and at one point was on the verge of breaking down before shouts of 'Alright, Phil,' helped him regain his voice.

The sight of tears welling in the eyes of hardened men during the singing of YNWA was as great an expression of humanity as I have ever witnessed. There was nothing mawkish or self serving. If anything, in a world that seems increasingly desensitized to violence and ever more forgetful of history's significance, the tears are refreshing. The ritual ensures that sense of continuity; keeping the bond intact between those living and those who have passed. Here, the words of Keats ring true, they 'will never pass into nothingness'.

At one point during a speech by a government representative a chorus of 'Justice for the 96' rang out amidst the 6000 people on the Kop. It didn't last long, but it was loud enough to be heard, and noted.

My final walk from Anfield was my first along dry streets. I was pleased to see the ashen skin of winter had been shed from Liverpool's buildings. I kid you not: sunlight bathed the city, softening the facades, permitting the sky to be blue and the grass to be green. I felt a fleeting urge to stick around, to extend my stay and see the city in its new light. But I thought of Erin, and knew only a prick would take such things for granted.

After a silent farewell at the foot of Bill Shankly's statue I took my usual route down Walton Breck Rd, verging left onto Everton Valley from which the clear day afforded a fine view across the docks to the low northern banks of the Mersey.

Kirkdale Rd turned into Scotland Rd, and aside from a dicey bit where you had to keep your wits about you (due to traffic hooning left into the Kingsway tunnel), it was an easy walk to the city centre. I stuck around, and the long sunset cast across the estuary wrapped the Three Graces in pink iridescent warmth.

My last night in Liverpool was with Kate and Graeme. A few of their friends dropped in to say goodbye, including their friend Matt and his new partner, Kaleel. They had both been drinking but it was more than a slip of the tongue when Kaleel, a native New Yorker who'd been living in Liverpool for a couple of years, said that Scousers ought to get over Hillsborough. He compared it to New York where, unlike Liverpool, people were able to joke about 9/11, use humour to nullify the devastation even though it was a lot fresher in the memory.

His comment didn't sit well. To make such an accusation before bothering to question 'why' was disingenuous.

To my recollection, no one ever accused New Yorkers of killing their own. Such an accusation could only come from the mouths of fanatics. I've heard the 'Truther' conspiracy theories that 9/11 was an inside job but it's a theory with holes even bigger than ground zero. It's also a far cry from the media vilification directed at Liverpudlians in the aftermath of Hillsborough. As I assembled my thoughts and weighed up the potential futility of challenging the point of view of a half-cut American, Graeme surprised the lot of us.

'Hillsborough is the biggest injustice in the history of Britain,' he said. Fuck me, I thought. Where did that come from? Before heading out that morning, I had asked Graeme if he was coming to Anfield. He had the day off but said he wanted to do something on his computer. No righteous indignation here then, I thought, heading out the door.

It never occurred to me that he, like Kaleel, had little idea of Hillsborough's significance in his adopted city. That morning the word Hillsborough didn't mean a great deal. By that evening, however, things had changed. Curious as to why I'd spend my last day in Liverpool going to a memorial service, Graeme typed 'Hillsborough' into Wikipedia. Primed with info after plenty of reading, he told Kaleel about the Sun's smear campaign against the fans and the cover up by the police in order to clear itself of criminal incompetence. He mentioned the Taylor report and explained how the subsequent inquests had been a sham because they deliberately ruled out any evidence that pointed to senior officers being accountable.

He mentioned how police had lied that a CCTV camera looking down on the crush had not been working, how it gave them the convenient excuse for their hesitation in helping the victims, as they couldn't see the extent of the disaster from the control room. And how, after a ground engineer dismissed these claims by signing an affidavit to say the camera had been fully operational, the police then changed their story by saying the tapes from the camera had been stolen and never recovered.

Graeme was on a roll. With his tongue burning red and the information still fresh in his mind, his argument was impressive. When he stopped to take a breath, I chimed in with how nearly two hundred statements from regular police at Hillsborough were changed by a team of solicitors so that anything criticising senior police management was either removed, or rendered unreadable. Police had even said how unhappy they were, and how betrayed they felt by the police force for doing such a thing. But even that was deemed insufficient to warrant a fresh inquiry.

Then there were the payouts.

While the majority of the victims' families barely received enough to cover funeral expenses, fourteen 'traumatised' police were paid €1.2 million. In order to receive that amount, their insurers had to accept that their trauma was caused by the negligence of their superiors... and that's the way it came out, more or less.

Perhaps it was a slightly sloppier version of the above, but the point was made: until the superiors are held accountable, the ignorance remains, and Hillsborough doesn't end.

'I had no idea,' said Kaleel.

He could well have conceded out of desperation to change the subject, but Kaleel seemed sincere in accepting there was a lot more to Hillsborough than he first suspected. In saying that, he and Matt wasted little time in heading for the door.

'That Kaleel,' said Graeme, looking puzzled. 'He really got on my goat.'

Epilogue

I've put off finishing this for as long as I could. It has to end now.

I have been hoping to end on a triumphant note but it seems I've been naïve. It's the 10th March 2012 and I've just turned off the TV before Liverpool's game against Sunderland has ended. I've turned it off because they're one-nil down and I just bloody well know they're not going to even equalise, let alone win. One measly goal against a middling team is beyond them.

I'm sitting on the edge of the bed in my hotel room in Wellington, New Zealand. I'm thinking that Shankly's idea of football success at Liverpool – based on a bond between players, manager, and fans – is outdated. It doesn't work any more. No one cares about authenticity. A constant tsunami of commercials, consumerism and fakery has flooded everyone and everything. Money is more vital than ever. Especially in football. Yet Liverpool holds on to Shankly's purity – the 'socialism without the politics' ethos borne from immaculate working class roots. We want to retain that purity as part of our recipe for success. No one can match Liverpool's respect for the old days, but when the right kind of success isn't happening, it doesn't amount to anything more than foolish sentimentality – and progress strains where sentimentality lurks. What has been Liverpool's strength could now be its greatest weakness. With every missed pass and wayward shot from the men in red, daring to hope for greater things seems trite.

Since I left Merseyside, the club has taken a battering.

It began with the American owners thinking they could make money at the club's expense by putting it into massive debt, and using its revenue to pay it off. Throughout the circus of their ownership, Hicks and Gillett turned on each other. All of a sudden the grand old club became, as Andy Dunn from *The Mirror* put it, 'a club riven by petty squabbles, soured by political in-fighting, and fraught with self-interested factions.' It was eventually brought to an end when three of a five-man board voted against Hicks and Gillett and won the club the right to be sold. Just a day shy of going into administration, it was bought by more Americans, albeit ones with better credentials. As you can imagine, much damage had already been done.

Rafa Benitez – mercurial, stubborn, and detail obsessive on a good day – finally succumbed to the pressure. Within the chaotic environment he became an utter control freak. Caught up in the outbreak of board room civil war, he soon lost the plot.

Games where Liverpool had everything to play for were squandered. Benitez seemed incapable of acknowledging any fault, and the club eventually committed financial *hari kari* by dropping out of the Champions League.

Decent players started leaving. Some were just frustrated by Benitez's perplexing decisions not to play them, some reported utter disillusionment at his obvious favouritism towards others, his tendency to screw minds and berate the players he didn't fancy. In defence of Benitez, it's hard to know who's being petulant and who's being pernicious in times like these. But the complaints were similar to those once levelled by top United players towards

Sir Alex Ferguson. The difference being, in spite of such controversies, Ferguson kept winning. Benitez didn't. He may have prospered if he'd been allowed to simply manage the team. Caught in the middle of the crap-flinging contest between Hicks and Gillett, he was denied the right. Regardless, the manager's capability was compromised. Benitez had to go.

It was a shame. And despite his mistakes, Benitez showed his heart was in the right place by donating €96,000 to the Hillsborough Family Support Group – a fine way to mark the end of his reign. The end of an era, however, did not mean an end to Liverpool's problems.

An amiable, owl-faced manager was appointed as Benitez's replacement. Roy Hodgson was never the right man for the job and Liverpool went on their worse run of results that anyone could remember. Under Hodgson, the team played without hope or direction. He bought a plethora of substandard players and the team got worse as the weeks went on. It physically hurt just seeing these wowsers wearing red shirts, let alone trying to play football. It's questionable if they were even trying to do that. To think they got to wear the same red uniform as the team that had pulled off the greatest victory of all time just five years prior - it makes you want to drown yourself in a bowl of cornflakes. The atmosphere at Anfield went from the inspired roar which I have described to a sullen silence broken by occasional outpourings of bitter lament. Virtually unrecognisable, they booed their manager and booed their own players. The spirit had gone. It was bad enough watching from the southern hemisphere. I can barely imagine what it must have felt like being one of the Kop or Annie Rd regulars, plodding along to every home game, knowing things were only going to get worse before they got better. If they got better.

It was a great relief when Hodgson was replaced by Kenny Dalglish. The King was back. He diagnosed the problem at Anfield to be one of high anxiety and brought unity back to the club, as only a living legend signed by Bill Shankly could. Within a few months he took them from being four points away from relegation to nearly sneaking qualification back into the Champions League. Things were looking up. Yet the winds of misfortune had dealt the club another shitty blow.

Torres wanted out.

Fernando Torres:

Senor 'I read Liverpool's history in bed with my wife.'

Senor 'I feel so at home here I walk my dog in the park'

Senor 'the Kop gives me wings'

Turned into:

Senor Sulk Face

Senor If I try to win it might kill me

Senor I only want to play the Champions League

Senor I want to go to Chelsea...

Chelsea. If a player wants to leave Liverpool you just have to stomach it.

But when a player woos you with great goals, undisguised passion, and charming little comments pertaining to the Liverpool way, and then decides to simply give up when things get a bit tough, then you have reason to feel aggrieved. And swapping it for Chelsea, the very antithesis of Liverpool? Very, very aggrieved.

Thankfully, I hadn't spent money on a Torres shirt like Craig had. He and so many others had little choice but to throw their once-cherished garments bearing the Spaniard's name into the bitter flames of betrayal. By the time Torres handed in his transfer request he'd filled every Liverpool fan with so much anguish it was almost good to see him go.

No it wasn't. It was terrible. He'd confirmed all our reasons for loving Liverpool and then pushed out an almighty turd which fell from a great height and broke Anfield asunder.

Dalglish had little choice but to let Torres go, citing the old school edict: no man is bigger than the club. The King's words had a steadying effect. The club would go on. Chelsea paid €50 million for Torres, a record-breaking transfer fee between two English clubs.

It gives me scant consolation to report that – at the time of writing – Torres has been terrible for Chelsea. He is currently on a stretch of twenty-four games without scoring a single goal. In fact, he has only scored five goals in all competitions since joining them. Pound for pound he is their worst signing ever. Poor management, the pressure of playing under a €50 million price tag, the lack of a Stevie G supply line of great passes, and no updraft of confidence blustering in from the Kop all play their part in his ongoing failure. Psychologically he's a completely different player, and seems reluctant to accept any responsibility for his lackluster efforts. I would love to sit back and snicker but when I look at Torres now I only see regret: mine and his. Chelsea may well be in the Champions League but Torres is nearly always sidelined – a few minutes here, a few minutes there – a bit-part bum. He even spoke of people being rude to him in London restaurants. In the city up north they used to respectfully admire him from a distance.

No matter how you look at it, Merseyside can't seem to shake its mode of one step forward, two steps back.

It made a success out of being European Capital of Culture, but like everywhere else in Europe, the recession hit hard. The government cuts are playing out like a mirror of the 'eighties, and with such a reliance on jobs from the public sector, the city's unemployment has reached chronic levels once again. According to the Department of Health, the Everton area next to Anfield has the most deprived population in England. With a dearth of opportunities, the official 'workless' rate is three times the national average. Statistics for education show the lowest grades in England, while any health funding they receive is diminished by council cutbacks. The sombre rows of abandoned terraces that were marked for renovation have run out of funding. They just sit there, looking more decrepit by the day. Like the city of Detroit in the USA, Merseyside is depopulating.

As far as employment is concerned, Kate and Graeme seem to be doing okay. But the downturn cost Eddie his job. With no luck finding a new one he had little choice but to sign on to the dole. The problem with that was the bit where they had to declare their rent, nearly all of which was being paid by the landlord. Declaring that would've caused all the problems in the world, so their only option was to move out of Harvey Rd.

With no interest in registering for email accounts, Eddie and Joyce are terrible at keeping in touch. Aside from a single phone call, I rely on news from Barry to know how they're getting along. True to form, Barry applies a positive spin to everything. Eddie's back driving cabs, and they're off on 'the big camp' in April.

Barry's been doing alright, although his employer and friend, Mr Heritage, passed away in 2010. He left Barry 'loadsa money' in his will, and, from what I can gather, Barry's been spending well; a month or two sucking back the do-dah and soaking up the rays in sunny Spain.

He was just weeks away from coming to stay with me until he was diagnosed with pancreatis. He's determined it won't get him down.

Barry never did get the Liverpool squad to sign the back of my picture of Anfield. After another trip to England Mike brought it back just as it was. Of course, the messages and scrawls from the Birkey regulars were all I needed, and I was glad just to have it back. Yet Barry felt bad for not delivering on his promise. What he did deliver – via Mike also – was a steel shield bearing the Liverpool crest – Liver bird and all. The story goes that some scally walked into the Birkey after pilfering it from a wall at Anfield. Barry got it for fifty quid and now it takes pride of place in the study of my flat.

It was hanging outside on the wall by the front door until I caught a young Asian guy attempting to steal my bike. Incredibly, the little punk was wearing a Man Utd top. I yelled that he'd better start running. He dropped my bike and bolted down the stairs and down the street. The shield was in plain view so he must've seen it.

I had a hunch, by the way he tore off, that the little Manc-loving misfit was gone for good – they scare easily, their lot. But just in case, I took the shield down and put it inside. If someone stole it, I'd be devastated because, yes, despite their apparent hopelessness, despite the utter turmoil and endless false dawns, I remain compelled.

I figure my undying love for Liverpool is a perfect example of how the unconscious mind rules our decision making. If the playing field represents the soul of man, then the esoteric significance of the game of football could be man's ongoing inner conflict between the tendencies of good and evil. Liverpool is the club that my unconscious mind initially recognised as being good, representing man's higher impulses. They were the side most deserving, the side more likely to play the game in the right spirit, and thus emerge triumphant.

This unconscious decision to support Liverpool can't be overridden, even if my conscious reasoning mind wanted to. So it's ongoing that when they do not emerge triumphant, I worry, because something's wrong.

If they win I barely think of them at all. Several reminders of their victory throughout the day to enhance my mood – that's it. Otherwise, it's hard work for a worried mind. I have to find valid reasons for why they didn't perform to expectation. I'm forced to trawl through all the match reports and analyses until I can find something that somehow excuses their failure. Only then can I get some peace. Lately, it's been really tough, but somehow I'll keep doing it, keep finding reasons. Against Sunderland, I'll rationalise that such an abject display is merely the psychological consequence of a season of bad luck. I will cite the incredible number of times Liverpool have shot and hit the goal post (twenty-one times so far this season). So many games we could've won if the ball had flown just an inch or two one side of the wood work. I will note the gale-force wind at Sunderland's ground to be a genuine leveller. And I will note that, even though the two strikers we bought with the money we got for Torres have hitherto produced more problems than goals, an inch of luck here and there could make a difference. It won't make much difference to this season, but it could provide hope for the next. Just like last year and the year before that, hope for Liverpool is a clean slate, a fresh start, a new season.

Just as well my personal life is on the up.

I'm in New Zealand for a friend's wedding but this is not where I live any more. I moved to Sydney to be with Erin, about a month after I got back from Liverpool.

We've had some major issues, but I'm glad to say it was the right decision. So thank you, unconscious mind; for the most part, you've served me well. Erin and I got married in 2010 and we're now expecting a baby, a little boy, in fact. I wanted to name him Stevie but that's the name we gave to the cat. It's difficult enough learning how to conduct yourself in life without your immediate namesake being the family member who licks his own arse. So with no disrespect to Stevie G, we think we'll name him Leo instead.

Not long ago, I asked Erin if my propensity for being distracted by Liverpool was part of the reason she left me in Auckland. She said it wasn't, and generally speaking, saw it as being healthy. 'We all need a distraction from ourselves,' she said. Very wise. But for some time now Liverpool hasn't *felt* like a separate entity. It's somewhere under my skin, and I wonder where that leaves me. A sense of detachment from all things is a Buddhist tenet. It's an important one, especially if you want to live well in a world of glaring faults. But when it comes to Liverpool's welfare, a sense of detachment all but deserts me. Detachment could so easily spare me from riding this horribly erratic, highly emotional red rollercoaster, but I can't seem to do it. Problem is, I love the red rollercoaster.

You'll be pleased to know that I love Erin more. The thing about her and me is, no matter how much we fought, we were still better together. And somehow, over the past few years we've given each other a better run of happiness than either of us had ever experienced.

I've learned that happiness isn't something that will necessarily come along and plonk itself in your lap, no matter how much you deserve it. Sometimes you have to get off your arse, find it, and protect it. Like everything else, it takes work. Even then it can be taken away. But you continue working all the same. Medication helps, but despite us having found our run of happiness in 'the land of the lucky', it's like luck itself, you really need to make your own.

My father and I are making a decent go at a good relationship, and I've improved a great deal with not interpreting criticism for Liverpool as reflecting everything that is wrong with the world. Instead of becoming indignant and stewing on why a person's errant remark makes them potentially fascist, I take it in my stride and can see that these things shouldn't be taken so seriously. That way, I can guarantee the Nazi isn't me. When you take away death and suffering, life is just varying degrees of silliness, after all.

One thing that hasn't changed is my inability to sing. When I arrived in Sydney, Erin and I house-sat an apartment just metres away from the lively Oxford St. At times the laneway beside our building seemed like an outdoor latrine to every greasy feral, bung-eyed wastrel, and underbelly bogan Sydney had to offer. One night however, there was a guy singing YNWA as he peed against the opposing wall. Sensing a kindred spirit, I poked my head out the window and joined in on the chorus. He stopped singing, pulled up his pants mid-stream, and took off around the corner. Didn't even look around. That's not the Liverpool way, I thought.

Epilogue Extra

In 2010 the Hillsborough Independent Panel was set up to examine previously undisclosed documents relating to the disaster. In September 2012, their report was released. It confirmed what many Liverpool fans already knew – that in an attempt to deflect blame for the disaster, senior officers and solicitors altered the statements of their officers to remove or change any comments unfavourable to the South Yorkshire Police. It also cited that the SYP and a local Tory MP had made slanderous allegations about the Liverpool fans to the media, yet there was (still) no evidence to be found among the documents, TV and CCTV footage to support claims of drunken and violent fans.

Moreover, the report stated that crowd safety was compromised at every level, and that a better emergency response could have saved 41 of the 96 victims.

The findings fully exonerated the Liverpool fans. The likes of the Hillsborough Families Support Group, who have pushed for the truth for so long, will — at the very least — no longer be chastised by those who bought in to the conspiracy against them.

Following the panel's report public apologies were issued from the highest office (Prime Minister David Cameron), through to the very lowest (former Sun editor, Kelvin Mackenzie).

Although bittersweet, this late affirmation is a sign of hope and a source of some relief to the Liverpool families and community. It has paved the way for further inquests and this time, surely, Justice for the 96 is the only possible conclusion. YNWA.

ABOUT THE AUTHOR

Glenn Bowden was born in Christchurch, New Zealand, in 1974. His first travel story won him a trip for two to South America. His novel, *Cutting Caleb Keys,* was published by Penguin Books in 2007. The publication of *Liverpool, for Real* was delayed due to the breakdown of his marriage. Never mind. He is happy being a dad, working on his second novel, and willing the reds to be mighty once again.

CPSIA information can be obtained at www.ICGtesting.com
Printed in the USA
BVOW04s2151010414

349484BV00002B/73/P

9 781482 680942